CULT FICTION

Also by Clive Bloom

THE 'OCCULT' EXPERIENCE AND THE NEW CRITICISM:
Daemonism, Sexuality and the Hidden in Literature
* READING POE, READING FREUD: The Romantic Imagination
in Crisis
DARK KNIGHTS: The New Comics in Context
(*with Greg McCue*)
* JACOBEAN POETRY AND PROSE: Rhetoric, Representation
and the Popular Imagination (*editor*)
* TWENTIETH-CENTURY SUSPENSE: The Genre Comes of Age
(*editor*)
* SPY THRILLERS: From Buchan to le Carré (*editor*)
CREEPERS: British Fantasy and Horror Fiction in the Twentieth
Century (*editor*)
LITERATURE AND CULTURE IN MODERN BRITAIN
(1900–1929) (*editor*)
* PERSPECTIVES ON PORNOGRAPHY: Sexuality in Film and
Literature (*co-editor with Gary Day*)
* NINETEENTH-CENTURY SUSPENSE: From Poe to
Conan Doyle (*co-editor with Brian Docherty, Jane Gibb and
Keith Shand*)
* AMERICAN POETRY: The Modernist Ideal (*co-editor
with Brian Docherty*)
* AMERICAN DRAMA (*editor*)

* *From the same publisher*

The Queen of Cheese descends . . . Betty Page, top pin-up model and the original Sweater-Girl, 6 September 1954 (Range/Bettmann/UPI)

Cult Fiction

Popular Reading and Pulp Theory

Clive Bloom

St. Martin's Press
New York

St. Martin's Press, Scholarly and Reference Division,
175 Fifth Avenue, New York, N.Y. 10010

First published in the United States of America in 1996
First paperback edition 1998

Printed in Great Britain
by Antony Rowe Ltd, Chippenham, Wiltshire

ISBN 0–312–16194–8 - clothbound
ISBN 0–312–21356–5 - paperback

Library of Congress has cataloged the hardcover edition as follows:

Bloom, Clive.
Cult fiction : popular readings and pulp theory / Clive Bloom.
p. cm.
Includes bibliographical references (p.) and index.
ISBN 0–312–16194–8 (cloth)
1. American fiction–History and criticism. 2. Popular
literature—United States—History and Criticism. 3. Popular
literature—Great Britain—History and criticism. 4. English
fiction—History and criticism. 5. Authors and readers. 6. Canon
(Literature) I. Title
PS374.P63B56 1996
813.009–dc20   96–8458
                                                        CIP

Clive Bloom, Cult Fiction, published 1996, "St. Martin's
Press, Scholarly and Reference Division," reproduced
with permission of Palgrave Macmillan'

CMID# 143402

Printed on
Recycled Paper

For James and Jonathan, Natasha and Kirsty, Zack and Charlie

Contents

Acknowledgements

I would like to thank Alan Durant, Michael Walters and Middlesex University for a sustained study leave in which much of this book was written; Charmian Hearne for her editorial support; Gary Day, Greg McCue, David Pringle and Helena Blakemore for ideas over the years; Vivien Miller for research on US Census Records; Kelly A. Cornelis for her research on Mills & Boon; Steve Holland for his help in making various contacts; Lionel Fanthorpe for his inside knowledge; Antony Smith for his help in tracking down the names of certain authors; John Wolf of the Open University, Judith Champ of Kings College, London; Eleanor Wordsworth at *Reader's Digest*; Maurice Flanagan for his supreme ability to supply rare paperback material; Steve Chibnall, chair of the British Association of Paperback Collectors; finally Lesley Bloom and Susan Tourick for getting my disordered notes into proper typographic order and Anne Rafique for her editorial assistance.

The chapter on Jack the Ripper originally appeared in slightly different form in *Nineteenth-Century Suspense* edited by Clive Bloom, Brian Docherty, Jane Gibb and Keith Shand (1988); the chapter on H.P. Lovecraft appeared in *American Horror Fiction* edited by Brian Docherty (1990); the chapter on Sax Rohmer appeared in *Twentieth-Century Suspense* edited by Clive Bloom (1990); the chapter on Harry Price appeared in slightly different form in *Creepers* edited by Clive Bloom (1993). The author wishes to thank Lumiere Co-operative Press, Macmillan and Pluto Press for permission to reprint.

Part I
Et In Arcadia Ego

1

'Scuse me Mr H'officer:
An Introduction

Cult Fiction is an exploration of pulp literature and pulp mentalities: an investigation into the nature and theory of the contemporary mind in art and in life. Here the violent, erotic and sentimental excesses of contemporary life signify different facets of the modern experience played out in the gaudy pages of sensational and kitsch literature: novels, comic books, tabloid newspapers.

This book offers the reader a chance to investigate the underworld of literary production and from it find a new set of co-ordinates for questions regarding publishing and reading practices; ideas of genre; theories of commercial production; concerns regarding high and low culture, the canon and censorship; and the nature of the theories we use to explore the above areas. Concentrating on many disregarded and forgotten authors the book provides a theory of kitsch art that radically alters our perception both of literature and literary values while providing a panorama of an almost forgotten history: the history of pulp.

Pulp is not only a descriptive term for certain forms of publishing produced on poor quality paper, but it is also indicative of certain attitudes, reading habits and social concerns. For the aficionado, this literature is exemplified by those forms of magazine and paperback publication which flourished between the 1920s and 1950s in America and which should be distinguished from both dime novels, paperbacks per se and comic books. For academics, the term vaguely expresses a field of popular publishing neglected through the overemphasis placed upon canonic texts, while for cultural critics it often has meant the exemplary instance of mass culture's propensity to debase everything and exalt the lowest common denominator.

This study attempts to explore all these concerns and definitions, traverse them, broaden them and deepen them. It is axiomatic of this study that artistic movements and aesthetic concerns are intimately involved with social, commercial and perceptual history and that the formal questions we might ask cannot be asked without some sense of *location* in questions necessarily not formal. As such, the study does not overemphasize the definition of genre nor that of production, nor that of social history but attempts to negotiate through these toward an opening out of the question beyond such narrow definitions of the subject.

I do, however, want to provide a dynamic model of cult fiction and of pulp – an aesthetic as well as a history of trash art which acknowledges its vibrancy and excitement and its own mores of taste, hierarchy and validity. In this way, trash art speaks for itself, but within those constituting frameworks of commercial necessity and ephemerality that mark all trash out for what it is.

One can see this book as attempting to outline a different literary history and provide a different set of aesthetic criteria in order to investigate the complexities of print as both entertainment and provider of information. Within this history of *information* I delineate a second tale of cultural and social negotiation and of Anglo-American reading habits in which the *suppression* of one form of literacy becomes a marked theme. Lastly I must stress my attempt to tease out the complex negotiations that occur within the publishing market, within literary forms and within class structures and human relationships that an investigation of this kind must take into account. Evidence for ephemeral enjoyments, including reading for pleasure (as against utility), is often thin and its assessment problematical, nevertheless I have conjectured only where a link is not available in evidence so much as in logic and where problems of structure required a paradigm offered by the evidence but ignored by other writers.

Literary history of the type found in these pages is a discipline which needs to remind itself constantly that literature is not merely historical evidence (far from it), but is of course, always itself and yet *in* history. Yet literature is a kind of historical evidence not merely for its own evolution but also for attitudes of mind. This is, therefore, a history of perception using literature as a highly specialized, highly attenuated and usually distanced evidence. Literature 'represents' only in a curiously non-imitative and non-representational manner. Thus it is itself and yet indicative of those wider movements it mediates and metamorphoses through the printed page. I have been conscientious to see literature both in and for itself and as a social force representing conditions of cultural change.

I have divided the following pages into three parts. The first part offers the work's central argument and deals with questions of taste, publishing history and definitions; the second offers examples across a limited range of texts and genres in an effort to suggest both pulp's aesthetic concerns and pulp's attitudinal concerns. Part III is a requiem not only for pulp but also for a certain theoretical adventure. As readers will see, I delineate not just a history of that underclass of literary production usually known as pulp but I also give some hints as to the wider context of pulp aesthetics or trash art with examples from further afield. Although a history of print, this also gives an opening into other areas which are related.

More ambitiously, so most problematically, I have attempted to suggest a model which incorporates Anglo-American history and reading habits to show how intimately both sides of the Atlantic have shared (and been divided by) a common language. Too many studies ignore the basic importance of this linguistic relationship in their concern for one country's literary heritage. This book is about another as yet unsung heritage and consists of a history, a general theory and a series of examples. The examples are drawn from as many areas as possible but it is inevitable that certain areas, favoured by particular readers, may be less well covered than those readers might desire. For this I excuse myself on grounds that the book is designed as an argument, not a compendium. Books and authors are referred to for their illustrative value, their significance for the argument and their intrinsic interest, and inevitably they can only act as a sample. My terms neither include nor exclude bestsellers and blockbusters but where these are better dealt with in other studies I have ignored them, unless to dispute a point or take forward an argument. 'Popular' here does not mean merely common and much of my argument is taken up with writers and books neither commonly read nor bestsellers, but nevertheless determinedly popular by definitions concerned with market forces, mass reading habits and education, class divisions and attitudes at once political, social, cultural and always aesthetic.

The reader of this book will be well aware by the time they reach the last page that it has been about the context and history of popular reading habits, but it has been more than that and I have tried to explore the hidden byways of a literary history rarely taught in academia, hidden in second-hand bookstores and often only collected by a small band of enthusiastic 'amateurs' or left even by them to be finally bought by someone like me to whom the eccentric connection may just be the right one.

In one sense these pages contain an unseen map of bookshop visits in and around London as well as phone calls to mail order dealers and an occasional trip to a convention (both as a participant and as a spectator). I am not a dedicated fanatic but a fascinated by-stander who is perhaps too ready to pick and choose, too *disengaged* ever to join the ranks of those whose life is measured in checklists, nevertheless my life too has been measured by popular fiction.

My life as an academic has divided itself between esoteric liter-ary theory and esoteric literary 'trash' – a term I use in the same way that the gay community returned to the word 'queer'. Critical essays on spy novels, thrillers, comic books and horror stories and a continued interest in the popular and ephemeral has kept me returning to the well, a loyalty I cannot shake. Years in dusty book-shops tells one, as nothing else can, that all art dies eventually and that it is indeed no less mortal than the ephemera that surrounds it and no less vulnerable to being passed over in silence by the casual browser. Only seek and you will find! Every second-hand bookshop and junk shop with its shelf of decaying and musty paperbacks is a catacomb of the undead. A visit is a type of Gray's 'Elegy', an archaeological trip into the past of the ordinary, a re-minder of one's mortality. In rereading or refinding long-forgotten and half-remembered writers one does a service not only to history but to a communal memory which is different from 'history' and which is shot through with an affection history does not feel.

But you need not get too mushy: there are huge numbers of books printed each year that are simply unreadable, some deserve forgetting and no longer exist as art but merely as history. In this book I have made choices, finding certain books either too dull or too empty for discussion; there is good and bad in everything and every pulp fan has his or her 'list' not only of the significant and worthy but also of those which keep their affection. I doubt if we can ever make the dead live again but we can give them a good send-off and perhaps in doing so learn something of the true place of the living in the schemes of social and literary culture.

I have not dealt with children's literature as a specific subcategory, indeed to do so would have been against the principles behind some of the ideas in this book. Instead, such literature is mentioned where it falls naturally within the argument in general or forms a bridge upon which adult and adolescent readers meet. It is a fact that all the arguments here rehearsed regarding adult reading matter can be applied to, or have already been applied to children's reading matter; debates over quality, taste, the canon, morality and ethical acceptability as well as questions of content and style mirror such debates elsewhere regarding literature, its cultural significance and social importance.

It is ironic that, as with publishing for adults, there has long been a tradition of wilfully refusing to acknowledge why children read certain things, in effect to rescue books from both their readers and their authors. This tradition of *denial* still prevalent today, but especially so from the 1950s to late 1970s, was in its most virulent form an unconscious equation between the reading interests of foolish middle-class boys and girls and those of the inarticulate, semi-literate adult proletarian, such imaginary creatures represented by Enid Blyton and Mickey Spillane. How else could one such critic make such an equation: '... I would as soon consider including [Enid Blyton] in a study of children's literature as I would consider including say Mickey Spillane in a literature degree course.'[1] One is inclined to ask, despite changes in current university curricula how much has, or would change?

A word must be said, given some of my later arguments, about the omission of detailed information concerning the unstamped radical press of the early eighteen-hundreds. After 1815 newspapers carried a stamp or tax duty of 4d. (four pence) which meant working people could not afford to buy them. This effectively removed the chance of such people, the working middle classes, also joining in any real political debate. From the 1830s onwards, due to internal political pressures and inspired by the July Revolution in France there appeared a new wave of illegally printed and distributed unstamped newspapers selling for 1d. (one penny). By 1836 such papers had far exceeded sales of the legitimate press, were read right across the country in both town and countryside and were driven by a dissident movement of printers, booksellers, authors and illegal distribution centres. Many hundreds of people were fined or imprisoned or both but the 'tax on knowledge' was repealed and reduced to a general rate of one penny. Thus finally ended this highly popular form of subversive publishing.

Effective as popular means of radicalizing the unenfranchised 'the Unstamped ... were [also] a colourful and strident step towards cheap journalism and cheap literature'.[2] They were designed by such means to bring their readers to 'political and economic self-awareness' of, on the one hand, the oppressions of aristocracy and monopoly, or on the other the newer oppressions of exploitation

and property.[3] In each case the attempt was to elevate the reader
and to provide self-improvement and education.

While these productions could be considered an abortive attempt
to create a *national* politicized consciousness among working people they were nevertheless a highly prophetic precursor of cost-
effective production – ironically the very system they opposed.
Reading was widened and encouraged if not elevated or overtly
politicized. The reading public of the middle nineteenth century
were still parochial in their political affiliations and it was only the
monopolizing of ownership in the later years of the century that
flattened out local divergence and nationalized the political attitudes of working people now able to participate, through reading,
in a commonality of attitudes.

This commonality of attitudes, which allowed working people to
participate in national affairs, occurred later in the century in the
United States where from the 1870s a virtual state of anarchy existed
between workers and their bosses. If the presses of Hearst and
Pulitzer provided one sort of news, packed with 'personality' and
'sensation-mongering' as Matthew Arnold sourly remarked in his
essays of the 1880s (collected 1888), then the growth of populism
and radicalism during the same period also provided ground for
cheap socialist and anti-capitalist newspapers, pamphlets and
broadsheets aimed at uniting working people. Where Arnold found
'a community singularly free from the distinction of classes [and]
singularly homogeneous', as well he might having been 'sponsored'
by Andrew Carnegie, there was, in fact, a country divided on class
and ethnic lines – divisions which proved irresolvable. Blacks and
Whites read in their newspapers of suppressions and violence,
reports reaching their climax in the collapse of 1893. Such reports
and the obvious hardship of workers and their families made
socialists of such as Eugene Debs and populists of Henry Vincent
who started a journal in 1886 called *The American Non-Conformist
and Kansas Industrial Liberator*, which aimed to 'tend to the education of the labouring classes'.[4] The *National Economist* found 100 000
readers among working people and in the South newspapers appeared with names such as *The Comrade, the Toiler's Friend* and
Revolution.[5] Lectures were organized and books and pamphlets provided at a prodigious rate:

> One gathers from yellowed pamphlets that the agrarian ideolo-
> gists undertook to re-educate their countrymen from the ground

up. Dismissing 'history as taught in our schools' as 'practically valueless', they undertook to write it over – formidable columns of it, from the Greek down. With no more compunction they turned all hands to the revision of economics, political theory, law, and government.[6]

All in all, these attempts paralleled and finally blended into the Democratic Party platform, if they were not already suppressed by other means.

The legacy of the early radical press in Britain was a public able to afford nationally disseminated ideas provided, ironically, by the monopolistic ownership of press 'barons', a situation paralleled later in America. It is therefore entirely to miss the point to argue that press ownership is merely conservative, manipulative and degraded.[7] While ownership was monopolized, consumption was always a matter of *local* negotiation – readers of popular papers were and are a peculiar mixture of gullibility and shrewd refusal (what Richard Hoggart might have called 'common sense'). The radical penny press did not simply vanish but rather it went underground, absorbed into the very sensibility of British reading habits. Opposed by temperament to the very nature of pulp, the cheap radical publisher's subversive nature modified into the illicit pleasures of gaudy literature – hardly, perhaps, educational or morally elevating, but effectively democratic for all that.[8]

Finally, the reader should be warned that I do not include a specific chapter on women's romantic fiction. This area has been a 'cause' among feminist critics and social historians for sufficient time for much of the argument to have become stale and commonplace. Such publishers as Mills & Boon are also self-reflexive in their attitudes and their promotional material itself has provided a wealth of information as to their aesthetic concerns. Thus, although some areas (the cheapest women's story magazines and film-story magazines) have been less explored by critics, I have let their testimony stand except where I take issue with their findings or believe they have insufficiently credited certain evidence.

Rarely is research work, even in the humanities, carried out in isolation. During the 1980s a number of significant studies emerged from the radical left which clearly showed the complexity inherent in working with 'popular' culture and the problematic discontinuities which emerge in such work.[9] The links between culture, politics, class, gender, race and economic realities found themselves plotted in a more sophisticated way than had previously been offered by many earlier liberal or left-wing thinkers. Ultimately, nearly all these writers went on a diversionary search for a supposedly authentic lost proletarian voice, at once both popular and radical. Through generalizations regarding the linked nature of capitalist publishing and patriarchy (a history of suppression and manipulation) and a consistent refusal to really get to grips with the specific nature of such publishing, its readers and the nature of capital's internal history, the Marxist studies which emerged against the background of Thatcherism upheld a project that ultimately fell back on the old clichés of an earlier leftism.

My admiration for their exploratory abilities is offset by my inability to accept such general statements as make simplistic equations without either theoretical or carefully tested empirical evidence. While these are still important books one cannot help but think that the writers were trying hard to understand lowbrow writing but could not rid themselves of the belief that there is a *conspiracy* behind mass culture which must be *resisted*. Like the penny press of old these writers still wanted serious licit reading, in a word, legitimation. They risked – so obvious in their examples of unread proletarian print (however interesting) – losing the very notion of the popular they wished to save, itself vulgar, intractable, Technicolor and consistently resistant to the patronage of such theory.

My own study is primarily an analysis of literature determined in its outlook by concerns which are both aesthetic, sociological and to a lesser, though significant extent economic. In using this mixture of approaches I have tried to 'get inside' certain literary problems which are seen either as unproblematic or which have, in my opinion, been prematurely closed off. Withal, this is not merely a study of literature and history for it is informed by Marxist debate on the relationships between structure and agency and class and community. My own work is Marxian rather than Marxist and my conclusions are far more determined by ideas concerning popular *accommodations* than popular revolution. I have seen the capitalist mentality in a kinder light than Marxist critics.

If it is true that explanations concerning production and class are necessarily central to the debate conducted here, nevertheless they are not sufficient in themselves as explanations of the complex range of perceptual nuances which may be encountered; what answers for humankind in the aggregate may not correspond at all to the peculiar circumstances of men and women individually and what has significance statistically may not signify for any one person (whose relation to the statistical norm will always be aberrant). The residue left after all else is exhausted by the discussion of production and class must give us a lived experience which cannot simply be reabsorbed into either of the two categories. Equally, Marx's jaundiced comments on the 'nightmare on the brain' of 'the tradition of all the dead generations' fails to recognize the positive significance of the plurality of traditions between individuals, families, communities and even nations and the constant remaking of history by the present generation in its own image and no longer in 'borrowed language' able, in a word, to liberate itself from the dead hand of the past. Yet to step into the absolute present is not a liberation but a futile attempt to step out of history itself and thereby into the real nightmare of a continuous contemporaneity where human destiny would be once and for all out of the hands of humankind and history itself cancelled. Curiously this is the dream of a rapacious capitalism and revolutionary Marxism. This book narrates one aspect of the tale of the continuous present.

My own claims and comments I hope add to the debate above, especially in terms of sectional groupings and with regard to urban and rural fantasies inter- and *intra*-class. If such grand claims are at all valid then they are only so in relation to the debate they may open rather than to any definitive answers they might give.

I am only too aware of the debt I owe to enthusiastic workers both academic and amateur upon whose efforts this book draws. In this regard I am conscious of the warning recently issued by Brian Stableford in his introduction to a work by one of Britain's best 'amateur' pulp literary investigators:

The Mushroom Jungle – or, more likely, a semi-sanitised, semi-plagiarism by some academic hack who specialises in repackaging the research of better men – will take its place on university reading lists.[10]

Suitably chastened, I hope this effort will be neither a semi-plagiarism nor a mere repackaging. The comments on academic authors I leave to the reader to judge.

2

Throwing Rice at Brad and Janet:
Illicit, Delinquent Pleasures

This is a book about popular fictions and pulp fantasies. At one level this is also a book which attempts to redirect a certain critical attention toward 'trash' art, situate it *within* popular culture generally and consider its aesthetic. On another level this is a book about taste and popular perception in a social as well as artistic history determined by commercialism and urbanization but lived in the sphere of the acutely personal and private. Just as with all popular arts, pulp is a moveable feast since it can be appropriated by and on behalf of the hierarchists of taste at any particular time and thus taken out of its pulp status. Pulp is both a desire for respectability and a refusal. As I argue later, its legitimacy as pulp is correlative with its illegitimacy as 'serious' art. Hence it is both forced into illicitness and is always illicit.[1] But the delights of trash art are always contrary – at once risqué and conformist – always out of the grasp of legitimation. When you have defined them, then, like street talk, they slip away to appear elsewhere in their own secret language of seduction.

If what is explored here is only partial the nature of the task is to some extent overwhelming, for a vast archaeological programme would have to be undertaken if the consequences of pulp and all its many contributing factors, not to say biographies of its mainly ignored and anonymous producers were to be fully explored and put into some sort of order. Such an exploration is one in which trash art is not seen as a mere sociological symptom nor is it reduced to a dull and inconsequential set of formal problems but is rather understood as vibrantly alive both socially and aesthetically. It also emerges as the aesthetic context within which much that is of consequence politically and otherwise is played out on a flickering and evanescent stage of ghostly ephemeral objects. If it doesn't live up to carnival, it does, at least make a spectacular parade. Pulp, like

12

'rock 'n' roll works as a common experience and private obsession',
as Greil Marcus, citing critic Jim Miller has pointed out.[2]

Any good critic of such ephemeral and fleeting material must be
alive to its nature and not try to redeem or rehabilitate; the canon
can take care of itself and is sufficient to itself. I do not wish to
widen the canon. I want the canon to define my own interests as
specific, different, and enjoyably *illicit*. We may again talk of pleasure and about the vulgar (in its original sense) – something alive
because crude and because totally contemporary. As such I am the
complete fan and the ironic spectator and I fully comprehend the
disjunction needed to uphold the aesthetic of temporality (the aesthetic of immediacy and the ephemeral) and the inquiry of the historical (finding continuities and moments of breakage and rupture).
Every fan knows this: that the cult following preserves the ephemeral traces of the newly forgotten. The cult is religiosity after the
fact, recognition almost too late – almost but not quite. At this
point, the cult itself re-enacts in itself the drift of that which it hopes
to preserve at its shrine. Which is only to say that pleasures that are
fleeting are hard to recall. If Betty Page is the queen of trash art
then she will return speaking Klingon.

Doubling back upon itself, the cult obsession provides for the ever-
present reinvoking of capitalism as personal destiny. Hence QVC,
the worldwide telesales channel, sells teach yourself Klingon tapes
to those whose personal destinies and most intimate expressions
are fully integrated into the anarchic capitalist loop. Nor does this
produce a bliss so moronic that it cannot also be self-reflexive. As
Nick Hornby has pointed out in a recent book about English soccer,
obsessives have no choice: they have to lie on occasions like this.

> If we told the truth every time, then we would be unable to
> maintain relationships with anyone from the real world. We would
> be left to rot with our Arsenal programmes or our collection of
> original blue-label Stax records or our King Charles spaniels, and
> our two-minute daydreams would become longer and longer and
> longer until we lost our jobs and stopped bathing and shaving
> and eating, and we would lie on the floor in our filth rewinding
> the video again and again in an attempt to memorise by heart the
> *whole* of the commentary, including David Pleat's expert analysis,
> for the night of 26th of May 1989. (You think I had to look the
> date up? Ha!) The truth is this: *for alarmingly large chunks of an
> average day, I am a moron.*[3]

Few critics, as will be seen in these pages, are able to maintain that ability to be both simultaneously inside and outside this trash art/popular aesthetic and also able to see the gradations within the popular itself. It is a difficult job to recognize pulp for what it may be (but so many incarnations) and to balance celebration with cerebration – to want to explore what to many is at best repetitive and at worst abject – and to find instead consequence in the fleeting and a sympathy for the mundane. It is banality which is in some ways most surreal, and pulp takes us into the most bizarre corners of the most banal worlds – freakishness, the irrational, morbid eroticism, pathological conditions of all sorts, Martians, crop circles, spiritualism, UFOs, vampires, costumed superheroes, love at first sight; money, success, revenge – in short a whole other universe which is at once commonsensical and crackpot. Readers are alive to the fantasies of money and sexuality in an S and F fantasy of the modern world and yet they are prepared to accept Fortean explanations for almost any natural or physical phenomenon. If the high priestess is the late clairvoyant Doris Stokes, then the age is forever Edwardian, the war always the first but the goal the glitz and razzmatazz of Hollywood consumer goods, *Hello* magazine, houses in the country and a wild promiscuity lived only and happily in the head. Pulp is essentially a benevolent, conservative and godless form determined by chance and luck.

Pulp is public expression lived out privately. If human nature is at once private and historical (that is, subject to change) pulp may have more than art to tell us about ourselves. Pulp is the child of capitalism and is tied to the appearance of the masses and the urban, mediums of the nineteenth and twentieth centuries. As such it is the embodiment of capitalism aestheticized, consumerized and *internalized*. Hence it is both oppressive and liberating, both mass manipulation and anarchic individualistic destiny. Pulp is our daily, natural heightened experience: a product and a channel for a moment in human self-consciousness and its aspirations lived in the banal and in the now.

Real pulp is a refusal of bourgeois consciousness and bourgeois forms of realism. It is capitalistic, anarchic, entrepreneurial and individualist and it found expression not only in the gaudy covers of pulp magazines, cheap paperbacks and comic books with their aliens, gangsters and silk-stockinged floozies in our century, but also in the flimsy chapbooks and ballad sheets of years before which celebrated the adventures of Jack Sheppard, Dick Turpin or Jack the

Ripper. Here fiction and fact are both fantasy. Here the *Police Gazette* meets the *National Enquirer* and neither fact nor fiction can any longer be trusted.

Here also, authors become entrepreneurial producers, as this characteristic but possibly apocryphal anecdote from the life of Jeffrey Archer illustrates.

> 'I've tried property', Jeffrey went on, 'and that didn't work. I've tried shares and that didn't work. I've tried all the things that everyone else has tried and they didn't work'. . . .
> 'The only thing I can think of is to write a bestseller'. . . .
> 'A bestseller', Jeffrey went on, 'which turns into a movie. That's the only way of making enough money to sort out my problems.'
> 'Jeffrey', said [Adrian] Metcalfe, 'you can't write!'
> 'Don't be ridiculous, Adrian. It's nothing to do with writing, I'll *produce* a bestseller. I can tell a good story. I'm convinced of it.'[4]

If authors become producers and readers become consumers this is neither a mindless slavery to the market nor a revolution in advanced taste. Rather it marks a style of negotiation and rapprochement in *democratic* mass experience. For instance, for Greil Marcus popular music offered both commercial opportunity and personal freedom within a mass consensus:

> The Beatles and their fans played out an image of utopia, of a good life, and the image was that one could join a group and by doing so not lose one's identity as an individual but find it: find one's own voice.[5]

No really authoritarian states can stand pulp culture – it reeks of anarchy and nonconformity and subversion. Thus authoritarian states ban such corruption and condemn rock 'n' roll alongside comic books, erotic literature, fast food, Levi jeans, James Bond, US soap operas and Coca Cola. No authoritarian state has produced a quarter decent rock group – anarchic, uncontrollable, open to cult status (a challenge to the ruling oligarchy), sexually explosive and ever youthful. For Marxist-Leninism, spiritualism and rock 'n' roll were one and the same thing, not surprising that authoritarians can find themselves in Shakespeare and Dante but cannot tolerate Batman comics read by the lightning flashes of rock technology.

Such accommodation as can be made with great Western art in authoritarian regimes leads them to overvalue realist, and by implication bourgeois, fictions — ones that can be incorporated into the body of the authoritarian aesthetic. Part of the internal contradiction of modern authoritarian regimes is that their artistic taste is abysmal, hierarchist and propagandist: the populace must be educated, moralized, always sit bolt upright. The result is bad art and bad faith against which pulp seems (and is) liberating and terrifyingly complex (bewildering to newly 'enfranchised' peoples released from subservience). Pulp acts as a corrosive and subversive force in totalitarian countries for it represents democracy and capitalism and individualism redefined within a new loose and anarchic collective. In democratic culture it has an essentially longer and uninterrupted history in which subversion is now an illicit behaviour always seeking accommodation within a progressively decentred consumerism. When it seeks bourgeois status (a rare event) it does so only by proxy and then only temporarily.

It is an interesting irony that pulp thrives on the fantasy *representation* of authoritarian, fascistic figures and situations, situations simplified into violence and erotica. Pulp never was the apparently totalitarian brainwashing that George Orwell warned against in his reading of James Hadley Chase's *No Orchids for Miss Blandish*. Quite to the contrary, pulp represents an anarchic edge on the margin of bourgeois propriety and at the centre of modern consumerist multiplicity. This, if anything, is the totalitarianism of an unrealized and groundless space of endless choices of *no consequence*.[6]

High art has since the beginning of this century attempted to assimilate pulp culture into its regime. T.S. Eliot's 'Fragment of An Agon' was, originally less pretentiously entitled 'Wanna go home Baby'.[7] In the field of the visual arts the work of Marcel Duchamp and Stuart Davis gave birth to those 1960s pop artists whose aim was to make pulp over in their image. They made themselves respectable but did nothing for pulp. Marcel Duchamp's found objects – the flotsam of pulp culture, were always irreducible, always 'wrong' – a continual refusal to assimilate into mainstream art consciousness; that same consciousness that Stuart Davis's *Lucky Strike* and *Odol* of 1921 and 1924 would attempt to bind to serious art and Western iconography.

It may not be surprising that Davis's successors, whether pastiching benday dots as with Roy Lichtenstein, or satirizing painting by numbers as in Andy Warhol, distanced themselves further

from the *irreducibily* popular, ending up as superior commentato
for bourgeois gallery visitors. The pulp psychedelia of 1960s London (of which the Beatles shop sported a considerable amount) was
irretrievably lost under layers of white paint. Andy Warhol's work
remained – a collector of pulp freakdom, but only an occasional
participant. Warhol's factory was art *refusing* its subject matter, a
true élitism from which all but the in crowd were excluded, the
public works acting merely to sanitize and control pulp and its own
internal aesthetic in order to repackage it as decoration and as safe
simulation.

In the realm of cinema and television, director/producer David
Lynch has endlessly explored the bizarre nature of smalltown
American banality. From the crazy schlock of *Erasurehead* to the
opening sequence of *Blue Velvet* where a man aimlessly waves to us
from his fire engine, to the television series *Twin Peaks* to *Fire Walk
with Me*, Lynch is determined to find the pattern in the Formica
of the roadside diner. For Lynch, pulp culture is essentially both
familiar and totally alien and in the complex mixture of these two
emerges an innocence of the banal, a type of transcendent good-
ness. Despite the evil that lurks in the angles of Lynch's imagination, innocence is continually proclaimed. At the end of *Fire Walk
with Me*, Lynch's prequel to *Twin Peaks*, Laura Palmer meets the
angel of love helped by 'spirit' guide Dale Cooper in the Black
Lodge: smalltown USA is returned to its innocence and each particular dark history rewritten or erased in love and salvation. The
last scene of *Fire Walk with Me* is itself schlock, sentimental and
pulp – Lynch stops being a commentator and joins in.

Like Divine, (but also obviously quite unlike Divine!) La Cicciolina
is pure pulp fantasy – an exotic and unlikely latin Betty Page (see
Chapter 7). But now Betty Page has married the foremost pop artist
of the *fin de siècle*. Jeff Koons is his own consumer durable. Koons
(and La Cicciolina no doubt – and Betty Page) understands the
relationship between art and the market. He knows that late
twentieth-century art cannot *be art* without the market. The subject of such art cannot therefore be otherwise than the market itself
– consumer culture at its most vulnerable and effective:

I have always used cleanliness and a form of order to maintain
for the viewer a belief in the essence of the eternal, so that the
viewer does not feel threatened economically. When under economic pressure you start to see disintegration around you. Things

do not remain orderly. So I have always placed order in my work not out of a respect for minimalism, but to give the viewer a sense of economic security [. . .] Where I see art going, its exchange value, its economic substructure, will be removed: it will function solely as a means of support and security. From this point of view, my work has strong biological implications: the encasement of the vacuum cleaners with the ideas of removal and protection, and the equilibrium tanks with water suspending basketballs – these are all very womblike.[8]

Such a configuration creates not tension but an essential innocence – the artist again speaks of spirituality, innocence and love *because* of market forces. Such consumer theology for Koons is essentially televangelism with Koons the Messiah of the ordinary.[9] 'Everybody grew up surrounded by this material. I try not to use it in any cynical manner. I use it to penetrate mass consciousness – to communicate to people.'[10]

Yet whether creating *Popples* (1988) or *Poodle* (1991) Koons's work in its heart is a refusal – a sleight of hand which, like all fakes, cannot sustain (oh, yes, pulp is always genuine – its fans are never fooled). The use of hard materials and shiny surfaces which reflect the viewer's helplessness deny the very claims Koons makes for universality and connection. Koons's works contain, indeed proclaim the pure surface of pop culture in the same way as Baudrillard's proclamation of seduction or Guy Debord's society of the spectacle where everything is shiny, surface, depthless and meaningless: a society for the mindless lost in a Disneyworld run by ad agencies and fuelled by Sprites. Yet pulp culture, when *lived*, is all depth, passion, erotics. If it is innocent, its innocence is that of the damned who don't yet know it, not of the saved who have been rescued by consumer artefacts in upmarket galleries. That's what makes Koons so sterile compared to, say the early graffiti of Keith Haring. When Koons declares 'Embrace your past' he knows there is only the present.[11] But all pulp cultures know their past – its lineage is preserved, protected and cherished but only for the initiated. All pulp has history – only complacent artists miss the point through the violence of benevolent pastiche. Pulp is all depth and depth as style – as that very surface drawn down into itself.

In *Manet* one of a serious of works completed in 1991 of the artist and his wife copulating, Koons is shown licking La Cicciolina's open thighs – Koons acts the outrageous artist but La Cicciolina, dressed in lace and white high heels, her pubis air-brushed clean, pouts the pout of the pulp queen she is – she alone understands the pulp impulse, its trash art aesthetic. Koons wishes to save pop culture and the pulp erotic by making it into safe, married love – innocent, spiritual, homely. His later work has puppies, children and kittens. Yet his work breaks the very respectability pulp craves (its own irony) – this is not pulp because it is too *crude* and too explicit. In La Cicciolina's fake orgasm and airbrushed nudity she alone understands the heart of trash art – (Think of the real eroticism and humour and innocence of the still available poster of a tennis player scratching her naked bottom). La Cicciolina is a symbol of the illicitness of pulp, while Koons is the benevolent authoritarian restoring order to his wife's tease. La Cicciolina is authentic cheesecake, whilst Koons is anarchic – entrepreneurial pop promoter. In their alliance is the very accommodation and refusal at the heart of pop culture and trash art.

It is this accommodation and uneasiness between commercial interest and aesthetic or ethical goal which marks literary works in a way that other forms avoid. The printed medium since the seventeenth century and certainly since the eighteenth has maintained the closest and most necessary links between entrepreneurial activity and cultural definition. The entrepreneurial act links the printer-publisher of the eighteenth century to the author-producer of the twentieth. It is no coincidence that Max Weber in his search for the spirit of capitalism found it in America during the eighteenth century and in the figure of Benjamin Franklin whose life was that of a printer-publisher (as was that of his brother) and who was responsible for the first major popular work of American literature *Poor Richard's Almanack* which was at once cheaply produced and widely consumed by a growing population. It was not a work of spontaneous folk art but of commercial, calculated material distributed for profit and determined by print. This was predicated on the *primacy* of reading and literacy and only secondarily on oral repetition. It is America's first work of mass literature for a large and largely heterogeneous society held together by printed news and factual information. It is therefore no coincidence that Franklin's autobiography moves medieval hagiography into the realm of personal anecdote and democratic remembrance. Franklin represents the movement from the craftsman-artisan to the individualist-entrepreneur and can be seen to be unaware of either monopoly capital or corporate capital in the modern sense. The individualist-entrepreneur could equally be a gentleman. Thus Franklin closes the gap between individual endeavour and mass aspiration – the personal and public spheres – through the matter of print.

The links between mass literacy and personal aspiration, eccentric desires and public requirements always proved unbridgeable when the medium was print – public duty being abandoned in favour of craftsmanship and inspiration. This was in no little part due to the essential intervention of capitalist activity in the realm of printed aesthetics. It should not be forgotten how many respectable publishers and proprietors began their lives in the underworld of publishing for a mass or 'semi-literate' readership. Rupert Murdoch, after all, financed *The Times* from profits earned at *The Sun*. A previous entrepreneurial newsman, Alfred Harmsworth, the future Lord Northcliffe, proprieter of *The Times* from 1908 and one of Britain's greatest media magnates, began as a journalist who dealt in anecdote and trivia and was the founder of *Answers to Correspondents on Every Subject Under the Sun* which specialized in sensationalist competitions and sold at a penny an issue. Nor should it be forgotten that his bedside reading was *The Newgate Calendar*, nor that his career began with George Newnes proprietor of both *Tit Bits* and the *Strand*.[12]

Through such publications the new reading public satisfied its curiosity about the world and itself; curiosity about self now competed with public duty. During the age of criminalization the world of Newgate already represented a sentimental nostalgia for a history determined by hero robbers and larger-than-life thief takers. Harmsworth's personality was already sentimentalized in parallel with and no less than his readers'. Where Marx and Engels saw the masses, Harmsworth and his brother saw also the individual. It was Marx, not Harmsworth, who opposed the popular – the two attitudes forged in the reading room of the British Library and in Fleet Street marked out the contest for the medium of print.

This contest, marked out by growing ethical and social qualms, can be seen enacted in the most unexpected places. Owners of middlebrow or even 'society' magazines might go downmarket to earn quick money. Even H.L. Mencken who was co-owner of *The Smart Set* was not indifferent to the mass-market sales enjoyed by *Detective Story Magazine* which had benefited from social trends after World War I.

The disillusionment that followed the war, the frustration over the mushrooming gangster control of the cities affected the detective story as much as it did mainstream fiction. And the 1920s occupation with the American language, the dissatisfaction with the Victorian rhetoric and polite exposition was nowhere more strongly felt than among the writers of private eye stories.[13]

Attempting to compensate for uneven sales Mencken began *Black Mask* in 1920. Highly successful and hugely influential, the magazine proved an embarrassment for Mencken who referred to it as 'our new louse'. He finally sold the enterprise and returned to defending culture.

This two-tiered publishing and reading system was repeated on both sides of the Atlantic. However, by the middle twentieth century even though many entrepreneurial and opportunistic Victorian publishers had consolidated their position and become large corporate enterprises they gave rise to a flourishing subsystem of pulp publishers which existed alongside them. Such publishers included Thorpe & Porter and E.H. and Irene Turney in Britain who between them ran a stable of extraordinarily named pulp authors who enjoyed universal success in the aftermath of World War II and the early years of the welfare state – years in which American imports were restricted.

Even the Booker Prize, established in 1968 in Britain to ratify the art of the novel was the consequence of a shrewd move made to establish a public profile and respectability for a long-time food business. The prize grew out of an idea by Tom Maschler and Graham C. Greene of Jonathan Cape. Cape had bought Ian Fleming's *Casino Royale* and Fleming had created a company called Glidrose to protect potential profits. Booker chairman Jock Campbell who was a friend of Fleming, bought the company and put Booker into the publishing business. Originally named Artists Services, Booker Books already represented a number of authors by 1968 and had also acquired 51 per cent of the rights to Agatha Christie. The entire sequence of events had been determined as much by commercial interest as by aesthetic concern.[14]

If significant authors were accorded the privilege of such prizes others had this recognition refused both by working practice and by social and cultural expectation. What recognition, and by what hierarchy of definitions can one begin to bring to visibility the writers who were refused canonic status and whose style was demoted to

mere technical skill? Such writers, even those who are popular
classics (a bizarre status), are refused a meaningful place within the
fluctuations of literary culture. At best, they become sociologically
interesting, at worst they become pathological cases.

If Robert Louis Stevenson, John Buchan and Arthur Conan Doyle,
Agatha Christie and Ian Fleming are second-league popular classics,
what becomes of Sidney Horler, Guy Thorne, William Le Queux
or Sax Rohmer who are remembered but rarely read, or Barbara
Cartland, Catherine Cookson or (from a quite different direction)
horror writer Shaun Hutson, who are all read but certainly not
recognized, or the likes of early Mills & Boon authors Joyce Dingwall
and Kathryn Blair who are totally forgotten alongside so many others
who nevertheless made a living out of print. Indeed, how does one
deal in any real sense with writers such as 'Bartimeus', 'Taffrail',
'Seamark'*, 'Seaforth' and 'Dam Buster' or the anonymous authors
of *The Man who Killed Hitler* of 1939?[†] Moreover, unless we are
driven to sociology or matters of taste it is only with difficulty that
we are able to speak 'academically' about such authors as 'Hank
Janson', 'Ben Sarto' and 'Paul Renin' (all pseudonyms), or the
multiple authorial enterprise of Nick Carter, or of 'Desmond Reid',
the name given to all stories needing editing for the *Sexton Blake
Library* and which linked a large number of writers including Michael
Moorcock.[15] Moreover, how does one approach those well-written
novelizations of the 1920s to 1950s, published by Dell among others
and based on successful plays and films or even those more recent
novels based on *Star Trek*, *Dr Who* or the Warhammer gamesworld?
Is 'bastardization' all we can speak of? And in such a light doesn't
the work of Ernest Hemingway or Nathanael West seem to have
more in common with Dashiell Hammett, W.R. Burnett, Cornell
Woolrich and the movies than with Henry James or Jane Austen.
And isn't it this which precisely locates their power and place as
literature?

What emerges is a fluctuating field, a set of possibilities rather
than a set of results: a network as well as a hierarchy.

---

* 'Seamark' was actually Austin J. Small. He was a bestselling Hodder & Stoughton
  author until the 1950s, yet he has not enjoyed any bibliographic attention even by
  compilers of encyclopaedias on popular fiction. He wrote thrillers and romances
  and contributed to the *Strand Magazine*. For information about 'Seamark' see the
  article by J.E. Miller, 'Mystery Maker' in *Million* (Nov–Dec 1991) pp. 28–9.
† The actual authors of this book were Dean Southern Jennings, Ruth Landshoff and
  David Malcolmson. It was published by T. Werner Laurie in London and sported
  a swastika on its title page. This book should not be confused with one of the same
  name by Robert Page Jones published in 1980.

After all Dashiell Hammett himself wrote the syndicated comic strip 'Secret Agent X-9' and (partially) the radio series 'The Adventures of Sam Spade,' while William Faulkner worked on the scripts of *The Road to Glory* and *Land of the Pharaohs* . . . It's easy for a critic to make a clean distinction between the accomplished art of *Red Harvest* and *Sanctuary* . . . and such expendable trash as 'Secret Agent X-9' or *Land of the Pharaohs*, but in the American cultural web they are interwoven densely and inextricably.

The paperbacks provide just such a stew of high and low, vigorous and decayed; . . . In short, they partake of the characteristic America. It is useless to speak of 'high art,' 'personal art,' 'folk art,' 'commercial art,' or 'exploitation'; in the living situation, they all float about in the same pond.[16]

We are then confronted with the question of why *serious* novels do not last. What life is left in Joyce Cary or Hugh Walpole?

Mackinley Kantor, a pulp writer turned respectable novelist, pointed out the nature of these pulp writers' lives and the immensely complex mixture of writing talents and temperaments that participated.

Of these, the first group is much the largest. These are professional pulp writers – men and women whose talents for simple story telling at a rapid pace are profound, and whose output is amazing. They write hundreds of thousands of words every year. Most of them never land in the big money, but average from two to ten thousand dollars a year. A very few, relying on dictaphones and batteries of stenographers, manage to make considerably more than that. But these are freaks – minor, unsung Edgar Wallaces, who work by graph and by chart, who manufacture stories at a sweat-shop pace.

In the second class come young writers on the way up: people whose capabilities do not as yet permit them entry to the better markets, and who regard the cheap magazine market solely as a means towards an end. They write with intent and ambitious gaze fixed upon the *Saturday Evening Post* and *Cosmopolitan* and the *American Magazine*. Even in their angry days of struggle and reluctant apprenticeship, they firmly believe that their stories are good enough for the more expensive magazines; unless they need a quick cheque for a few dollars in a great hurry, they will send their manuscripts around to all the better markets before they have any truck with the pulps. As their skill improves, more and more frequently these writers have their stories accepted by the better magazines and eventually the one cent, two-cents-a-word crime and detective and adventure story magazines become stained little steps in the ladder beneath and behind them.

Then there's the dismal third group: a few unfortunates who may have achieved a certain popularity in slick paper at one time, or perhaps in the book world, but now – unable to continue meeting the excruciating demands of the 'class' editors and the 'class' public – are compelled to slide back into the pulp field from which they had once fondly imagined themselves forever emancipated.[17]

And then there are those entirely marginal writers who earned a living or a part living through writing, whose work sold regularly, who themselves were neither merely eccentric nor spurred on by simple vanity and who must be accounted for if a theory of literature is to have any meaning. In these writers can be found traits which may confirm or question the nature of the literary *per se*. By any account these writers need to be situated both in regard to the canonic and in regard to the *popularly* canonic. Excluded in *all* accounts of literature's history, disregarded by critics and usually unknown to academics such works and their authors belong to a twilit existence where their very act of writing and their publisher's commitment to market their work seem, as if by magic, to cancel by those acts their value either as books or even as products. Removed from the land of the living the readers of such books are ignored or spirited away as the 'masses'. Through such means a wider aesthetic, much cruder and racier at its margins but possibly more vigorous, is duly impoverished.

These 'invisible' writers and their forgotten publishers produced an imaginative space at once banal and luxuriant, naive and yet oddly complex. Somewhere between the written culture of the nineteenth century and the visual culture of the late twentieth, these writers act as an historical link which is also and at the same time an aesthetic link in its appeal to readers sophisticated in the media of film and television and perhaps only merely competent in the realm of the written. In the marginal world of the pulp magazine and the throwaway paperback is the essence of the imagination of our times. Far more. than in the stylistic contrivances of the modernists here exists, warts and all, the core of the modern sensorium – our imaginative life lived in the instant and the contemporary as well as the moral and the conservative.

> the pulp-created genres – science fiction, horror, private eye, Western, superhero – now dominate not only popular literature but every sort of mass entertainment, from movies and television to comic books. This legacy will remain long after the last of the pulp magazines themselves – haphazardly saved and physically unsuited for preservation – have all turned to dust.[18]

One genre above all others exists to explore the contemporary and the futuristic and here too in the interstices of the mainstream popular the marginalized writer can be found. Two such are Robert Lionel Fanthorpe and H(orace) B(owne) Fyfe and their respective books *Phenomena X* (*sic*) and *D-99* which may stand as examples both of the work of these authors and as indices of some of the issues suggested in this brief discussion.

Lionel Fanthorpe turned 60 in 1995. A resident of Cardiff, but born in Norfolk, Fanthorpe's writing career began when he was only 17 with the publication of his first novel in 1952. Contracted to publisher John Spenser, Fanthorpe was to produce considerably more than a hundred books on science fiction, fantasy and the supernatural using 17 house 'names' including John E. Muller (the name may be a corruption of Johnny Weissmuller), the one under which *Phenomena X* appeared. Indeed, most of his output appeared between 1957 and 1966 with book titles being generated by the publisher or the author, the tape machine replacing the typewriter, speed dictation (which sometimes saw a book produced within days) and a total disregard for proof-reading or professional checking. Fanthorpe's career coincides with and is an integral part of the pulp fiction publishing world in Britain in the late 1940s and early 1950s in which small-scale publishers (the 'mushroom' publishers) flourished. With an astonishing ability to produce exciting and readable ephemeral literature, Fanthorpe's works appealed to a broad, (probably young male and often working-class) readership, although they also would have appealed to more literate middle-class school boys. Stocked regularly at Smith's Station Book Stalls, such literature also sold well at seaside resorts in Britain especially as holiday or escapist reading as a recent novel by Gordon Burn, *Alma Cogan* recreates, and as the central character comments:

Books, like churches and classical music, have always made me feel turned in on myself and involuntarily gloomy. It gives me no pleasure at all to say it, but there's hardly a book that I've started at the beginning and read all the way through.

The only exceptions are the American pulps, the paperback shockers which circulated on ... long train journeys ... in the fifties. They completed my education.

Like violets, and small saucers of prawns and whelks, they were sold by men with trays around the pubs in Soho and the equivalent areas of the bigger towns, and this contributed to the sense of illicitness I always felt about them. 'Any health mags, love stories?'

I always picked them up from where they were lying in a studiedly casual way and read them with a growing feeling of guilt and a packed hotness behind the eyes. . . .

Sin Circus, Shame Slave – She knew the little tricks that fan lust in men and women. *One Hell of a Dame* – The naked story of lusty-bodied Sheila whose uncontrollable desire put her name in lights. *Resort Girl. Diamond Doll. She Had To Be Loved. Gay Scene* – Every time a man had her it was rape. But with other women it was love. Gutters of lust ran wild in this *Sex Town.*

Along with the American magazines you found on sale at some station bookstalls – *Zipp, Abandon, Caress, Hollywood Frolics* – these were titles which struck me then as a kind of concentrate of eroticism. (And recalling them now, I have to say, still give me a certain frisson.)

(chapter 4)

It comes as a surprise to find that many print runs of these cheap paperbacks were often in excess of 10 000 copies (although returns are not accounted for), such figures far exceeding the print run of 'respectable' novel-writers unless they were lucky enough to have become bestsellers. High publishing runs were normal within the pulp industry regardless of the author's name, indeed house names acted as substitutes for author's names, replacing them with *brand names* – markers of product identity, clues to a book's contents and guarantors of excitement and escape. Here the author's name is a controlled trade mark, the name of the actual author effaced in order to give them a house identity which would repay them by prolonging their writing life.

By 1966 when Fanthorpe had finished with John Spenser he had produced, under a series of names, most of their fantasy and science fiction list and he has produced to date almost 200 novels, technical works, studies of unsolved mysteries, Celtic mythology and ecclesiastical studies (Fanthorpe is an ordained priest in the Church of Wales). Much of his vast output was produced part-time when he was a teacher.

Horace Bowne Fyfe was born in Jersey City in 1918 and began his career as a pulp writer in 1940 with the publication of his first short science fiction tale for *Astounding Science-Fiction*. Thereafter he produced 60 tales, many about the 'Bureau of Slick Tricks', a terrestrial secret organization set up to defeat alien plots. The only novel he produced, *D-99* (1962) continued these tales in a light-hearted manner in which 'a host of confused, outsmarted, and frantic aliens' prove no match for human ingenuity.[19] In *D-99* aliens are all referred to as 'BEMS', shorthand for bug-eyed monsters. Unlike Fanthorpe, Fyfe produced no more stories and seems to have stopped writing soon after.

In many ways it would have been impossible for Fanthorpe to flourish without the foundations having been laid a decade previously by Fyfe and the pulp science fiction produced in the United States. Fanthorpe and others 'translated' this work into an English setting. The fascination with alien civilizations, BEMS, ray guns, technological innovation and futurology (for good or ill), flying saucers and distant galaxies was a product of and a stimulus to the notion and nature of modernity in the 1930s to 1950s: The future was engineered, technological, progressive and *endless*, tempered only during the late 1940s and 1950s by a Cold War mentality. (Could it not also be said that the propaganda of dehumanization aimed at the Soviet Union during the Cold War was at its foundation a replotting of the alien empire pulp magazine stories of the 1930s and 1940s, a re-coordination of the popular imagination?)

Behind such writers as Fyfe stood figures like John W. Campbell Jr. Technologically educated, although an unsuccessful scientist, Campbell was an enthusiast of modernity, a technocrat and a futurist. As editor of *Astounding Science-Fiction* he discouraged the 'gothic' and promoted tales in which scientific prediction had a logical imaginative setting within tales of electronic innovation, social engineering and the exploration of the possibilities of a harnessed physics. Nevertheless Campbell was intelligent enough to recognize the potential of Fritz Lieber Jr.'s satiric rethinking of the Conan tales of R.E. Howard. It is to Lieber we owe the term 'sword and sorcery'. Among Campbell's other authors could be numbered Isaac Asimov, Arthur C. Clarke, Theodore Sturgeon and A.E. Van Vogt and it is no coincidence that L. Ron Hubbard, then a successful pulp author, should first publish his ideas on *Dianetics* (space-age therapy) in the pages of Campbell's magazine.

By the mid-1950s, during the heyday of both British pulp writing and science fiction and as Lionel Fanthorpe and H.B. Fyfe were respectively pursuing their careers as authors, the very nature of the genre and its broad inclusiveness were being questioned. 'Serious' science fiction as a type of 'white' propaganda for technological change (an educational tool) would now be separated from the pulp dreams of *Phenomena X* or the Bureau of Slick Tricks: The debate reached international proportions, as Patrick Parrinder has pointed out:

> Typical of the time was a paper by the astronomer Patrick Moore which inspired a lengthy debate at the 1955 UNESCO conference on the dissemination of scientific knowledge. Moore argued that each country should set up a science fiction selection board, so that novels distinguished by 'scientific soundness' (together with a category of scientifically unsound novels thought to possess 'wholesome' qualities of literary merit) could be given a stamp of approval. If this were done, science fiction could play a useful part in the propagation of knowledge, thanks to its ability to reach readers in urgent need of instruction who seldom if ever read a factual work.[20]

By the time C.P. Snow came to give his lecture on 'the Two Cultures' writers like Fanthorpe and Fyfe had already joined the aesthetically unmentionable even within their own chosen genre: the fictionalized dreams of scientific progress. By a twist of fate the exclusion of such writers did little to promote science *within* the genre, indeed by the late 1980s: 'the aspiring science fiction writer, a contributor to *Fantasy and Science Fiction, Interzone* or *Isaac Asimov's*, is more likely to be an English teacher than a research student in physics.'[21]

Phenomena X is a ripping yarn concerning Dolores (yes, Dolores!) Foster who works in an electronics laboratory as a computer operator with her bespectacled colleague Garth (yes, Garth!) Hainforth. Walking along the road one day Dolores finds a mysterious brooch in the gutter. The brooch seems to contain within it myriad shifting patterns and she decides to wear it to a cocktail party thrown by the weirdly sinister Tony Delmont. A stranger with bizarrely translucent features takes a particular interest in the ornament and Dolores and Garth follow him home. Dolores gets too close and she and the stranger vanish through a wall. Garth finds himself arrested, convinces a government psychiatrist and a chief inspector he has not murdered Dolores and an adventure ensues in which it is shown that the mysterious stranger is an alien. Delmont and other humans, including a conniving politician, all have implants in their heads in order to obey the game rules of the 'Engineers' as they orbit (sic) the dark side of the moon. Discovered at their diabolical plans the aliens are threatened with destruction by earth missiles and agree to depart as Garth and Dolores are reunited. The story is foolishly overwritten and naive but it is also amusing and enjoyable, while if its style is unfortunate its metaphors are more satiric than incompetent, as this example suggests: 'the brooch inside her bag was as incapable of influencing her as the writings of an Oriental philosopher of the Ming dynasty whose work she had never seen.' (chapter 2)

Conversely D-99 is a competently written but dull piece in which a number of short stories are poorly woven together through the simplistic device of having them all related to a secret earth ('terran') rescue organization. The tales include a woman sentenced on a puritan planet for being too sexy (she ends up having a weightless sex scene!), a man kidnapped by aliens and implanted with a control device, a couple of space explorers shipwrecked on a planet where it is illegal to crash and an underwater explorer on a distant planet imprisoned by alien crustaceans but befriended by a telepathic fish who relays messages to the terran rescuers. It is hardly surprising that the last story is never resolved. Back on earth, the rescue organization itself has suffered a power failure and fears run high that Lydman, the mad scientist and chief gadget-maker has gone crazy. Even here, in this foolish and boring tale you are aware of a satiric self-awareness: 'What did you say?' demanded Smith. 'Telepathic? A telepathic fish? ... Don't ask us to – Well what I mean is ... well, how do you know they're reliable?' (chapter 1) Isn't that unfinished sentence aimed at the reader? The universe of bug-eyed monsters and half-civilized galaxies peopled by 'crazy savages' (chapter 3) collapses into itself and marks the limits of its own fantasy with telepathic fish.

The definition of such books by reference to concepts of formula or genre is itself often refuted by both the peculiarity of the contents and the strange direction of the narrative. Indeed, part of the nature of these books is the bizarre direction 'genre' is forced in and the unrestrained and yet clearly self-conscious and manipulative way genre boundaries are crossed and so-called formulas mixed in order to produce hybrid plots. Readers have expectations which include a desire for consistency and an unspoken request for going to the limit. Reference to formula can in these circumstances only properly be applied as a crude starting-point or mythic origin in order to explain what these books actually contain. Formula becomes for such authors a mythical point of reference in the game of mix and match.

Far from acting as a limit or restraint, the idea of a formula is merely the point of departure for the writer's imagination. While John E. Muller's, *Phenomena X* seems (from internal evidence) to be set in 1966 it makes no effort to be contemporary, rather, with its electronics boffins, satiric cocktail host, kindly chief inspector and alien humanoids it reminds the reader (and that's as strong as it gets) of a mixture of 1920s English villains, 1940s pulp science fantasy, 1950s British television police tales (especially Inspector Lockhart), late 1950s English cinema (with its endless cocktail parties, smart addresses and sports car drivers) and the vogue for alien tales (for instance *Quatermass* and *Dr Who*) – in short, it reminds but does not copy and it mixes ingredients into a tale rather more suited to Edgar Wallace or E. Phillips Oppenheim than Arthur C. Clarke or Isaac Asimov despite the publishers listing the book as science fiction.

Equally, Fyfe's *D-99* appears to have greater affinities with both the pulp smart detective tales of the 1940s (especially in the description of the office secretaries who are *all* 'babes'), and the colonial adventures of Edgar Rice Burroughs than the science fiction that is its subject matter. In its confirmed emphasis on the secret department's office routines (despite the obligatory mad scientist) the story comes closer to the contemporary (the book appeared in 1962) Hollywood and television portrayal of the corporate man as hero. Here is the world of Rock Hudson and Doris Day, *Bewitched* and *The Man from U.N.C.L.E.* The inset series of tales about the problems of interstellar travellers are sealed from this main narrative into a series of self-contained colonial adventure stories, quite able to stand outside the central narrative. But even here one is finally less reminded of Edgar Rice Burroughs than a prefiguring of a meeting between Gerry Anderson's *Thunderbirds,* or *Planet of the Apes* and Steven Lucas's *Star Wars*: colonial space opera with humanoid enemies and instant rescue facilities provided by a fabulously rich and benevolent secret organization.

Here ideas of genre are simply meaningless. This is where a theory of popular literature based on generic explanations breaks down. The revisionist chant that *all* literature is simply genre based, a chant designed to challenge canonic views is as unhelpful here as its opposite, both avoid the question of what cannot be accounted for in actual texts. That such writing may be recognizable, and therefore in some sense consistent, is only to say that consistency is one necessary factor among others in fiction, such writing being no less consistent than that of the classics.

It is equally unhelpful to shift genre definitions. Both books are labelled science fiction but neither concerns itself with the truths of science fictionalized, as it were, in the style of Arthur C. Clarke, nor are they versions of that type of space opera so consistently satirized by L. Ron Hubbard, nor for that matter are they totally of the space serial style exemplified by Flash Gordon, although both have more in common with the last type than with the previous two. This qualifies neither book as space fantasy *per se*.

These books are themselves a type of sub-branch of one sub-branch of the science fiction community. This particular route would necessarily see an unbroken line of authors and editors stretching back through the pulp magazine tradition to Hugo Gernsback, founder of *Amazing Stories* – a man dedicated to putting science (that is technological progress) into fiction. Such a 'tradition' may be said to be characteristically American with an emphasis on technology, contemporaneity and future progress – a fiction bound for the 'final frontier' and one which had a resonance even for American defence policy in the 1980s. Gernsback was to popularize what Marconi, Edison and the Wright brothers had achieved, not directly, but through an attentuated literature in which the past was left behind and science fiction was freed to explore a fantastic extrapolation from the present. In so doing Gernsback and then Campbell moved away from an earlier European science fiction tradition which had predated the pulps by many years and which was essentially *literary* in nature. Thus disengaged, science fiction changed from a variation of romantic literature into a subcultural lifestyle based on 'the future'. When Isaac Asimov dedicated *I Robot* to Campbell, who, he said, 'god-fathered the robots', he did so by ignoring the rich vein containing European tales of automata that led to the coining of the term 'Robot' in the 1920s by the brothers Čapek.

The problem of definition and explication becomes even more acute when dealing with literature that has changed its genre and status over the years. This is the case with work that falls into other categories such as propaganda or pornography but which uses the rhetorical devices of fiction. A curious example of this concerns an anonymous Canadian tract of 1836, *The Awful Disclosures of Maria Monk* which began life as a dramatized piece of anti-Catholic propaganda following Emancipation in 1829 and continued to be reprinted in 1837, 1854, 1860, 1875, 1939, 1948/49, 1965 and 1971, not as propaganda but as pornography.

The story itself is easy to summarize. Maria Monk, having been given a rudimentary education by Protestants asks her mother if she can learn French which she is taught by nuns of a local order in Montreal. Despite the fact that the nuns appear uncouth and ill-educated our heroine joins their order and thus a Monk becomes a nun! Virtually held a prisoner, Maria is forced to endure the drudgery of a nun's life until she realizes the frequent visits of the local priests are motivated by the fact that the nunnery is being used as an official Catholic brothel run by a masculine and ugly mother superior cum madam. Infanticide is the usual means of contraception, the babies' bodies disposed of in a cellar/*oubliette*. Any nun causing problems is faced with or endures torture – two nuns being held in dungeon cells – and at least one nun is tortured to death in Maria Monk's presence. This routine of violence, superstition, rape and drudgery is Monk's daily ordeal until she finally escapes to tell her tale. To relieve the dark and melodramatic atmosphere there is the character of Jane Ray, an eccentric, vulgar and violent madcap who is tolerated by the authorities for reasons never revealed.

By 1948, the Modern Fiction company's edition could boast that the book had been 'for over a hundred years ... a bestseller', the cover of this particular edition being a four-colour picture of a nun in full habit whose large emerald green eyes, plucked eyebrows and voluptuous red painted lips suggest a book at once erotic and pruriently moral, in a word: *kinky*.

Of course, the potential for erotic and kinky violence in religious bigotry has always been a recognizable feature of its central theme. These can be found in attacks on Catholicism, where nunneries become bordellos, and priests perform satanic rites, on Judaism with its supposed 'white slavery' and ritual child murder, and on Islam with the emphasis on harems and decadence. By the 1948/9 edition we are also invited by the publishers to purchase *Lolita in Soho* by Scott Morley, 'the intimate story of what happened to a young girl who fell for the illusions of security offered by a married man'. The high cover price suggests less a hardback edition than a risqué read.

No information seems to exist as to the author or authors of 'Maria Monk' whose style nevertheless suggests professional or semi-professional writers of those broadsheets, melodramas or chapbooks so popular at the time among working people in both Britain and America (See Chapter 3). This book has the sensationalism of popular expression but puts it to the service of middle-class (that is, respectable) bigotry, combining as it does the vogue for tales of exotic mayhem and gothic horror. The title itself also suggests continuity with other older forms of ephemeral tractarian literature of which 'An *Awful* [emphasis mine] Memorial of the State of Francis Spina after he turned apostasy from the Protestant Church to Popery', printed in Falkirk in 1815 stands as one example. Even the heroine's name suggests reference to 'Monk' Lewis's bestselling work.

Purporting to be a *true* account and thereby utilizing the style of the universely popular 'confessional' literature of the time, 'Maria Monk' is nevertheless a blatant forgery – a clever fiction which declares both 'what I have written is true' and all characters in this novel are entirely fictitious' (1948/9 edition). The theme itself was not a new one and the equation nunnery equals brothel is an old literary theme. Moreover, the strange and eccentric character of Jane Ray seems modelled, borrowed or plagiarized from a now lost or forgotten fictional source known to the authors yet not known by readers of 1836. The exact meaning of the character 'Jane Ray' may indeed be lost to us entirely although she is suggestive of a cross between the later figures of Nellie Dean and Crazy Jane.

An assertion that the whole book was a plagiarism was hotly refuted though an open letter published in the *Protestant Vindicator* in March 1836.

We . . . declare that the assertion, originally made in the Roman Catholic newspapers of Boston, that the book was copied from a work entitled 'The Gates of Hell Opened' is wholly destitute of foundation; it being wholly new and not copied from anything whatsoever.

The letter was signed by a number of Protestant activists: W.C. Browntree; John J. Slocum (of whom more later); A. Drew Bruce; D. Fanshaw; Amos Belden; David Werson; Thomas Hogen. These same signatories were convinced of the truthfulness of Maria Monk's tale, having met her *in person*. Who they met or what her fate was is lost to us.

Soon after the book's publication in New York it was circulating among gullible middle-class Protestant activists and ministers in both Canada and the United States. In New York it was taken up by those fearful of Irish immigration and a popish conspiracy while in Montreal it formed the basis for Anglo-Scottish fears of French superstition. By May 1836, *The Dublin Review* had refuted the book as a forgery but this did not prevent continual reprinting and trans-lation, a version in Dutch being printed in Newcastle, England, for export during 1836. The attack by the *Dublin Review* reveals the probable class of reader anticipated by the book's authors and publisher. Indeed, one can imagine the book as a basis for sermons on popish ways both in America and Britain throughout the early nineteenth century where other sensational tales of nunneries and debauchery similarly circulated (for example, the case of the Mercy Nuns of Hull in the 1850s).

The history of the book's reception is nowhere better shown than in the changes in its title. By 1948 the book was simply 'The Awful Disclosures of Maria Monk' but it had begun life as 'The Awful Disclosures of Maria Monk as exhibited in an narrative of her resi-dence of five years as a novice and two years as a Black Nun, in the Hotel Dieu Nunnery at Montreal'. In, 1837, an appendix had been added (suggestive of the original book's popularity) giving 'further disclosures of Maria Monk conerning her visit to Nun's Island' and a reply to *The Priest's Book* by J.J. Slocum who we previously met as John J. Slocum in the *Protestant Vindicator* from the spring of 1836. Re-emerging every ten years or so in new editions the book's title had been modified to 'A True Account' by 1860 but had been embellished with illustrations which were then omitted by the present century. A version printed in 1971 contained an account of the 'Ladière Case' as a further modification.

What all this suggests is that the work known as 'The Awful Disclosures of Maria Monk' was continuously subject to modifica-tion and embellishment for over a hundred years of publishing and that there is a *tradition* of reprinting and reading exemplified in this work which is undocumented and disregarded. By the twentieth century the book was read not as 'factual' Protestant propaganda but as pornographic fiction. Its own internal structure had aided this process of metamophosis. 'Maria Monk' shows us clearly that pulp fiction is a matter of *process* and that there is no clearly fixed text (although there is an *original* one) in which its essential nature can be described. Instead, the work develops, mutates and spawns over history, being both monstrous (in the nineteenth century) and almost homely (in the twentieth century).

In marked contrast to Shakespeare's work which moved from fluidity into fixity in the nineteenth century and became *the* signifier for cultural literacy for the middle classes thereafter (see Chapter 6 for the complex history and problematic status of Shakespeare), the anonymous 'Maria Monk' lost its respectability, became subject to flux and ended up acting as a signifier for a banal plebeian and titillatory eroticism. Pulp is literature as process: unfixed, illicit and 'anonymous'. Such work may thrive but will only have a half life (that is, as a form of recognized fiction) because of its unclassifiable nature.

'Maria Monk' is marketed as pornography or religious tract – it is all one, as the book is both these things simultaneously as well as being an 'autobiography' and a gothic novel. The book is hardly a candidate for critical applause and one need not treat it with respect either as good art (which it is not – except as a convincing tale) or good pulp (it is neither very erotic nor very exciting – the narrative is virtually non-existent). However, the book's presence and longevity does demand our attention because it has enjoyed longer continuous production than many popular classics and its aesthetic outlook acts as a bridge between respectable genres and disreputable genres – the gothic and the pornographic. It is these 'bridge' texts that rarely get attention and yet which force us again to reconsider concepts of a formal and aesthetic nature (style and genre) as well as resiting the nature of the literary.

Maria Monk was the nineteenth century equivalent of Linda Lovelace, her book is a pornographic adventure: what do you do with a problem like Maria? Adverts at the back of the 1948/9 edition offer for sale Edwin J. Henri's *Kiss of the Whip* which for 25s. (twenty-five shillings) presents: 'a veritable cavalcade of notorious methods of self-abasement and corporal punishment – particularly with the *whip*.' Alternatively there was *Erotic Love* by 'Sardi' a snip at 30s. (thirty shillings) in which, 'Individual orgies, such as those of the Marquis de Sade and Jack the Ripper, send a chill down one's spine, reminding one that many a man is but the victim of "a twisted nerve, a ganglion gone awry".' These two books could be purchased 'post free' alongside *Your Destiny* and *Astrology and Sex* or 'How the Stars Control your Sex Life'.

Steven Marcus has suggested the way nineteenth-century pornography operated and in so doing he is able to expose some of the rhetorical structures of 'Maria Monk'. Marcus tells us that: 'Pornography . . . typically undertakes to represent itself not as a story or fantasy but as something that "really" happened.'[22] He then continues:

> Pornography, as I have mentioned earlier, moves ideally away from language. In its own way, and like much modern literature, it tries to go beneath and behind language; it tries to reach what language cannot directly express but can only point toward, the primary processes of mental energy. This is a partial explanation of why pornography is also the home of the forbidden, tabooed words. These are the stubborn, primitive words of the language; . . . The very deadness of much of the language of pornography, even its clichés and meaninglessness in a verbal sense, demonstrate to us that its meaning is to be found in some other area. . . . Its intention is, rather, unmetaphoric and literal; its aim is to *de-elaborate* the verbal structure and the distinctions upon which it is built, to move back through language to that part of our minds where all metaphors are literal truths, where everything is possible.[23]

On one level this appears to pinpoint the pornographic nature of 'Maria Monk', it certainly catches the nature of the *culture* the book exists within, nevertheless, at the risk of becoming pedantic, these comments miss the essential *avoidances* of the text. At each and every point of erotic contact, the mechanics of such contact are replaced by either lacunae or by a secondary discourse of violence and incarceration. An example of such description is offered with regard to Jane Ray.

> I received a great shock one day when entering the room for the Examination of Conscience, for I saw a Nun hanging head downwards by a cord from a ring in the ceiling. Her clothes were kept in place by a leather strap tied around them, and her head was some distance from the floor. Her face was dark and swollen by

the rush of blood; her hands were tied and her mouth was stopped by a large gag. It was Jane Ray.

This is itself followed by a comment put in the mouth of Maria Monk but too knowledgeable to be something she could have known: 'I could not help noticing how similar this punishment was to those of the Inquisition.'

Such writing hovers *between* fiction and pornography and acts as a primitive bridge between the two: a type of pseudo-pornography born out of gothic prejudice. In this culturally ignored backwater all literature becomes anonymous, processed and fluid. Here the expected boundaries of fiction and of pornography are breached and the fixity of print disestablished.

Here, in these texts is displayed the essential instability in a system which is fluid and protean. The creation of a stable canon was a necessary component of this system, an attempt to codify and taxo-nomize an anarchic situation. Thus the canon was entirely artificial and entirely necessary – an attempt to retrieve the personal and communal from the social. The canon is *the* determinant in a system which allows the self-validation of hierarchy but at the same time provides an escape mechanism (the refusal of legitimation) for the vast majority of printed material. In the offensive against the canon, academics have not 'opened' the canon to fresh air but made the canon itself the mere product of socio-pathology. The needs of the canon (which are dealt with in detail later) defined an area for debate which gave a language to pulp while refusing it a voice. What we need to do now is retrieve pulp *without* reference to the canon and thereby avoid a debate in which definition is already decided. Pulp literature demarcates that fluidity, protean nature and simple abundance in language in which excess is key. The canon allows us to see clearly why pulp was historically excluded and made as 'other' but it also allows us through such grounding to comprehend pulp's social, cultural and *aesthetic* functions in *their own right* and conditioned by their own productive and consumptional complexity. Blinded by distaste for the canon, liberal- and left-wing critics have failed to assimilate the popular arts that they tend to distrust: pulp is inherently unstable and this is pulp's power and why it is feared.

The vast majority of writers who had to earn their living by writing, that is proletarianized writers, were, and are, part of that congruence of money, work and art and are always the victims of canonizing and exclusion. The voices of writers, mostly working class it should not be forgotten, thus doubly excluded, equals the denial of a real living history (messy, contradictory, problematic) represented by the world of publishing and authorship. Most critics simply recreate the canon in mirror form. This has nothing to do with retrieving the half-forgotten history of pulp and its aesthetic conditions. It again simplifies history and art and ignores the archeological recovery required if we are to do justice to real men and women who earned their livelihoods through printed artefacts and who contributed to a significant portion of the information media. To do so is simply to seal the coffin twice. To rediscover these voices is to find a scandal by scandalous methods.

The circumstances surrounding the creation of the modern canon were such that various interest groups – some establishment and others opposed to the establishment – were able to agree on the conversion of Arnoldian ethical propositions into Wildesque functional propositions. 'Is it right' was corrected into 'is it well done'. This movement, modernistic in temperament, led anti-establishment figures such as F.R. Leavis, for instance, in the 1930s, to look to a canon antithetical to upper-class interests. In separating the divisions of fiction, which he saw as the supremely democratic medium, he attacked the control of culture by upper middle-class interests at Cambridge, and especially those of Bloomsbury.

Whether defending or refusing democratic reading rights, canonic creation managed to turn political and ethical issues into aesthetic issues. The question of the canon is in essence an ethical question determined by moral right. Thus canonic texts could both widen and control access to Literature (*not* access to literacy or access to ordinary print forms which circulated regardless). Such control coincided with the progressive appearance of Great Books programmes in the United States and the origins of the Norton Anthology. Such programmes consolidated a certain history of America, as the widening of the educational programme in Great Britain coincided with the explosion of pulp literature but acted to suppress it or ignore it in favour of an undeclared great books 'Eng Lit' programme. In the United States this trajectory was activated by the influence of such factors as the movement of Blacks into Northern cities, mass peasant immigration from middle Europe and fear of White degeneration. In Britain it coincides rather with a widening franchise spearheaded by a consensus politics more and more in the moral and cultural hands of a lower middle class distrustful of other groups and anxious to claim the moral ground of culture. Corporate capitalism and welfare statism both helped create the grounds of cultural debate. Art's moral focus would now be the necessary depiction of the *real*: all else would be sacrificed, not only on moral, but on aesthetic grounds – bad art would be bad for your health – a point already being made in the 1920s on both sides of the Atlantic.

A later chapter on taste will detail some of the essential history and characteristics of canon-making and the cultural debate that followed. Now it is sufficient to note that the creation of a modern canon coincided with the appearance first of a protean new print medium based on industrial production, intensive capital investment and monopolistic practices (themselves parasitically preying on entrepreneurial inventiveness), which gave way to a further information explosion with the appearance of photography, cinema, radio and television vertically and horizontally integrated into the previous print culture. The result was cultural confusion and lost social coherence of a sort unexpected and unwelcome by many:

Our emergent world society, with its particular qualities of speed, mobility, mass production and consumption, rapidity of change and innovation, is the latest phase of an ongoing cultural and social revolution. It has few historical precedents as a cultural context. Industrial technologies, now approaching global scale, linked to an attendant multiplicity of new communication channels, are producing a planetary culture whose relation to earlier forms is as Vostok or Gemini to a wheeled cart. World communications, whose latest benchmark is Telstar. . . . This interpenetration, rapid diffusion and replication is most evident in the position of fine art in the new continuum. Transference through various modes changes both form and content – the new image can no longer be judged in the previous canon. The book, the film of the book, the book of the film, the musical of the film, the TV or comic strip version of the musical – or however the cycle may run – is, at each stage, a transmutation which alters subtly the original communication. These transformative changes and diffusions occur with increasing rapidity. Now, in the arts, an avant garde may only be 'avant' until the next TV news broadcast or issue of '*Time/Life/Espresso*'. Not only pop but op, camp and super-camp styles and 'sub-styles' have an increasingly immediate circulation, acceptance and 'usage' whose feedback directly influences their evolution. We might formally say that they become 'academic' almost as they emerge, but this notion of academy versus avant-garde élites is no longer tenable, and may take its place with the alienated artist and other myths.[24]

The denial of legitimacy to certain forms of publishing, authorship, subject matter and reading practice left reading habits little changed in reality – what changed was educational practice and *the allowable limits of debate*. The other of the canon was pulp and pulp was also its bastard offspring.

The pulp purchaser was now the same as the enthusiast of industrialized artefacts – mass men and women were transformed into *Kitsch-mensch*, the *Untermenschen* of urban life. The result was a denial both of the modern, of the manufactured and of the multiple – a point made explicit in Walter Benjamin's famous essay 'The Work of Art in the Age of Mechanical Reproduction' of 1936. Pulp, like kitsch, was the worst pandering to an infantilized, sentimentalized, blind consumption; narcissistic and vicious. For Harold Rosenberg 'There [was] no counterpart to kitsch. Its antagonist is not an idea [i.e. art] but reality'.[25]

For Herman Broch, kitsch lovers are born of Romantic extreme narcissism and industrial abundance – comfort and sentiment and conformity all become symptoms of individualism (rather ironically) and the neurotic. The religious impulse ends for Gillo Dorfles in the fetishism of empty objects. For Clement Greenberg, pulp as a form of kitsch is a 'rudimentary culture' which imitates in empty form the 'genuine' effects of high culture:

If the avant garde imitates the processes of art, kitsch, we now see, imitates its effects. The neatness of this antithesis is more than contrived; it corresponds to and defines the tremendous interval that separates from each other two such simultaneous cultural phenomena as the avant garde and kitsch. This interval, too great to be closed by all the infinite gradations of popularized 'modernism' and 'modernistic' kitsch, corresponds in turn to a social interval, a social interval that has always existed in formal culture, as elsewhere in civilized society, and whose two termini converge and diverge in fixed relation to the increasing or decreasing stability of the given society. There has always been on one side the minority of the powerful – and therefore the cultivated – and on the other the great mass of the exploited and poor – and therefore the ignorant. Formal culture has always belonged to the first, while the last have had to content themselves with the folk or rudimentary, culture or kitsch.[26]

This rudimentary culture is a second level reality but a reality which points away from the 'truth' towards an empty factuality – it coincides with journalism and conformity. If kitsch, and therefore, pulp fiction, equal falsehood, then it is because they aim at effect not reality. They aim to make beautiful not make more 'real'. Broch argues that, 'In science and art alike the important thing is the creation of new expressions of reality.'[27] Indeed, he goes further in arguing,

Kitsch is certainly not 'bad art'; it forms its own closed system, which is lodged like a foreign body in the overall system of art, or which, if you prefer, appears alongside it. . . . The enemy within, however, is more dangerous than these attacks from outside: every system is dialectically capable of developing its own anti-system and is indeed compelled to do so.[28]

Kitsch is a cancer within the aesthetic appreciated by people who form themselves into cultural and social viruses. But bio-medical social analogies are thrust aside for quasi-theological ethical considerations.

[A]n ethical system cannot do without conventions . . . Can the same be said of a life inspired by kitsch? The original convention which underlies it is exaltation, or rather hypocritical exaltation, since it tries to unite heaven and earth in an absolutely false relationship.[29]

From such musings Broch concludes pulp/kitsch to be a 'neurotic [i.e. unhealthy] work of art' and that one expression of it, radio, is 'a volcano vomiting a continuuous spout of imitation music'.[30] His conclusion: universal neurosis and spiritual death.

What underlaid these fears, played out against totalitarianism in Europe, the Far East and elsewhere was that pulp was the cynical, conspiratorial link between corporate capitalism and state monopoly

capitalism. As in the paradoxes of Orwell's *1984*, slavery was freedom and escapism was true conformity. This concern was founded
on fears regarding the State's possible total control of information,
whether in the United States, Britain or Russia, and that this *exter-
nalization* of control was effected through the manipulation of *ephemera* constituted in an ever-elongated contemporaneity. Now, 'now'
lasted forever and history was at an end: Yet, as J.A. Sutherland has
pointed out with regard to modern publishing and reading habits,

> In fact culture would seem to be more resilient and resourceful
> than we habitually take it to be. Indices of production and con-
> sumption have all multiplied, rival media have installed them-
> selves, without the feared collapses. The reading public has not
> been reduced to the condition of denatured Epsilons; nor has it
> stratified as it should have done to fulfil pessimistic prophecies.
> These facts have lent strength to more recently fashionable theo-
> ries which oppose gloom and argue that the problem of the fu-
> ture will not be cultural regimentation in a consumer manipulating
> society, but the bewildering diversities and cultural opportuni-
> ties of a post-industrial, technocentric world.[31]

Such pluralism in reading habits needed not merely new packaging
but new ways of understanding print consumption.
    In 1935, Allen Lane launched Penguin. Penguin Books continued
a tradition of good quality books at cheap prices: quality content
yet inexpensive packaging. As yet, in Britain, cheap was not exactly
nasty.

> Yet Penguins needed the most aggressive and Americanised of
> the multiple stores to break into the market. They needed mass
> sales, above the bestseller threshold (13,000–17,000 was the initial
> break-even range; Lane calculated that he would need an annual
> volume sale of 2 million. . . . And they exploited a new, techno-
> logically transformed kind of book.[32]

Pulp publication was in every sense except expectations based on
similar concepts of production (if not economies of scale) and newspapers and paperbacks of all sorts were the *sine qua non* of mass
reading habits.
    The publishing revolution brought about by Allen Lane did not
occur spontaneously; other British companies had experimented with

limp-cover or paper-cover books of which Heinemann (challenging the monopoly held by Tauschnitz) and Hodder & Stoughton (who were producing a large format paperback series as early as 1905) were leading examples. 'Heinemann had even set up a separate company to do so with co-directors Bram Stoker (*Dracula*), Arthur Waugh (Evelyn's father) and W.L. Courtney (a leading journalist) and even this company had the precedent of Hutchinson's 6d. (sixpenny) 'Blacks' of the previous century (in which such leading authors as Charles Garvice appeared) and limp or paper-cover books produced sporadically in the United States by publishers such as Arthur Westbrook in Cleveland.[33]

Lane's genius was one of *application* and American publishers were not slow to relearn the marketing and packaging techniques Lane borrowed. In 1939, Robert De Graff founded Pocket Books based on the Penguin concept, mixing popular and classic titles, soon others followed: Popular Library (1942); Dell (1943); Bantam (1945); Graphic (1948); Pyramid (1949); Lion (1949); Checker (1949); New American Library (1949) which was Penguin's own US imprint.[34]

From now on fiction and other human interest material would feed directly into paperback production, just as it had done previously with the pulp magazines which paperbacks had mainly replaced by the 1940s. Aggressive marketing, lurid covers, violent and erotic stories about money, drugs, the city, teenage delinquents, mobsters and action combined with a very low price gave these paperbacks as air of sleaze, and cheap soon stood for nasty. Many pulp authors transferred their loyalties to paperbacks and for a decade the paperback ambivalently represented good reading at cheap prices and 'cheap' reading at low prices.

The paperback author remained resolutely on the edge of that 'sensationalism' which had been so noticed by nineteenth-century commentators and which was the constant target of the censor's vilification. But the paperback pulp author also united the exposé of the earlier muckraking journalist with the exploitative fictionalizing of the pulp-magazine writer. Just as the censorious were shocked by the revealing nature of the paperback so the paperback itself traded on shocking revelations; journalism and fictional authorship both rewrote and yet also reported the banality of 1940s and 1950s America. This introduction, for instance, to *The Man Who Rocked the Boat* (1956) (later renamed *Slaughter on 10th Avenue* (1961)), a book about New York assistant district attorney Bill Keating, begins,

I believe many readers will be *shocked* by the *revelations* in this book. It is an 'inside' story in every sense of the word, based on a remarkable man's experiences as an assistant district attorney and as counsel to the private, citizen-supported New York City Anti-Crime Committee. I find it *far more exciting than any fictional detective thriller* I have ever read, because it deals in reality. Bill Keating has resisted the temptation to romanticize or *sensationalize*. The facts of his career are *sensational* enough.

(Emphasis mine.)

This is the *ante* in the age of Spillane, in which Spillane competed with the revelation and the exposé.

Spillane's early novels, with their libido, violence and gangsterism were both a commentary and a pulp prophesy. When John Kennedy was assassinated by unknown gunmen it seemed to confirm the existence of a gigantic and hidden conspiracy involving gangsters ('The Mafia' now steps onto the stage), the red menace (Lee Harvey Oswald), union corruption (Jimmy Hoffa) and paranoid secret agencies (The CIA); Kennedy's death and the subsequent revelations about his libidinous adventures (especially with Marilyn Monroe) reconstituted the nature of the office of president and in so doing confirmed the growing cult of *celebrity*.

The older interest in the extraordinary nature of the banal had been noticed as early as the 1880s by Matthew Arnold in his comments on the American Press.

> The Americans used to say to me that what they valued was news, and that this their newspapers gave them. I at last made the reply: 'Yes, news for the servants' hall!' I remember that a New York newspaper, one of the first I saw after landing in the country, had a long account, with the prominence we should give to the illness of the German Emperor or the arrest of the Lord Mayor of Dublin, of a young woman who had married a man who was a bag of bones, as we say, and who used to exhibit himself as a skeleton; of her growing horror in living with this man, and finally of her death. All this in the most minute detail, and described with all the writer's powers of rhetoric. This has always remained by me as a specimen of what the Americans call news.[35]

This interest in the bizarre nature of the ordinary, which had been the mainstay of mass publishing and had become enshrined in such papers as *The News of the World* and magazines such as *Reader's Digest* was now paralleled by a fascination with the bizarre nature of the celebrity, libidinous, wealthy and corrupt, connected with power (finance/politics) and with Hollywood, dead too soon, by violence either accidental (Jayne Mansfield's decapitation in a car crash; James Dean's 'haunted' Porsche); self-administered (Marilyn Monroe's nude suicide; Judy Garland's death in a toilet bowl); or by assassin (John Kennedy; Bobby Kennedy). Kennedy's death was history re-enacted as pulp fiction, a Technicolor world (remember the Zapruder tapes) of lasciviousness and violence in Camelot.

The world of the celebrity also narrowed the gap between the bizarre and the banal (the two extremes of reality). Whereas previously the interest had always focused on the revelation of weirdness just below the surface of normalcy (the banal as extraordinary – a type of transmogrification of the mundane), now the bizarre was merely ordinary. By the late twentieth century, New York had become its own pulp scenario, superseding Spillane, in a hyperreal displacement of the imagination. 'I've been doing crime work a while, and I've been doing it in New York a while, and New York stories are just so off the wall, so crazy – the mayhem is beyond belief.' Such were the thoughts of the Deputy City Editor on the New York *Daily News* in the late 1980s – the pulp fiction atmosphere duly brought out by the use of 'mayhem', recalling the machine-gun mayhem of 1920s Chicago.[36]

The market which provided a living for Spillane later buoyed up the work of Generoso Pope Jr. A graduate of MIT and a Cold-War warrior in the US psychological warfare programme, Pope bought the New York *Enquirer* in 1952.[37] With a change of name to the *National Enquirer*, circulation increased from 17 000 to one million on a diet of violence, gore and the bizarre. This was a paper devoted to an almost Fortean view of human nature and a presentation at once horror comic, Spillane novel and *Twilight Zone*. Fictional pulp which had dealt in the self-same subjects had now been replaced by reality *as* pulp: an endless carnival of the extreme.

> Pope based his appeal on the public's prurient interest in violence. [He combined] the world of bizarre and horrific tales of shark attacks, decapitation, white slavery, . . . lunatics, and the occasional . . . special.[38]

Nevertheless by 1967, 'the newspaper had passed reluctantly from the profitable "gore era" into a kind of schizoid phrase which incorporated a bit of the old tried-and-true horror with personal beauty tips, celebrity chit-chat and reader-oriented human interest stories'.[39]

With the market's obsession with television stars and the sales-stand in the supermarket guaranteeing a captive female audience, the *National Enquirer* soon took off, backed by the new tabloid style of British emigré journalists weaned on crime, sex and celebrity – a mixture intrinsically British since the founding of papers such as the *News of the World* in the previous century. By 1991, S.J. Taylor could point out:

> The only genuine profit centres left today in the American press are 'the supermarket tabloids' – bizarre hybrids which combine magazine layout and design with investigative news gathering techniques. To a large extent, they have been manned [sic] by Brits, imported either by the late Generoso Pope in Florida or by Rupert Murdoch operating out of New York. In unsynchronized movement, and with the full cooperation of Hollywood's 'hype' machine, the supermarket tabloids succeeded in inventing and exporting the cult of celebrity that encircles the globe today. It is the last outpost of the tabloid mentality in the US . . .[40]

Yet, for Taylor, the message is also positive, for her the tabloids prevent conformism, complacency and conformity, an attitude refreshingly opposed to the orthodoxies one expects. 'The lesson from America is that, without the tabloids and their spirit of irreverence, the press becomes a bastion of conformity'.[41]

The gap between reality and fiction is closed and widened, a ploy successfully used again and again in both popular fiction and journalism and one in which the everyday is seen as both inconsequentially dull and mind bendingly bizarre *all at once*, with the ephemerality of the paperback mirroring in its very form the transience and also the essential nature of the society it serves.

What shocked in the paperback's form was the knowledge that printed material (of whatever nature) was now transient, ephemeral, trivial, without history or a future, disposable, degradable, escapist and *anonymous*; neither Shakespeare nor Tolstoy was spared and Shakespeare was now as available and as disposable (because of the very form in which 'He' was packaged) as any 'hack' writer of science fantasy or crime fiction. What shocked was the very *lack* of hierarchy, the free-for-all refusal to differentiate through packaging, marketing or purchaser. Printed fiction had begun in a mercantile age and the age of mass reading had confirmed that literature from the eighteenth century onwards was always essentially a commodity at the heart of which lay an unresolvable ambivalence over the nature of creativity, authorship, imagination and genius.

The two, product and producer, could never be disentangled but they were always required to exist in mutual antagonism (many paperback authors stood for principals opposed to the very commodity they helped produce). What paperbacks did for a brief period between the 1940s and 1950s was to conflate this antagonism: authorship again became anonymous, quixotic – simple labour. The mystique was removed and it threatened every sector with its violence. Moral outrage and social concern recognized not a refertilizing of the literary imagination *from below*, nurtured in the pre-war pulp magazines but, rather, a decadence in which print was unrestrained and unclassifiable. The containment of paperbacks was in the final analysis not a cultural cauterizing but a type of quartering in which morality may have won a spurious victory but art and creativity were partially lobotomized, brought in line with an authoritarian but paranoid age.

It is ironic therefore that when George Orwell was finishing *1984* during the paper shortages and import bans on print of the post-war years, a whole new print industry had grown up in Britain, which forged the modern publishing of paperbacks and which, consumed by print-starved ordinary people, helped widen, cheapen and democratize reading habits in the UK, a fact which most standard histories of publishing elide or ignore. That the initial impulse for a new mass market was not the sudden withdrawal of American pulp offerings after the war but was, rather, the appearance of quality paperback printing before the war began is ironic. Far from being totalitarian such offerings as British post-war pulp and American pre-war pulp were anarcho-capitalist, anti-establishment and popular.

Pulp consensus was now at the heart of democratic culture-making and decision-taking.

3

Turning the World Round: The Print Revolution

Raymond Chandler was a Victorian. To be exact, his youthful aspirations and ideals were formed in England, at Norwood in South London with his mother, grandmother and aunts in genteel middle-class surroundings and at Dulwich College for Boys, designed to prepare middle-class males for a professional and civil-service life serving the Empire. A.E.W. Mason, author of *The Four Feathers*, had taught at Dulwich College and its headmaster was A.H. Gilkes. Chandler began school there a year before Victoria's death, some forty years before his first novel. An aspiring poet and satirist he learnt those late Victorian verities and inherited those late Victorian doubts that later emerged in his fiction. Schooled in English history, passing the civil service Classics exams with extraordinary ability, Chandler was the model of an English gentleman, bred of the Edwardian rapprochement with its immediate past.[1]

When Chandler began writing it was this inheritance that returned in an American context. Marlowe, originally named Malory after the author of *Le Morte Darthur*, that quintessential influence on the image of the gentleman in the Victorian age (think of Tennyson or Morris) is an Arthurian knight (looking for Mrs *Grayle* and the *Lady in the Lake*) who smokes a pipe, wears pyjamas, acts graciously towards women, believes in honour, plays chess and looks nostalgically backward to a golden age. Like Chandler, Marlowe is reserved, fastidious and élitist.

A product of an English education and an American lifestyle, Chandler was a true product of the late nineteenth century and early twentieth – oilman and novelist, corporate executive and gentleman. In this sense, Chandler was the perfect late Victorian contradiction and his famous detective adventurer reworks that contradiction in print. Marlowe lives on the edge – he is a relic of the late Victorians' legacy to the Edwardians – a thoroughly modern character whose first-person narrative (itself reinvented in late

Victorian adventure fiction) echoes Matthew Arnold's worst fears about democracy: if not looking on Dover Beach, then on the worst of Los Angeles and Bay City, the 'remnant' could say with Chandler 'I have lived my life on the edge of nothing'.[2]

The crime novel seems an apt vehicle for someone for whom modern democratic man is either utterly alone or utterly criminal and the first-person narrative an appropriate vehicle for the doubting voice which both upholds old-fashioned certainties and knows that they have not merely passed but never really existed. This is the voice of the nineteenth century, a voice often both startling and unfamiliar – it is a voice without anchor: a voice on the edge.

This excursion into the work of Raymond Chandler should serve to remind us of the breadth of the term Victorianism and of its consequences. If the railway is at the centre of Victorian modernity then the aeroplane is a consequence of the restlessness of that century: much of the modern world having come into being in the last century is still around us and still part of our daily lives – refined perhaps, perhaps disguised. Indeed, it may be argued that the uprisings of 1968 were the last moment of a Victorian belief in radical change, psychological and existential longing and a socialist and Marxist dialectic based upon Germanic idealism and a belief in liberation through struggle. This takes us to the heart of the matter – the Victorian age was an age dominated by the radical disestablishment of an older sensibility and a continuing revolution in another and newer sensibility which lasted until 1968.

Through looking at Victorian literary publishing, purchasing and reading habits we can see the appearance of a new literary sensibility produced by, and a consequence of, market forces and commodity production. Here the book is both product and work of art, decided both by unit cost and critical taste, an object of purchase and a process of reading. Books were not new, fiction was not new, what was new was the emergence of new fictions, new types of books and a new reading public. The novel and short story (the tale), poem and journalistic essay were the creation and driving force behind new ways of perceiving in a literate democracy.

In this way, a new information industry emerged which coincided with the world of entertainment, bringing with it new forms of professionalism (authors and publishers), new distributive networks

(Smith and Mudie) and new forms of presentation (part publications, three-deckers, serials). The power of widening literacy and
the emergent market-driven literary world created a demand for
new forms of expression and therefore new forms of content – the
woman's question and the demands of women readers created the
content of many works whose structure was designed to optimize
the potential sales from new areas of representation.

The field was volatile and expansive. A greatly expanded industry brought about a new meaning to representation. The forms of
this new literature were created experimentally in the crucible of
a market constantly testing its products until it could stabilize
not merely the product's form but the ways such form could be
consumed. Once established, these products were again quickly
destabilized by the publishing demands of newly discovered publics
whose reading habits and purchasing ability aided the pursuit of
both publishing profits and product excellence but also led publishers to create different aesthetic forms and different artistic subjects.
New readers were found as the forms developed to *make visible*
otherwise invisible subject areas (the genres of horror, detective or
science fiction). Forms and contents, authors and publishers, readers and markets emerged together to create the literature of the
nineteenth century. As such this history is one not only of process
and change, but above all one where there are moments of uncertainty in an alliance between profit and art, democracy and
modernity. Victorian literature was conditioned by exploration and
uncertainity.

Novelty dominated Victorian literature; the literary arts were
firmly rooted in, indeed one *condition of*, the Victorian entrepreneurial business spirit. To talk of *Victorian literature* is, as the Victorians well knew, to fantasize about a stable entity and therein a
set of fictitious stable values. Victorian literature was conditioned
by doubt (the gamble of the market) and was determined by doubt
(the moral dimension of the narrative). Furthermore, its shape was
also determined by doubt. Victorian literary production and consumption owed its vitality to this doubt, this instability in the very
conditions of its making. The growth of Victorian reading and the
extraordinary momentum of the publishing machine were the uncontrollable virus of Victorian liberal democracy. The authority of
the printed word was guaranteed by its ungrounded nature in
democratic (and therefore unpredictable) mass reading habits. It

was the triumph of Victorian reading and publishing that they were both eclectic and protean and it was the tragedy of Victorian literature that the authors, publishers, academics and critics who were made by this new world also sought to hierarchize it, restrict it, stabilize it and divide it: in a word, to tame the very forces that made Victorian literature come alive.

At the beginning of the nineteenth century the concept of a vast reading public and a publishing industry would have been little more than a dream to contemporaries: relatively few published books existed; fewer were published each year; fiction was rare and read by only a few; libraries were even rarer and expensive; distribution was virtually impossible while travel was dominated by poor roads; publishing houses were still mainly printers; authors, as yet mainly unrecognized, were undervalued and disorganized.

By the third quarter of the century this situation had completely changed. New printing techniques emerged as publishing houses grew in size and sloughed off their old printing associations while incorporating new business attitudes. Marketing and distribution became possible with the appearance of trains, railway bookshops, library purchase and the ubiquitous bagmen; passengers could now read in a train compartment whereas before the coach was simply too shaky. Added to this, the power of authorship had grown, allowing some to grow rich in the trade because of the vast increase in the consumption of fiction and newsprint encouraged by and part of a new mass literacy. This also spawned new markets especially in children's literature and magazines for adults. As markets grew they split and created specialist genres both in fiction and in the appearance of hobby or sport journals. Finally authorship became a professional business about to be protected by an author's union: the Society of Authors. If at worst it was a free-for-all, at its best this protean growth meant that the English-speaking world, both sides of the Atlantic and beyond was one that read and discussed the central issues of industrial democracy. As such the trade in information and in books (including piracies) was truly international.

Louisa May Alcott's *Little Women* stands as a perfect example of the evolution of the novel. Published in 1868 it was read by adults and children in England familiar with American prose since the success of *Uncle Tom's Cabin* which had arrived in 1852 and been bought by Mudies and others in such considerable quantities that it soon passed the million-seller mark. At the time, the question of abolition had been *the* moral issue for British readers of all ranks. Thus American political issues were already British moral conundrums.

Alcott's book is a veritable encyclopaedia of the evolution of the novel form from its early days in Walter Scott and Charlotte Yonge to its development by Dickens. Encased in chapter headings and moral reminders borrowed and adapted from Bunyan, Alcott manages to incorporate not only Shakespeare (*Hamlet* and *Macbeth*) but also Richard Brinsley Sheridan and Fanny Burney as well as *Undine and Sintram*, which so influenced Newman and the Oxford Movement; but here too are large numbers of contemporary authors central to the development of fiction. Into *Little Women* come the already mentioned Charlotte Yonge and her *Heir of Redclyffe** (chapter 3); Sir Walter Scott's *Ivanhoe* (chapter 5); *Uncle Tom's Cabin* (chapter 4); *Vanity Fair* via both Thackeray and Bunyan (chapter 9); Dickens's *Pickwick Papers* (chapter 10) and *Great Expectations* (chapter 11) and Elizabeth Wetherell's *The Wide, Wide World* (chapter 11). To add to this, references are made to novel-reading, poems are written by the sisters and plays of a melodramtic and gothic nature produced. At the very end Alcott points to the contemporaneity of her chosen genre:

> So grouped, the curtain falls upon Meg, Jo, Beth, and Amy. Whether it ever rises again, depends upon the reception given to the first act of the *domestic drama* called
> LITTLE WOMEN
> (chapter 23; italics mine)

Far from being unaware, this writing is self-conscious and only too aware of the evolution, importance and development of the novel both as entertainment, art and moral instrument. Moreover, this is a work calling for a new market – young people's reading, and, as here, the domestic novel for young people was aimed at women. Thus central to the evolution and uncertainties of the nature of fiction was the equally uncertain moral education of a household of women, left to define themselves during the American Civil War.

---

* Accredited by some as being the first women's romance.

The definitions of women's roles and the fictional form in which their roles were dramatized and rehearsed were inexorably linked: the publishers answer to the first being the structural answer to the second. It is no coincidence that Jo wants to be a journalist and her frustrations as an emerging adult (which mirror her mother's) are as 'unresolved' as the 'clear' moral of this edifying Christian text. The irresolvable nature of the moral may be linked then to the required subject of the novel – the domestic setting. What is meant by a Christian moral and therefore a proper role for women is as unresolved as what is meant by a novel and its true subject – in moving from Bunyan through Charlotte Yonge and temperance tract to Dickens, Alcott's book, in its very structure, tends toward secular action: neither its subject matter nor its temperance roots can return it to Bunyanesque allegory. The novel refuses its allegorical role in the pursuit of the secular fact. From whence did this instability *and* power emerge?

Although publishers, printers and booksellers all existed before the turn of the century it was the new rationalisation of these areas plus the appearance of new forms of print enterprise and new methods of selling printed material to an expanded reading public that marked the emergence and domination of fiction and newsprint.

The case of fiction is instructive. Without the monopolistic control of Mudie and his library system and W.H. Smith and his sales system working in alliance with the publishing houses of John Murray, George Routledge, Chapman & Hall and many others the very *shape* and form of fiction would have been different. The importance of the three-decker novel to the industry and to Mudie's, the appearance of the serial form through Chapman & Hall and the new reading matter (part work or short novel) aimed at train commuters and pioneered by Routledge (in order to avoid Mudie), made the imaginative space which determined the *art* of the novel. This cannot be ignored. The art of the novel, even that of George Eliot and especially that of Charles Dickens, was a product of a commercial alliance which was rarely other than productive.

Publishers had since the late eighteenth century been reorganizing their businesses in such a way that they may be taken as the first great appearance of the capitalistic method of production. It should not be forgotten that Benjamin Franklin, Max Weber's archetypical proto-capitalist, was both a publisher and a printer. Through legal, administrative and technological changes, the primitive proto-capitalist publisher/printers of the previous century had by the nineteenth transformed themselves into modern businesses, although it is also true that, until the 1870s, publishers that had not evolved could still flourish

The new middle-class entrepreneurial (gentleman) publishers succeeded because of their willingness to learn from the older, more primitive popular printer/publisher entrepreneurs whose family businesses stretched back, at least in spirit, to Tudor times. It was from these crude presses that almost all working people gained their reading material in the form of broadsheets and chapbooks – a literature that died out only in the 1870s and which, as children's publishing, had a half-century of life longer.

Such businesses, although organized on a small scale in terms of management and productive functions, were able to pour out vast amounts of printed material: fiction, half-fiction and news, which covered the printing of popular 'folk' tales, confessional crime, reports of superstitions and the supernatural, of recent battles, of births, marriages and royal scandals, as well as reprinting jokes, anecdotes and comments on political questions. Many chapbooks (folded and cut to produce 24-page booklets) contained a mixture of topics, fillers and woodcuts. Stories were recycled, 'true' tales invented, true confessions made up; the emphasis almost always was to make stories *contemporary*; history, as the rural past, was never popular, the popular subjects being up-to-date sex, crime and murder.[3] The result was a thriving popular publishing industry in which there was no discernible difference either philosophically or commercially between fact and fiction.[4] Such publications flourished both sides of the Atlantic and if tales of Robin Hood were mutually enjoyed by Americans, so tales of Indians, scalpings and abduction also enjoyed popularity with the British working population.[5]

Fiction fed fact and both fed profits. Seduction and betrayal, a central theme of gothic and popular fiction, gave structure to the true crimes of men like William Corder whose murder of Maria Marten at the Red Barn in Suffolk and subsequent trial, confession and execution in 1828 led to a veritable orgy of fascinated reading. One broadsheet sold over a million copies, a figure not to be surpassed until 1897 when the circulation of *Pearson's Weekly* reached one and quarter million after it ran a competition.[6] This particular broadsheet, containing the murderer's confession (in quartrains), was penned by the sharp–eyed publisher, James Catnach, a man who gained great wealth from such writing and publishing. As one street hawker said to Henry Mayhew 'there's nothing beats a stunning good murder after all'.[7]

Catnach is one of the better-remembered names among the scores of anonymous penny-publishers, although others such as the Worrals of Liverpool, Bebbington of Manchester, John Harkness of Preston and John Pitts of London, James Kendrew of York, John Cheney and J.G. Rusher of Banbury and Isaiah Thomas of Worcester, Massachusetts, are recorded or gained posthumous fame through biography.[8] The vast number of authors working in this industry themselves remain biographically silent although some are known because of later fame or because Henry Mayhew spoke to them: one such was John Morgan who complained to Mayhew about Catnach's unwillingness to pay up.

Catnach's works printed all sorts of ephemera from his premises at Monmouth Court in London and it was here that street hawkers would settle their accounts for wholesale broadsheets and chapbooks and from here that they would travel the country selling their wares in markets, at street corners or door-to-door in remote farming communities. With a staff of only four, rapid turnover and the quick reflexes of a later tabloid mentality, Catnach was able to command considerable profits.

> Catnach almost cornered the market in a wide range of publications for children that sold at a halfpenny or even a farthing and, as he was not over-particular concerning type or the choice of relevant illustrations, he was able to print rapidly and at small cost. He was also adept in putting out broadsides at the right moment on any crime or scandal that occupied the public's attention, as well as historic occasions such as a battle or a royal event. In addition, there was a steady income to be gained from printing tradesmen's cards, posters, theatre programmes and other fugitive items; and there was a very brisk trade every Christmas in the sale of carols.[9]

Such a publisher/printer could die a rich man, as Catnach did in 1841.

John Pitts was the son of a Norfolk baker who made his way to London and trained as a printer. He too became wealthy with the publication of halfpenny ($\frac{1}{2}$d.) ballads. One historian has labelled these men and their class 'rough, tough and uncouth opportunists'.[10] Nevertheless, there were no popular newspapers written at a level to suit [working people's] background and interests. The chapbooks and the broadsides ... filled a gap. While they might have heard of a criminal's being brought to trial, they might hear little of the outcome, until the broadside arrived with the whole of the story. This applied to historical events as well – the details of a naval victory, a royal event or a political squabble must wait on the arrival of the broadside, which not only reprinted the details in the press but relayed it in ballad form as well. The latter point was especially important: illiterate people often have remarkable memories – aided by the recommended and familiar tune at the head of the ballad, many a listener would effortlessly commit the verses to memory after hearing them only two or three times. The language was simple, the rhymes crude but memorable. To a large mass of the population the chapbooks and the broadsides filled a need that was not otherwise met until the introduction of the popular press in the 1850s.[11]

Furthermore, the reading habits of the poor fed directly into those of the richer classes. Crime, sex, royalty – in a word sensation – filled respectable newspapers, and sentimentality and vulgarity could feature in articles in *The Times*, without the readers of such articles realizing the continuum of earthy vulgarity and language that linked them to the poor.[12] Here was a true democracy of the vulgar, latterly to be swallowed up in publications like *Tit Bits* and in the juxtaposition of Sherlock Holmes stories in the *Strand Magazine* with another regular feature: curiously shaped fruit and vegetables, contained in illustrations of oddly distorted garden produce. Such juxtapositioning was the life blood of popular reading, something quite lost when we anthologize literature by such as Conan Doyle.

Vulgarity filtered *upward* and hence it is far less instructive to notice sources of influences in 'serious' or 'classic' literature than to notice parallel developments and contemporaneous *cross-fertilization* (not to say plagiarism). *Sweeney Todd* stands between the modern serial and the archaic chapman and his wares just as Edgar Allan Poe stands between the hack and the 'serious' fictionalist.[13] It is not merely in terms of imagery that we can follow 'the continuing process of cross-fertilization between the "highest" of high art and popular genres', but also in terms of their forms as commodities (that is structures within a market and a community of readers based on that market).[14] As such, productive techniques changed and modified subject matter as subject matter enlarged the possibilities of production. To cope with these changes popular 'serious' publishers rapidly modernized to take advantage of the sales potential exposed by the 'older' methods of broadsheet hackdom.

Changes incorporated capital-intense investment, partnership with banks, divisions in labour and production (i.e. Marx's 'means of production'), specialized management functions, new means of marketing, advertising, wholesaling and retailing; authors were treated as contracted professionals as books became commodities, essentially ephemeral and determined by a reading public (the market). Large-scale production was helped by new means of creating paper (first by the Fourdrinier machine) and mass printing (the steam press) even if other methods including modernized typesetting lagged behind. Thus with the book seen simultaneously as *moral vehicle* and *commodity* the publishing, lending and retailing empires progressed in mutual alliance.

The British book trade in the nineteenth century was a modern industry in every way. It took advantage of mechanised systems of production, developed highly efficient distribution arrangements based on the most up-to-date means of transport, and evolved a division of labour both between and within its various branches. Many firms were still family businesses, but they were large and well-organised, and many of their owners were employers of labour on a substantial scale. Millions of pounds of capital investment poured into the trade, much of it generated directly from profit. It was inevitable that attitudes within the industry also underwent a profound change. The parochialism of the battle for literary property and the restrictive practices of the congers and the trade sales vanished into history; the trade was in the marketplace, and the first consideration was economic success in the face of competition.[15]

Moreover, the three-decker novel, with its high price and stable form acted as the 'gold standard for an otherwise shaky market'.[16] This form acted to give depth to art and breadth to sales, indeed 'It is probable that the artificial maintenance of the thousand-page novel in this way made for greater as well as bigger fiction'.[17] Yet at the same time it acted to define other versions of fiction, in which the production techniques of penny-dreadful publishers were put to the service of middle-class reading, where 'huge figures were involved. In 1847, for example, Chapman & Hall printed 2 290 000 'parts' of Dickens's novels.[18] Thus was Charles Knight, the nineteenth-century printer, able to state with a considerable level of conviction that 'the penny magazine produced a revolution in popular art throughout the world'.[19]

Three further points need to be emphasized here. The first is obvious but little noticed, that the 'novel is the only literary genre to have been invented since the invention of printing, and its literary history is inseparable from the history of its publication'.[20] The second is that the continuing and lucrative trade in reprints of non-copyright work made older literature itself into an infinite resource for new literature of all kinds, and thus the content of such literature was a cheap and conveniently renewable resource both in its own right and as a prompt to new fiction using it as a basis. Lastly the new literatures slowly undermined the 'older' moralities (already worn thin in the eighteenth century).

The secularization of fiction (which meant it merely had to *represent* and *entertain*) was to form the backdrop for a slowly developing movement which led from the Christian moral tales of Charlotte Yonge and the tractarians to the sentimental, mystical Christianity of Marie Corelli and her populist and highly popular ideology to the growing body of literature in which the subject matter was society and the individual represented naturalistically. The moralism of Mudie, Smith, the Macmillan brothers and many publishers such as John Cassell had finally been defeated by their very success. Moreover, the centrally important need to lower both production costs and purchase price in order to widen ephemeral print's distribution, which had originally been intended to increase access to radical unstamped (i.e. untaxed) news, and revolutionary opinion was itself a highly moral crusade. That too was defeated by the very success of its technical and costing methods and the absorption of its politics into mainstream liberal debate.

Finally, it is amusing to reflect that the dramatic increase in publishing brought an equal rise in pornography during Queen Victoria's reign.

Such an alliance brought into being the new age of information without which the later industrial revolutions would not have succeeded. By the end of the nineteenth century almost all of Britain's workforce could read (see next chapter) and by the 1840s Britain was already a 'print-dependent society'.[21] It is no exaggeration to say that William Henry Smith and Charles Edward Mudie were the first information moguls whose monopoly on printed information was virtually impregnable in Britain and whose 'editorial' or purchasing decisions were decisive in the production and shape of British literature, especially fiction. When publishers were avoiding Mudie they had to devise new forms to do it, although until the decisive intervention of William Heinemann very late in the century these forms were often supportive rather than antagonistic towards Mudie's standardized form.

> Serialisation by no means threatened the three-decker in which the majority of lesser novelists continued to appear. The *Publishers' Circular* listed six times as many in 1887 (184) as in 1837 (31). A prime factor in its survival, and increased prosperity, in the mid-century period was the dramatic growth in the circulating library business. In the 1840s and 50s Mudie's library in particular expanded to control a major section of the metroplitan market and a sizeable portion of that in the country and overseas. At his zenith, in the 1860s, he earned up to £40 000 a year in subscriptions. . . . Mudie's triumph was the outcome not of cautious whittling down of costs but of slashing them dramatically, so short circuiting the gap that existed between high book prices and low income. . . . One reason that fiction tends to gravitate towards the cheapest form of publishing is that in most cases it is read once only, and then quickly. In America this economic logic led to books of incredible cheapness, designed to be thrown away after use. In Britain it was not the book which was cheapened but the reading of it.[22]

The essential point here is that unless purchased as part works and then privately bound or purchased as serials and possibly lost or lent to friends, bound books were not bought in the nineteenth century by *any* class. They were *borrowed* and it is this habit which made reading what it was.[23] It was the library, the reprint and the home-bound book which established the classics of the nineteenth century.

The collapse of the firm Constable & Ballantyne in 1826 had suggested that the publishing of inexpensive books could not succeed and yet the industry was soon joined by young entrepreneurs who did not see money-making and morality as mutually incompatible and sought ways to enlarge the former while promoting the latter.[24]

John Murray began his rise to fortune when, on coming of age, he bought out his partner and left retailing to become a phenomenally successful publisher. Dickens was only 24 when he began with *Pickwick Papers* and still in his thirties when he began *Household Words*. In the case of all these young men there was a felt need to stabilize and control a changing market place – to find a common currency from which all could prosper. To a large extent Mudie provided such stability as well as upholding the inherent conservative moralism of most respectable publishers.

Charles Edward Mudie's own career began, when in 1840 he opened a shop in King Street (now Southampton Street) in London to which students from the newly created London University would go. Having realised the potential of *lending* rather than selling Mudie's career took off. Unlike other library/booksellers Mudie soon professionalised his approach and taking as his mainstay the newly emerging novel helped create both a reading public in the middle class and the very form of their enjoyment: the three-decker novel which they borrowed in ever increasing numbers at affordable rental subscription. Such fiction at 31/6 was a luxury happily borrowed, rarely bought, 'it seemed to me in those days that the patronage of Mudie', recalled Mrs Oliphant, 'was a sort of recognition from heaven'.[25]

Mudie's vast purchasing power kept many publishers and novelists in comfort so no one needed to 'rock the boat'. However, even Mudie outdid himself and had by 1864 relinquished some of the shares in his business, although not control.

In 1861 it was estimated that the library included 800,000 books, and that 10,000 passed in and out of its walls every day.

The cost of building the hall proved, however, too great for Mr. Mudie's resources, and in 1864 the library became a limited company. Half the shares were held by Mr. Mudie, and he retained the sole management, so that there was no change in the conduct of the business. He still bought freely all such books as seemed to him suited to the tastes . . . of his large public.[26]

Through this 'moral' control and his censorious conduct, Mudie created a middle-class, middle-brow readership which still exists and which later began to change its allegiance to public libraries, where fiction could be had with somewhat less, though not always much less, censorship.[27] It was in the Croydon Public Library in 1908 that D.H. Lawrence, that archetypical man of the masses, found a copy of Nietzsche and first formulated his thoughts on the destruction of the very class from which he had emerged.[28]

While fiction helped define the age it did so in the context of many other forms of literature. Of the taste for encyclopaedic knowledge and the search for facts nothing fitted better than the newspaper. The newspaper was central to the spreading of mass literacy as it predated both the educational reforms of the 1870s and the appearance of the 'modern' novel. For some, the thought of a public reading newspapers alongside the new literacy which followed the Education Act of 1870 was just too much, as George Bernard Shaw lamented, 'The Education Act of 1871 [*sic*] . . . was producing readers who had never before bought books, nor could have read them if they had. . . . I, as a belated intellectual, went under completely'.[29] Of course, this did not prevent him from indulging in a journalistic career. Yet a much more optimistic picture arises concerning the new mass literacy if we turn elsewhere.

The cheap newspaper and periodical cannot perhaps be defined strictly as educators. Yet for good or evil, and probably on the whole for good, they are very powerful ones. Notwithstanding the many sins and shortcomings of the newspaper press, the working man of today, with his broadsheet for a penny is by its aid a man of fuller information, better judgement and wider sympathies than the workman of thirty years back who had to content himself with gossip and rumour, and whose source of information as to public events was the well-thumbed weekly newspaper in the public house.[30]

It is significant that this was noted *before* the Education Act, by social commentators in 1867. It may therefore be assumed that a great many working people could read before the implementation of the Act; that they read news, sport and popular fiction is proved by the print runs of broadsheets, chapbooks, almanacs, newspapers, special journals, serials and part works aimed specifically at that market.

One consequence of [the 1870 Act], however, was the creation of a myth about literacy in nineteenth-century Britain. The Act was supposedly to turn out hundreds of Board School literates. It was, therefore, easily assumed that the previous level and extent of literacy must have been very poor. The years before 1870 thus came to be seen as a dark age. Recent work has shown up the myth for what it is, but it is equally important to remember that for generations after 1870 it was a very widely accepted version of the past, and judgements and analyses of the relationship of education to the press were made in its light. By the 1890s at the latest it had become a cliché to link the large circulation of the popular press with the effects of Board School education.[31]

What might be said, is that the Act *redirected* literacy for the lower reading classes, created new patterns and provided a greater means of creating homogeneity in print and *controlling* print for certain sectional views. Shaw's claims against the new literacy were not on behalf of an old élite being pushed out but a new élite created in antipathy to current trends. Matthew Arnold's 'remnant' was a new 'faction' which defined its own role as one of opposition. Thus the ills at the end of the Victorian era could be blamed respectively on centralization, philistine taste, monopolistic interest and 'tabloid' journalism. Together, they spelled the end, for many commentators of the older liberalism of the early nineteenth century.

W.J. Fisher, sometime editor of the *Daily Chronicle*, wrote in 1904, 'the provincial Liberal press has become feebler and feebler, and in the smaller towns has almost ceased to exist'. The young liberal historian G.M. Trevelyan wrote in 1901, 'the Philistines have captured the Ark of the Covenant (the printing press), and have learnt to work their own miracles through its power'. L.T. Hobhouse, social philosopher and leading 'new liberal' journalist, wrote in 1909, 'the Press, more and more the monopoly of a few rich men, from being the organ of democracy has become rather the sounding-board for whatever ideas commend themselves to the great material interests'.[32]

The newspaper was in all respects the *sine qua non* of a modern print industry and a society defined by printed material. 'As early as the 1870s suburban trains were left strewn with the litter of thousands of newspapers every morning'.[33] Indeed, in the 1860s, noisy commuter trains had forced travellers into the privacy of reading – a situation credited with saving them time at their work.[34] Admittedly such habits were middle class in the 1860s but all literate workers spent time reading and Sunday became the day when such activity was especially sanctioned.

Like the publishing industry before it, the newspaper industry had, by the later nineteenth century tended toward a stabilized oligarchical structure. The protean world of the 1840s had become concentrated in the hands of newspaper 'magnates' by the 1900s. In 1910 the London Metropolitan press was controlled by Northcliffe, Pearson and the Morning Leader Group; the Sunday Press was divided by H.J. Dalziel, G. Riddell, F. Lloyd and again Northcliffe between whom 80 per cent of the market was distributed.[35]

Such concentration was cause for infinite doom-laden predictions from a disaffected intelligentsia and constant carping about the poverty of culture not just in the working people (who were disregarded anyway!) but in the real enemy: the philistine, suburban, middle class. If it was true that earlier patterns of local social life had been partially erased by this concentration of newspaper owners, and if the older local politics had been pushed out too, it was also true that the new journalism created a wider view of the world, thus uniting the British into a nation with common interests, common national politics and a homogeneity (in the 'ordinary') which gave the class system its definition and the classes their communal self-identity. There was no real or coherent industrial proletariat in Britain before there was a reading public aware of national affairs, and in this the middle class came to a consciousness of their role only with the appearance of print designed for them from the 1840s onwards. Self-definition learnt through the newspapers and educational processes of the latter part of the century was always a negotiation between the reader and the pressures exerted by school boards, library committees and editors. Print monopolies with their moral and political biases were not simply matters of evil but also causes of a thriving national culture capable of serious debate, as well as the creative forces behind the communal dreams of a literate consumer society. By 1957, Richard Hoggart could regret the passing of this world of industrial communities and urban villages which was based on the common pleasures and knowledge derived from the popular press of the later Victorian period.[36]

Print was intrinsically connected with the various strands of the concept of Victorian modernity. It was essential to educational, technological, and business change as it was also essential to the pursuit of knowledge, the demands of the daily news and the world of printed entertainment.

My argument, that the great perceptual movements of the nineteenth century were the result of a spreading and protean literacy, also suggests that any study of all *literatures* of the period must be aware that commercial demands and market forces were constantly creating and modifying literary forms, whether they be novels, text books, newspapers or even the smaller world of poetry. In mid-century the serialized works of Dickens were always 'works in progress'. Furthermore, the movement and growth of significantly Anglo-American reading publics led to constantly shifting forms. The publishing of fiction changed across the century to allow new forms to appear, the short story being the most notable, suited as it was to new consumer demands. Thus another group of writers got their chance to publish. Similarly subgenres were created which embraced spy thrillers, westerns, women's romance, imperial adventures and, of course, detective stories.

More than this the very nature of authorship changed. Writers became celebrities – toured America and thrilled packed houses. A long time before the end of the century a writer's name meant money, although many writers were keen to be known as 'the author of' rather than by their real names, the use of *noms de plume* being widespread (see Chapter 5). Author's names and styles were their fortune and their stock, part of the common ownership of readers.

Writers had finally become Carlylean heroes. To further this new heroism, a new technology was born. The typewriter allowed for rapid mechanical processing, and duplication of precious manuscripts came with the use of carbon paper: 'Mark Twain boasted of his willingness to use this curious new machine, and *The Adventures of Tom Sawyer* is reputed to be the first typewritten manuscript to be set into a book'.[37]

Forged on this metallic alphabet was something even more peculiar than this mechanical means of expression. Authors were now becoming aware that they owned a unique form of invisible goods – intellectual property. Copyright had for authors the same status as patents for inventors. Walter Besant's Society of Authors became, by the 1890s, their protective agency and it helped to create the proper atmosphere for those agreements which protected British authors from the piracies of foreigners (especially Americans).

Such changes encouraged both artistic creativity and popular entertainment and often the two happily combined, but tensions at the end of the period already revealed the neurotic nature of this continued expansion.[38] Yet, whilst Trollope and George Eliot and their publishers and readers were well aware of the distance between 'high seriousness' in fiction and simple entertainment their attitudes were not quite the same as those held by both the early and later Bloomsbury in defiance of popular literacy and antagonistic to its implications.

Daniel Boorstin has pointed out, in his monumental study of the rise of American modern consumer society that, 'Democracy required a new lexicon, a redefinition of what was excellent, of what was good, and – most significantly – of what was good enough.'[39] This new lexicon of good and 'good enough' (that cheap luxury of books offered by Mudie to the middle classes) was fought out in print and formed by print, especially advertising print and the language of consumption. This new lexicon more and more provided 'extravagant possibilities in the language of the commonplace'.[40]

The language of the commonplace was itself undergoing radical changes. This was especially so when new methods of transcription impinged upon the very sentiments transcribed. By the 1880s it had already become possible to mass produce steel pens, and once problems concerned with the corrosive effects of the old inks had been overcome with the production of new non-corrosive dyes, the steel nib was to become the standard instrument of transcription. Later in the century, this nib allied to an internal reservoir allowed for more rapid transcription using fountain pens filled with *synthetic* dyes such as nigrosine (patented in 1867).[41] The creation of the fully practical typewriter in 1874 (with continuous improvements from 1892) further aided rapid transcription, but it also marked a decisive break in the act of writing which now came closer to a form of rapid typesetting.

Authors were quickly organizing their expression to fit a new imaginative and structural space between the physicality of the fountain pen and the technological distance of the typeface of a typewriter. Rapidly changing the constituents of the old sentence structure such instruments created a substituted expressive form in the 'organic' paragraph.

> In 1860 . . . the average English sentence had half the words of an Elizabethan sentence. [But] the penny press and tabloid journalism would further shorten . . . sentences. . . . No story longer than 250 words, guest editor Alfred Harmsworth demanded for the January 1, 1901, issue of Joseph Pulitzer's newspaper *The World*.[42]

The 'new' concept of the paragraph was a substitution inherently 'modern', combining a belief in technological integrity, organic fluidity and the psychosomatic correspondence of thought and gesture. In a word, here was a new harmonics.

> A prime determinant of the pattern of gestures accompanying speeches read from written texts, . . . the paragraph . . . was generally ignored by rhetoricians until Alexander Bain's *English Composition and Rhetoric* of 1866. . . . Bain had developed a sophisticated associationalist psychology whose laws he applied to the structure of writing. . . . [He] drew from the Laws of Similarity, Contiguity, and Compound Association a systematic theory in which paragraph structure should be anticipatable from sentence structure (Similarity), thoughts within a paragraph should flow from one sentence to the next (Contiguity) and, together, the concordance of sentences should yield a powerful resultant (Compound Association). In other words, a paragraph truly expressive of one's thoughts should have Unity, Coherence and Mass (Emphasis).

In less than 40 years writers of American textbooks such as John S. Hart, author of *Manual of Composition and Rhetoric* (1870), had moved from an emphasis on the sentence to an insistence on the primacy of the paragraph. Charles Sears Baldwin, Assistant Professor of Rhetoric at Yale, had by 1902 produced his *A College Manual of Rhetoric*, which took the totality and unity of a composition as its starting point.

> By 1916, William D. Lewis, a high school principal, and James F. Hosic, instructor at Chicago Normal College, were explaining in their *Practical English for High Schools* that a paragraph is 'a unit of thought'.... Writing in paragraphs was at once the organic statement of coherent ideas and a training toward clear thought.
> This organic paragraph ... stood in trust of the link between mental activity and physical movement ... following not only the laws of associationalist psychology but also of psychophysiology.[43]

For popular fiction authors the combination of typewriter and dictation machine allowed for the creation of rapidly produced stories to feed the new reading public's tastes. Such innovation and demand became especially important for those professional authors who made their living as writers and had no other means of support, nor could afford to dally between titles. 'The popular storyteller, part of the working population, became the writer employed by the press owner – poised between the tastes and outlooks of employer on the one hand and customer on the other.'[44]

Working-class authors such as Edgar Wallace became intermediaries between two groups and two classes: to both they owed an allegiance and yet from both they remained separated. Wallace, himself the son of a Billingsgate porter, seemed to have little time for the 'working man', his targeted reader.

If Charlotte Yonge and Raymond Chandler have anything in common then it is that they and hundreds of other authors acted as witnesses and dramatists of the heroically mundane: the morality of spirit having become the necessity of ownership. By the late 1890s the Sears catalogue was the best-selling book of the nineteenth century.

Some have called the big mail-order catalogues the first characteristically American kind of book. Since colonial times, Americans had been more notable for their almanacs, newspapers, magazines and how-to-do-it manuals than for their treatises: the relevant, the topical, the ephemeral, had been more expressive of American life than the systematic and the monumental. The Sears Roebuck Catalogue was the Bible of the new rural consumption communities.[45]

In such a bible was the morality of ownership – a book for democratic peoples held together by a common language of consumption – peoples thinned by distance but joined by print. The Sears Roebuck catalogue is the quintessential book of the modern age. In its illustrated pages the concept of object information and consumer anticipation was heralded and advertising and print circulation came of age.

By the twentieth century, the very act of shopping itself was a fit subject for Anglo-American fictional representation, Virginia Woolf, Edna Ferber, O. Henry, Hugh Walpole, H.G. Wells and James Joyce all understood that shopping was a crucial activity in the definition of self in the modern world.[46] In the Sears catalogue people were introduced to the universe of things and from their newspapers to that of facts. What united these two areas was a curiosity about neighbours who were also 'strangers'. Their needs and desires were also the needs and desires of others in the community who also looked to purchase the universe of things and consume the universe of facts.

Learning from the marketing methods of the Sears catalogue and obsessed with the 'problem' of facts, DeWitt Wallace, founder of the magazine *Reader's Digest*, proved himself the inheritor of a tradition of popular publishing stretching back to *Poor Richard's Almanack*.[47] Wallace had been a failure in his attempts to be a university lecturer and a copy writer, but it had been this very failure, and his autodidactic beliefs that made him a successful publisher when he combined the little magazine format with an approach more reasonably associated with pulp presses.

Wallace's almost neurotic obsession with printed material, facts, tabulation and memory coincided with a general concern for such things and the growing popularity of that mind-training technique called 'Pelmanism' which had become a major cult between the wars. The new owner and editor of the *Reader's Digest* (which began publication in 1922) exemplified in his character the commonly held beliefs about modernity, change and business which he was able to commodify in his magazine of self-improvement and self-education: progressive in its contents, it proved populist in its attitudes. The central theme of the *Digest* became 'change itself'.[48] Here were factual articles condensed to their essentials for those who believed themselves to be too busy to spare too much time to read but who needed to be 'up to date' – the reader would be a practical person, business-orientated, mobile, domestic, conservative, family-centred, someone wanting 'knowledge of rather than knowledge about'.[49] Thus it was that *Reader's Digest* was at once middle-brow and plebeian, a product of America's belief both in endless progressive change and the conservative homely values of small-town communities.

The factual contents of the *Reader's Digest* and the pocket-book size of the format made it at once an 'essential' almanac and an escapist compendium, each condensed article being some titbit to store away in a moment of leisure and a possible clue to future business success to be remembered later when needed.

In 1950, a new departure led to the *Reader's Digest* Condensed Book Club in which new middle-brow literature was stripped of inessentials and reproduced in abridged form. The novel now was changed into its bizarre other: knowledge of rather than knowledge *about*. Stripped of its *style* (its nature as 'art') the novel became pure information as escapism, a practical guide to relaxation for the overworked. In retaining the 'essential' elements of character and narrative, the Condensed Book Club editors succeeded in losing the very 'writerliness' of the originals – that upon which the writers had worked longest, the very opposite impulse to that invoked by the enterprise of the avant garde. Popular fiction was thus proved a type of process of 'rewriting' within a framework of data converted into practical knowledge. The *utility* function of fiction was no longer in its moral trajectory but in its offering practical aid towards relaxation and escape.

While vilified by intellectuals, such escapism was embraced by the vast majority of popular writers. In the 1920s, for instance, writers like Ethel M. Dell catered for 'women with tiring and monotonous jobs; housekeepers, governesses, lady companions, maids [and] nurses' and this was certainly not due to incapacity or mere venality on the part of the writer.[50]

That Ethel [Dell] never aimed her cultural sights higher was not due to any lack of education, since, like her sister, she was well read and cultured. Her sympathics, however, were with those who were forced to work in uncongenial jobs; to them she set out to bring glamour and excitement.[51]

It is hardly surprising that in such a world the old certainities were redefined and that for some this meant a crisis in the very nature of meaning: the neuroses of high literary modernism were the neuroses of the age of print itself.

4

A River So Deep:
Literacy, Language

The massive social, economic and technological changes which allowed the new print industry to circulate and flourish could not have ocurred without a continuously increasing rate of literacy amongst the new democratic masses. While figures cannot prove particularly accurate in terms of how people read, why they read and at what level they understood the material, they offer a foundation for any further conjectures on the form and nature of literature *as is was consumed*.

Investigations into literacy have often taken the marriage signatures of men and women in parish registers as at least indicative of functional literacy. In 1867, one of the first British investigators, W.L. Sargant, found that 51 per cent of couples in England and Wales could sign the marriage register between 1754 and 1762 and that this had risen to 54 per cent by 1799–1804.[1] Nevertheless, this gradual rise took a dip while rural communities moved into towns and came to terms with factory life and urban communities. Despite regional variations and the fact that the universal literacy of all classes is not essential for industrial growth, literacy levels did continue to rise as did educational opportunity before 1870.[2] By 1851, the SPCK had 23 135 schools and approximately three quarters of all five to fifteen-year-olds were gaining some sort of organized education regardless of whether the institutions they attended were benevolent or coercive.[3]

Hobsbawm, in an interesting variation of literacy testing, has pointed out that if two letters were posted per person in the 1790s, then by the 1880s, 42 letters per head were being sent and that this may be taken as another indicator of growing literacy.[4] Whatever the case, by 1831 a quarter of the 14 million population of Britain now lived in towns and general literacy was increasing regardless of regional variation or industrial disruption to a point where 75 per cent of men and 50 per cent of women were literate.[5] By the end of the nineteenth century and with the institution of compulsory

education literacy became almost universal. In 1891, 94 per cent of
men and 93 per cent of women could read.[6] By 1910, only 5 per cent
of the British population was considered illiterate and by 1914 that
level had dramatically dropped to 0.8 per cent, measured by marriage registers signed by 'mark'.[7] It was only in the worst slums
between the 1900s and 1940s that literacy could not be taken for
granted and a call from the School Board Man could upset the pre-
carious system of earnings and family structure of the very poorest. Even the British Labour Party would not court the illiterate and
avoided recruiting them, in favour of literate *respectable* working
voters.[8] Nevertheless the very poorest still read newspapers such as
the *Daily Herald* or *Daily Chronicle* and retained a totemistic respect
for books.[9] Katherine Mansfield tartly observed in 1914 when creating one of her lower-class characters that:

> Henry was a great fellow for books. He did not read many nor
> did he possess above half a dozen. He looked at all in the Charing
> Cross Road during lunch-time and at any odd time in London;
> the quantity with which he was on nodding terms was amazing.
> By his clean neat handling of them and by his nice choice of
> phrase when discussing them with one or another bookseller you
> would have thought that he had taken his pap with a tome
> propped before his nurse's bosom. But you would have been
> wrong.
>
> ('Something Childish But Very Natural')

Books played a part within a complex web of social and economic relations and ownership helped to define status amongst the
humblest. Literacy was always literacy within a *context*, as one resident of a poor London street makes clear in talking of his father's
concern for family repectability and the correct façade to adopt
when cadging a charitable handout:

> And this is where my old man displayed both his contempt for
> the higher-ups – the *toffs* as he used to call them – and his natural
> con-artist's appreciation for the suitable stage-setting. . . . Shabby-
> genteel was my old man's *forte*: impoverished rather than hard-
> up. . . . [My] old man organised my mother to scrub and scour, to
> create the general image of poverty, hunger, and sparkling clean-
> liness – to show that Jack's little brood had no intention of

succumbing to the squalor and lethargic helplessness abounding on all sides of this little oasis of culture. To emphasise the cultural angle, Poppa had painstakingly cherished the dozen or so reminders of our former happy state of affluence before falling from grace in the shape of his library . . . Odd titles which the old villain had culled discriminately from totters' Sunday markets in which they displayed the gems and plums of their weekly gleanings from the totting with their barrows. They'd put them on the pavements outside their houses. Titles like *The Mill on the Floss* . . . *Cricket on the Hearth*, Marie Corelli's *The Sorrows of Satan*, Hall Caine's *The Christian, The Manxman* and *The Bondman*, etc. Predominance of place . . . was given to titles . . . with biblical connotations – *The Way of the Transgressor* would have been most appropriate. The book-case itself had been painstakingly crafted from an eggbox, lovingly finished in two pennorth of mahogony-stain varnish. . . . When old Goodrum [the Relieving Officer] knocked at the street door, two knocks for us on the first floor, not for him the bald invitation to 'Come on up!' No, the old man went down in person, to escort this distinguished visitor. . . . Short of pinning a poster with 'Down With Drink!' on the door, old Jack went through the card.[10]

The situation in the United States was somewhat different from that of Great Britain. Even from the earliest years a premium was set on literacy. John Adams, writing in 1765, could be proud of the fact that 'a native American who cannot read or write is as rare an appearance as a Jacobite or a Roman Catholic, that is as a comet or an earthquake', instead 80 per cent of men were literate in the colonies.[11] Women's literacy lagged behind but demands for cultural participation from 1790 onwards greatly improved the 40 per cent literacy rate of the 1760s.[12] By mid-century, literacy rates stood at 67 per cent for men and 51 per cent for women (accounting for immigration) and this was before compulsory elementary schooling was introduced in Massachussetts (1852), the District of Columbia (1864) and Vermont.[13]

Such an increase in literacy and education in mid-century America did not however have a direct relationship with industrial processes nor urbanization as in Britain. Indeed, while American technological practice was designed to *eliminate* expertise, generate consumer goods and spread general wealth, human management was generating a literate class of its own.

The scarcity of legal learning did not lead to a scarcity of laws or lawyers ([America] soon became the most lawyered and most legislated country in the world), but instead of a new kind of legal profession and a new concept of law; the scarcity of specialized medical learning soon led to a new kind of doctor and a new concept of medicine; and a scarcity of theological learning led to a new kind of minister and a new concept of religion. Similarly, the scarcity of craft skills set the stage for a new nearly craftless way of making things. And this prepared a new concept of material plentitude and of the use and expendability of things which would be called the American Standard of Living.[14]

Alexis de Tocqueville, that assiduous nation-watcher, found literacy well rooted in America when he visited in 1847. If an 'industrial spirit' had crept into the tastes of 'the industrial classes', nevertheless the democratic 'classes' of America showed a taste for literacy and a desire for reading matter.[15] 'The ever growing crowd of readers' were well catered for by numerous bookshops with 'American books crowding the shelves' even if few of those works were notable or their authors known to an educated public.[16] Thus, while Americans lacked a classical education, nevertheless one could still find plenty of books from England which were printed or plagiarized and de Tocqueville was happy to offer this encomium to the reading habits of ordinary Americans:

> The literary inspiration of Great Britain darts its beams into the depths of the forests of the New World. There is hardly a pioneer's hut which does not contain a few odd volumes of Shakespear. I remember reading the feudal drama of *Henry V* for the first time in a log cabin.[17]

If 'Americans [had] not yet ... got any literature' of their own by which de Tocqueville meant poetry and drama, then they had found a voice in the political pamphlet and in journalism.[18] 'Only the journalists strike me as truly American', de Tocqueville wrote, sharing as they did an appetite for information as entertainment, a concentration on the individual and a new more fluid use of the English language.

Progress in eliminating illiteracy sped up as the century moved on.[19] The introduction of an eight-year compulsory education programme (delayed in the South to disenfranchise the Black population) had led by 1900 to 22 per cent of the population being in elementary schooling and by 1940, in a population of 132 million, 7 million were regularly attending high school.[20] Between 1870 and 1940 the population had trebled from 44 million to 132 million and high school attendance had now risen from 5 per cent of the total possible school population in 1900 to 42 per cent in 1940.[21] Equally, illiteracy had progressively fallen from 20 per cent in the 1840s to 11 per cent in 1900 and thence down to 4 per cent in 1930 and 2 per cent in 1950 (of the population over 10 years old).[22] This was against European rates of 15 per cent illiteracy in 1930 and 8 per cent in 1950. But if America's population was more literate it was also differently literate.

By 1941 in his preface to the revised *American Language*, H.L. Mencken could point to the appearance, rise and conquest of a new form of English language, similar to, but different from the English of the British Isles.

[T]he pull of American has become so powerful that is has begun to drag English with it, and in consequence some of the differences once visible have tended to disappear. The two forms of the language, of course, are still distinct in more ways than one, and when an Englishman and an American meet they continue to be conscious that each speaks a tongue that is far from identical with the tongue spoken by the other. But the Englishman, of late, has yielded so much to American example, in vocabulary, in idiom, in spelling and even in pronunciation, that what he speaks promises to become, on some not too remote tomorrow, a kind of dialect of American, just as the language spoken by the American was once a dialect of English. The English writers who note this change lay it to the influence of the American movies and talkies, but it seems to me that there is also something more, and something deeper. The American people now constitute by far the largest fraction of the English-speaking race, and since the World War they have shown an increasing inclination to throw off their old subservience to English precept and example. If only by the force of numbers, they are bound to exert a dominant influence upon the course of the common language hereafter.[23]

It seemed to Mencken, as it did to the ancestors he cites, that the *experience* of America needed a new language, one more loose or fluid than the English of the English and as adaptable to circumstance as the language of the Elizabethans. By 1778, a Congressional Committee was demanding replies by foreigners be in the language of the United States and by the later eighteenth century, John Witherspoon, president of Princeton, could coin the term *Americanism* for the divergent language of the nation.[24] Witherspoon, writing as 'The Druid' (from 1781) contributed a series of articles to the *Pennsylvania Journal and Weekly Advertiser* on the nature of American speech and its need of *reform*.[25] To this end he noted:

1. Americanisms, or ways of speaking peculiar to this country.
2. Vulgarisms in England and America.
3. Vulgarisms in America only.
4. Local phrases or terms.
5. Common blunders arising from ignorance.
6. Cant phrases.
7. Personal blunders.
8. Technical terms introduced into the language.[26]

Happily *un*reformed, the American language continued to adapt to the experience of nation-making and it was Noah Webster in his *American Dictionary of the English Language* (1828) who began to provide a formal framework for the speech, spelling and grammar of the continent. In so doing he anticipated Mencken by a century.[27]

As an independent nation, our honor requires us to have a system of our own, in language as well as government. Great Britain, whose children we are, and whose language we speak, should no longer be *our* standard; for the taste of her writers is already corrupted, and her language on the decline. But if it were not so, she is at too great a distance to be our model, and to instruct us in the principles of our own tongue. . . . Several circumstances render a future separation of the American tongue from the English necessary and unavoidable. . . . Numerous local causes, such as a new country, new associations of people, new combinations of ideas in arts and sciences, and some intercourse with tribes wholly unknown in Europe, will introduce new words into the American tongue. These causes will produce, in a course of time, a language in North America as different from the future language of England as the modern Dutch, Danish and Swedish are from the German, or from one another: like remote branches of a tree springing from the same stock, or rays of light shot from the same center, and diverging from each other in proportion to their distance from the point of separation. . . . We have therefore the fairest opportunity of establishing a national language and of giving it uniformity and perspicuity, in North America, that ever presented itself to mankind. Now is the time to begin the plan.

Alexis de Tocqueville also noted the appearance of 'American' as a distinct branch of English.

Educated Englishmen, better able to appreciate these fine nuances than I, have often told me that the language of well-educated Americans is decidedly different from that spoken by the same class in Great Britain.

Their complaint is not only that the Americans have introduced a lot of new words (the difference between the two countries and the distance between them would have been enough to account for that), but that these new words are generally taken from the jargon of parties, the mechanical arts, or trade. They also say that the Americans have given new meanings to old English words. Finally they maintain that the Americans often mix their styles in an odd way, sometimes putting words together which, in the mother tongue, are carefully kept apart.[28]

He put this change in usage down to the need in a democratic country to respond to new things and relationships not covered in a traditional, conservative and autocratic setting.[29]

The changes in linguistic usage were the vital element in giving national identity to the United States because they encapsulated American political, legal and moral values and gave expression to the contractual nature of participation. To these ends English was adaptable, absorbing, as it could, the language usage of waves of immigrants, whether Irish, Jewish, Polish, French, German or any number of others, as well as being responsive to native American words and place names, and open enough for the creation of a lively vulgate, the slang of ordinary speech. New concerns demanded new structures of expression. By the 1920s, the gangster novel (curiously unlike the western) with its 'low' character and emphasis on speech over narrative placed the slang of the street in the context of the literary. Slang was no longer a curiosity (as with Sam Weller in *Pickwick Papers*) for middle-class readers – a language of a foreign race – *but the very heart of literary expression*.

William Fowler in 1850 could find in American words and us-
ages from foreign languages reworked and jumbled together with
new technical, professional, ecclesiastical, and legal words while
nouns were turned into verbs, spelling was rationalized and different compound words had begun to appear.

The expansion of the language of Americans accompanied the
increasing population and changes in industrial and agricultural
practice. By 1851, the population of the United States exceeded that
of Britain by over 2 million, by 1890–91 it had doubled the population of Britain with comparative figures of just over 33 million for
the United Kingdom as compared with just over 63 million for
America and by 1951 it was three times the size of Britain's population of 49 million.[30] The labour force also grew accordingly and
although it did not exceed Britain's workforce until the 1880s it had
exceeded it by 75 per cent during the 1930s.[31] Nevertheless, this
hides the fact that until the 1860s the labour force available in the
United States was approximately 2 million less than in Britain (i.e.
at the height of Britain's prestige in the nineteenth century) and of
the total population a much greater proportional movement into
towns and industrial centres can be found between the 1850s and
the 1950s for Britain than America.[32] America retains an agricultural
base and culture throughout the history of the industrialization of
the continent. Of the total workforce, by 1900, 27 per cent were in
industry and that proportion has not shifted much in America.

Bagwell and Mingay in their comparative economic study of
Britain and America between 1850 and 1939 point out:

> The relatively low proportion of the labour force engaged in
> American industry at the end of the nineteenth century reflected
> two important differences: the greater (but diminishing) role of
> agriculture in the American economy, and the already higher
> output per head of the American worker. It was only about 1890
> that the absolute numbers employed in American industry passed
> those in British industry, but in the output of certain key prod-
> ucts such as coal and steel, the United States had forged well
> ahead by 1900.

> With industrialization came urbanization. In Britain, as early as
> 1841 only 39 per cent of the population was living in rural areas,
> and by 1911 this figure had fallen to 19 per cent. In the United
> States, in 1850 only some 3.5 million people (15 per cent of the
> population) lived in places having over 2500 inhabitants, and

only 2m people (9 per cent) in places having over 25 000 inhabitants. As late as 1910 the rural population of the United States still outnumbered those living in urban areas, and it was only after that date that the urban population came to form the majority. But the tendency for large industrial centres to be created had been marked since the middle of the century, and by 1910 nearly 15.5m people (17 per cent of the total) lived in towns with a population of over a quarter of a million.[33]

Whereas in Britain writers tended to avoid or attack the twin concepts of business and technology, in America, writers embraced the conditions provided by both to explore and concentrate their language *as* writers. If Alexis de Tocqueville could notice as early as the 1830s that Americans were already obsessed with business and commerce, then Wallace Stevens could unapologetically write many years later that 'money was a kind of poetry',[34] and William Carlos Williams (attacking the Englishness of T.S. Eliot) could point out the industrial side of the American language, both its nature as raw material and its potential as representative of modern commercial exchange (that is as a mode of *communication* between people):

what we are trying to do is not only to disengage the elements of a measure but to seek (what we believe is there) a new measure or a new way of measuring that will be commensurate with the social, economic world in which we are living as contrasted with the past. . . .
It is as though for the moment we should be profuse, we Americans; we need to build up a mass, a conglomerate maybe.[35]

Williams continues, 'we [are], loose disassociated (linguistically), yawping speakers of a new language.'[36]
Both e.e. cummings and later Charles Olson found in the technology available to authors the definition and liberation of American 'speech'. The typewriter became both a form of convenience and a structuring device for the 'looseness' of the American tongue.

The irony is, from the machine has come one gain not yet sufficiently observed or used but which leads directly on toward projective verse and its consequences. It is the advantage of the typewriter that, due to its rigidity and its space precisions, it can, for a poet, indicate exactly the breath, the pauses, the suspensions even of syllables, the juxtapositions even of parts of phrases, which he intends. For the first time the poet has the stave and the bar a musician has had. For the first time he can, without the convention of rime [sic] and meter, record the listening he has done to his own speech and by that one act indicate how he would want any reader, silently or otherwise, to voice his work.[37]

Later this machine would itself become an item of nostalgia, an icon to the concept of real authorship and authentic inspiration in the face of the increasing use of computerized typefaces (see Chapter 12).

If poets were able to notice this configuration of commerce, technology, language and *space* so too were popular novelists. The American language became a kind of cartographical space to be mapped over and over again by each new writer in order to capture afresh an 'essence' forever evasive and forever mythically distant. James M. Cain writing of his style could point out in his preface to *Double Indemnity* that,

> I make no conscious effort to be tough, or hard-boiled, or grim, or any of the things I am usually called. I merely try to write as the character would write, and I never forget that the average man, from the fields, the streets, the bars, the offices and even the gutters of his country, has acquired a vividness of speech that goes beyond anything I could invent, and that if I stick to this heritage, this logos of the American countryside, I shall attain a maximum of effectiveness with very little effort.

What was at issue was the definitions of both a country and the *subjectivity* of its citizens in whose individual identity the national identity took shape. The American publishing industry was primarily engaged in a dialogue with speech patterns that print would both conventionalize, define and liberate.

Despite the fecundity of the American language and the generous inclusiveness and expressiveness of its nature, the English spoken in the British Isles remained and still remains relatively untouched by Americanisms. If critics from both sides of the political divide have deplored the influence of American culture they are not supported by anything other than superficial and emotional arguments. It can be shown that only relatively recently did American language usage make any real impression on spoken, written or literary English. Richard Hoggart, for one, amply demonstrated the vitality of colloquial English in his *Uses of Literacy* and Orwell's 'Newspeak' is concerned less with the *expansion* of language in the American model than with the closing down of language suggested by 'Basic English'.

While it is true that American business practice had been noted early in Britain, it made little impact except in retailing, where F.W. Woolworth stores were thoroughly Anglicized from the 1930s onwards; Ford and Woolworths are as British as they are American. Ordinary language too has proved resistant to America and it cannot be claimed that English became either a dialect of America nor that, on the whole, Americans and Britons cannot understand each other perfectly well through both spoken and printed media. Even the advent of the 'talkies' did not immediately subvert ordinary English language patterning, the taste for Chicago slang was not reflected in English youth slang to any great extent and American authors play an insignificant part in the everday reading matter of most Britons between 1900 and the 1950s. Indeed, the attempt to capture slang idioms in such diverse works as Colin MacInness's *Absolute Beginners* (1959), Anthony Burgess's *Clockwork Orange* (1962) and *Richard Allen's* 'Skinhead' books remain obstinately *English* in tone and *literary* intention.

Of the top 130 bestselling authors read between 1900 and 1960 by British working people only 10 were actually Americans, although both James Hadley Chase and Stephen Frances ('Hank Janson') who were English assumed a voice to appear authentically American and 'tough'.* Equally, many authors in Britain included an American character in their work to gain greater sales both sides of the Atlantic. Arthur Conan Doyle has Jefferson Hope as the true central character in 'A Study in Scarlet' ostensively a detective story but in actuality a cross genre mixing the western and the desert tale (where Mormons have 'harems'), while Bram Stoker, another transatlantic traveller like Conan Doyle has Quincey P. Morris help out in *Dracula*. Long before these writers, Dickens had added an American episode to *Martin Chuzzlewit*. In each case the American features were *reinvented* in acordance with English linguistic and conventional needs: America is Anglicized. This pattern holds good today even

---

* Compiled from various sources. By the latter half of the 1980s the figures for most-read authors (as opposed to most sold) had changed by only a few per cent in favour of American authors.

if many of our own authors have 'internationalized' themselves and chosen to live in America (such as Jackie Collins in Hollywood or Barbara Taylor Bradford in New York) On the whole, the English used in Britain has absorbed, changed and attuned American patterns to its own rhythms. America stood as icon for modernity, style, and the future. For the British reader America is a 'style' of *doing* and an imaginative stage. In this sense, it holds a meaning not too different to the meaning is has for American writers. The languages of the western and the gangster genres are, to that, extent, neither American *per se* nor English, but literary conventions acceptable both sides of the Atlantic.

A number of crucial points follow this survey of language and of levels of literacy. The first is simply that what is at stake is not literacy levels as such but levels sufficient for and widespread enough for the sustained growth of a viable industrialized print industry viewed as a whole, however small each individual unit may be. Only then can the conditions for a growth in literacy rates be created and a mutual dependence exist. Such sustained levels of growth were the products of continual negotiation, revision, expansion and attempted restraint of that which could be printed and read in the first place. Secondly, the industry tapped into a never ending *and* commerciable resource: the abstract space of language itself. The industrial revolution so demanding of raw material found its material even in the substance of human interaction, self-renewing and infuriatingly wasteful. Literacy in its necessary relationship with the various stages of the industrial revolution was the essential resource for transmitting information and for providing the worker with both the ability to follow orders *and* to question them. Social progress and democratic reading habits (for entertainment and instruction) go hand in hand as structural co-requisites of technological progress. The profusion of printed material denies ascendancy to any one ideology or platform. All viewpoints are provided for and none more or less applauded in terms of their mere existence as print. The dominance of one viewpoint would destroy the necessary circulation needed to maintain continuous consumption and growth.

Thirdly, the common language itself began to break up and come under the growing pressure for hierarchization and differentiation. Until the middle eighteenth century the vernacular and its written or printed form had been largely disregarded by polite society except for news, gossip, opinion and entertainment. Rules were few, spelling and grammar erratic. The printed languages of culture and science were often still the 'dead' classical tongues. The democratization of print (and therefore opinion) led to a demand (often unconsciously demonstrated) for a restratification of linguistic use *within* the vernacular. Serious literature was now carefully fenced off from mere entertainment or instruction. This hierarchization was a relatively slow process and is traceable across the nineteenth century and into the first half of our own. It accompanied a further division of the common language into that used respectively by the new professionals, technocrats and the 'lay person'. The appropriation of certain discourses cut across and excluded all not otherwise involved regardless of class or position. Theology was replaced by 'expertology'. And of all the professions to elicit an ambivalent response from the lay person none was so powerful as medicine, combining as it does intimacy, secrets, biology and technology with a moral and physical discourse regarding the healthy and the diseased. The very designation doctor comes to stand for expert and technocrat, possibly benevolent or evil. Again and again the 'doctor' becomes the focus of popular imaginings whether good like Dr Watson, Dr Petrie, Dr Kildare or Dr Finlay or evil like Dr Jekyll, Dr Fu Manchu or Dr No or ambivalent but 'mad' like Dr Strangelove or Abraham Van Helsing M.D.

Professionalized and hierarchized the common language was now irrevocably split against itself.

Fifthly, hierarchization and professionalization in the common language also cut deeply into the special language of literature. Those not wishing to compete in the marketplace or have their work viewed as mere entertainment created a recategorization of narratives in which serious fiction was differentiated from escapist literature by its thematics and truth-telling functions. Works of entertainment had for Henry James and the avant garde that followed,

in common with many literary artistic compositions the fact that they presented an invented subject-matter. The term 'fiction' could thus be used as the lowest common denominator for two modes of discourse that were outwardly similar, but essentially different in purpose.[38]

A cordon sanitaire around serious fiction effectively turned an aesthetic question into a moral one: the question of the health of fiction (differentiated by them, and by their technique).

Sixthly, the new print industry and the appearance of universal literacy could be used as a political weapon. From the 1850s onwards first in Connecticut (1855), then in Massachusetts (1857), literacy tests could be used to exclude undesirable foreigners from full citizenship. Between 1889 and 1924, seventeen states adopted such rules to exclude Blacks against a background of rising White literacy levels. The tests consisted of the ability either to read a page of English prose or read such a page and discuss it. In Louisiana between 1896 and 1900 Black voters dropped from 130 000 to just over 5000. Illiterate Whites were helped by 'grandfather' clauses. Despite Woodrow Wilson's second use of his veto in 1917 against the Literacy Laws (which he saw as unconstitutional and against the democratic principles of the United States), the matter of literacy and enfranchisement remained a live issue.[39]

To write of the growth of a 'reading *public*' is a misleading shorthand, although just acceptable in its most generalized sense, but to use the term as a historical concept is genuinely misleading, except to show up the marked tendency toward aggregation (into class, mass, urban, etc.) that affected all social analysis from the early nineteenth century onwards. This tendency to aggregate blends and distorts the conclusions placed upon it. Questions of gender or class or ethnicity cannot adequately be dealt with as questions of the mass, nor indeed, must it be said, can the *eccentricity* of individual examples be disentangled from some attempt to view such activity as a social tendency. Between the two methods lies a delicate negotiation.

Instead of the term 'reading public', I shall substitute the idea of *constituencies of readers* not only determined by class, gender, ethnicity and economic grouping but also classed by reading habit. Altogether these constituencies make up reading *publics*, general entities incorporating specific activities and attitudes. Such a movement towards disaggregation allows us a unique view of different communities of readers determined by their specific interests and bound by their places in history. No continuous history of development emerges. Rather we are confronted with parallel and contiguous developments that often but not always overlap and that run to their own timetable and that rarely have any relationship with canonic taste.

5

Outlaws Against the Law Badge: Readers Reading

What might constituencies of readers look like? The following examples may act as guides.

In the eighteenth century, a new and powerful group had arisen which would be central to the subsequent industrial revolutions in Britain and America. The men of the merchant marine represented a vast labour force of skilled workers, proletarians without machines, who plied the trade of the Atlantic ocean.[1] Conspicuous as figures in later seagoing narratives this group has a mystic, *anti-industrial* character for both British and American authors of the late nineteenth century. Yet these sailors were not merely mute exemplars for later fiction, for they were also, and more especially, the conveyors of ideas between the two countries: *international* in composition, metropolitan in nature, and articulate. What the signing of parish registers does not signify for these mariners was their literacy or their reading matter. Although such details are often consigned to mere speculation, it can be shown that at least some sailors approached or surpassed levels of literacy as high as the officer class they served and in conditions far more harsh. Henry Fielding's belief that all sailors were 'savages' ignored the fact that those like Isaac George and John Cross, though hanged as felons, were both educated enough to read.[2] One sailor, Olaudah Equino was conversant with *Paradise Lost* and had translated the Koran while in the American colonies.[3] What may come as a surprise is that all three were Black, part of a multiracial male nation sailing between Britain and the American colonies: a community in which reading was one of many methods of escaping the dullness of a voyage.

In the radical days of the unstamped penny press, soldiers regularly purchased and discussed seditious popular literature. In 1819, there were reports returned to Lord Sidmouth on all non-commissioned officers reading *Black Dwarf* and one man was

85

apprehended for selling material to a private.[4] Soldiers were recorded being punished for reading radical material during 1832 and at least one newspaper seller was prosecuted for selling such material to soldiers in a public house.[5] The Police informer 'Popay' reported that one soldier in the Foot Guards read *The Guardian* regularly and freely discussed his views with other recruits.[6] Fearful of being caught reading such material, the probable result being flogging and a possible drumming out of the service, soldiers are recorded as 'tearing up such reading material and chewing it into actual pulp!'[7]

While in port or on home duty, these sailors and soldiers would have mixed with the city 'mob', a boisterous, articulate, anti-authoritarian and largely free community. Within this group literacy also seems to have been higher then the parish registers would suggest, with pamphlets and ballad sheets freely circulating until the mid-nineteenth century. These loosely affiliated metropolitan groups, especially in London, were avid readers of the personal lives and deaths of those who had risen above the community and for a brief time disturbed the sleep of the magistracy. Jack Sheppard quickly gained mystic status during his lifetime and two weeks after his death was the subject of a Drury Lane play, John Thurmond's *Harlequin Sheppard*.[8] Dick Turpin also became a legendary figure – a modern-day Robin Hood – and the legacy of both these figures passed into the subliteracy of pamphlet, 'blood' and penny dreadful. By the nineteenth century, Ned Kelly was being compared to Jack Sheppard and Frank and Jesse James signed the letters they sent to the *Kansas City Star* as 'Jack Sheppard'. Sheppard became part of the vernacular landscape for sailors who used his first name as a nickname, for gypsies who retold his 'story' and for the urban proletariat of industrial cities in the 1840s.[9] Dick Turpin's name, his famous horse and his equally famous ride to York captivated those in Australia, as well as the Alleghenies and Ozarks.[10]

Turpin's deeds inspired many episodes in cheaply produced mass literature throughout the nineteenth century and his name and heroic attributes rapidly became a resource for fiction itself.

There were scores of highwaymen stories, in both penny and halfpenny parts: *Dick Turpin, Tom Turpin, Captain MacHeath, Captain Midnight, Moonlight Jack, Gentleman Jack, Black Hawk, Black Wolf, Black Highwayman, Sixteen-string Jack, Turnpike Dick* and *Tyburn Dick*, to name but a few; and, on the distaff side, *May*

Turpin, Starlight Nell and *Nan Darrell*. Consistently the most favoured character was Dick Turpin. Any similarity between the facts of his life and the fancies of his chroniclers was purely coincidental; and the liberties the authors took with the facts of Turpin's career (even his schooldays became a theme for highflown adventure) were as nothing compared with the liberties they took with time and space.[11]

Of all the tales of Dick Turpin, the first and most 'respectable' was W. Harrison Ainsworth's *Rookwood* of 1834, poured out at an extraordinary rate (the equivalent of one hundred printed pages in 24 hours!) in which Turpin's heroic ride to York was a major factor in promoting the legend.[12] By the 1870s, Turpin had gained in moral authority; if his deeds were illicit, he was still a true 'gentleman'. In *The Blue Dwarf*, the author clearly contrasts Turpin's lifestyle of highway robbery to that of mere commercial chicanery.

The sum realized by some highwaymen in those days was something fabulous. The money spent in riot and debauchery in a week would often have provided for fifty families.

'Light come light go' had always been the motto of those whose money came to them in a nefarious way. But many modern ways of making money are infinitely more nefarious than taking it by force. . . .

The cheating done by lawyers and brokers whose clients trust them, the hundred and one ways of levying blackmail by men in power and with influence in any place of trust, the disgraceful sweating exercised in professions where such mean tricks were never supposed to have been heard of, are infinitely more despicable than highway robbery.

At all events, the man risked his neck, and was always amenable to the laws of his country. . . .

But for the mean, crawling thieves we speak of there is no punishment – not even that of their consciences, for they have none.[13]

In the age of *criminalization* the romanticized bandit now stood for freedom, the individual, justice and, above all, honour.

The figures of Jack Sheppard and Dick Turpin, alongside lesser figures like Claude Duval were central to and developed by the growth of mass printing and mass urban reading habits long before such reading habits should have *statistically* existed! The newer popular presses printing millions of words and hundreds of thousands of part works and serials thrived on the legacy of eighteenth-century proletarian heroes, and were the descendants of the considerable circulation of popular ephemeral urban literature in the previous century, especially that concerned with the dying confessions of those going to Tyburn. In contrast, Jane Austen's lampoon of the gothic novel in *Northanger Abbey* was an attack on a limited, class-tied female readership. Quite another group, by far the larger, wanted tales from their *own* world, not that of the aristocracy or gentry, but human interest tales of unlawful doings and illicit heroes. It was these characters who gave that readership its thrills and its hopes and it was the taste for the *facts* in these characters' lives (as opposed to gothic fancies), that was the immediate ancestor of the fact-filled and personality-filled journalism of the nineteenth-century yellow press.

The reading population of London was large and cut across the classes. It was, perhaps the result of greater self-dependence and contractual relationships than elsewhere and those that moved to the city tended to be urban refugees from other cities (especially Dublin) and therefore themselves, literate. In cities generally it was found that some book ownership was not infrequent.

> In 1839 there were books in 73.2 per cent of the homes; Grays Inn, West Bromwich, Trevethin and Blaenavon in Monmouthshire, Kingston-upon-Hull and St. George's, Hanover Square in London produced findings of 78, 85, 86, 75, and 89 per cent. Of the twenty-three investigations of book ownership in a total of over twenty-five thousand working-class homes carried out in this period, only one, a Central Society for Education survey of an Irish slum in Marylebone, found more than half to be devoid of any literature.[14]

Thus only the very poorest were without access to books or unable to read them.

Literacy in the British countryside was lower than in London and disruption during the 1840s as people moved into provincial and northern cities may have lowered urban literacy rates. Whatever the case, recovery was swift. Nevertheless, the country labourer would have had less access to urban printed materials and may have felt less need to read. This can be examined through the reports of those sent among the rural poor (usually after some civil unrest) as agents of religious or other improving societies.

What these early nineteenth-century explorers of darkest rural England found were orderly homes and a keenness for education. Many homes had small collections of books which were treated with care and respect, and researchers were impressed with the number of rural homes with books, a figure that ranged between 50 and 75 per cent of all households visited.[15] They were equally impressed with the sober and religious nature of the books owned, with an overwhelming preponderance of religious works (unlike the reading habits of their urban fellows) and few of the new 'newspapers, cheap novels and penny magazines' were to be found.[16]

Modern historians have accepted this argument of reading habits both sober and self-improving among the literate urban poor, and their findings bear out the earlier comments by statistical and religious observers. We are told, for instance, by one modern commentator, that:

> it was still very unusual to find a working-class domestic library composed solely of secular items. Taken as a whole, the surveys bear striking witness to the comparative literariness of the traditional popular culture. The statistical societies had proved beyond question that the written word, most frequently in the form of the classic prose of the Bible and Prayer Book, was no stranger to the homes of the labouring poor.[17]

This type of continuity of Bible reading among working people can be traced to our own century where books like *The Pilgrim's Progress* and the anonymous *Hours with the Saints* were selling well before the First World War.[18] The rhythms of the *Book of Common Prayer* and chapel worship can also be detected in D.H. Lawrence's early work.

The movement away from overtly church-based reading for working people continued across the nineteenth century although the publishing of popular theological books was still strong before 1914 especially with publishers such as Hodder & Stoughton who otherwise were known for their adventure and thriller lists. Secularization of reading matter among working-class readers by the early twentieth century may be attributed not only to antagonism toward the recommended reading matter suggested by those who were seen as belonging to another class (teachers were a special case) but also to:

the deep disaffection from religious values shared by many work-ing-class boys and girls in their early teens and derived from the feeling that religion was unrelated to the daily struggle for sur-vival, which demanded a practical and opportunistic code of conduct that conflicted with the absolute moral dictates of the Bible. This contradiction between esoteric Christian dogma and a practical morality rooted in family and community relationships, is often hinted at, yet rarely articulated.[19]

What all this disguises is what was read when the do-gooder had no longer to be impressed by your piety. How many 'Bunyans' and *Saints* came home later in the century as prizes and were never read is again open to opinion. If the Bible was democratically read, then school prizes from religious missionaries would be less likely as popular reading. Indeed, the failure of Religious Tract Society pub-lications was in direct proportion to the success of *novels* with a Bible or religious theme.

The reasonable literacy rates of the rural poor (excluding the poorest field labourers) and the growing provision of elementary education in villages meant that reading was often the province of the children of labouring families. It was hardly the Bible and Bunyan alone that interested them.

At all times informal instruction by parents or friends or even by unaided self-help must have been almost as important as sys-tematic instruction in schools. Since Tudor times popular litera-ture in the form of ballads, broadsides and pamphlets had formed part of the stock-in-trade of the travelling bagman and furnished means of self-instruction. In the eighteenth century there was a great increase in the output of popular reading and didactic material intended primarily for juveniles, though also for their elders: spelling books, writing sheets, fairy stories, moral tales, fables, histories. Hack-written, crudely printed and illustrated, chapbooks of this kind were produced in great variety in numerous towns, and peddled round the fairs, villages and farms of the countryside by the 'travelling stationers'. The publisher John Newbery, who died in 1767, was the father of the children's book trade. Many intelligent but unschooled labourers and their children must have learned to read by puzzling their way through *The History of Tom Hickathrift, Jack the Giant Killer* or *Tommy Trip and his Dog Jowler*, bought at the door for a few pence.[20]

As the representative of the statistical society stood on the doorstep perhaps the chapbook hawker hid behind a convenient hedge! It is necessary therefore to place Bible and self-improving reading within the context firstly of children's education and the fact that often it was they who read to their (non-reading) parents and secondly, that the adult reading matter that followed consisted of a diet of sensation, superstition and political agitation.

The polite middle-class visitor at the door of the agricultural worker who approved the *conservative* nature of their bookshelf nevertheless had less liking for the interest they may have taken in the work of Tom Paine or the interest taken in William Cobbett's *Weekly Political Register* read aloud or in groups at gatherings at local public houses and then, when available at prices workers could afford, in people's homes.[21] The damning relationship between political unrest and alcohol could hardly have been missed and was condemned on the one hand while praise was heaped on Bible ownership on the other. Yet the two were inexorably connected within English working-class political thought and found their expression in the programme of the emergent Labour Party. Furthermore, these political views found readers in both women and children.[22] As a further sidelight, it is interesting to note that where reading took place at home it was often the woman who read out loud for her either illiterate or too tired husband at a time when women's illiteracy rates were supposedly a third to a half higher than that of men.[23]

Bible, political and childhood reading can all be viewed as a continuum that included almanacs, horoscopes and superstitious leaflets and booklets. If, as E.P. Thompson has pointed out, Bunyan and Paine were the key texts of the emergent working class then the reading of the prophecies of Joanna Southcott mark a moment of crisis both in political and millenarial thought. The artisan readers of Southcott saw politically in their practical life and apocalyptically in their imagination.[24] With the tide water of revolutionary zeal flowing away under the oppressions of the 1800s to 1820s, the anti-establishment millenarial writings of latter-day prophets turned into the practical and *political* adjustments of the middle of the century. What remains of this millenarial desire is a landscape of images and a deep conservatism and distrust of change in a certain superstitiousness that political action could not fully shift.[25]

Moreover, the religious engagement of Joanna Southcott's writings marked a peculiar *dis*engagement with the everyday (even as they suffused the everyday with magical portents). Existing only as a half-hidden subliterature (Southcott's box was still a matter of newspaper advertisements in 1994), this type of writing feeds into the secular wish-fulfilment fantasy of a later age, in which the *engagement* of otherworldliness is abandoned for the escapism *into* otherworldliness of secular working-class fiction. While working-class readers throughout the nineteenth century enjoyed reading about the personal details of contemporaries from their own class (especially from police reports) they also enjoyed indulging a parallel fascination with fate, spirits, freaks of nature, signs and portents, (and later in our own century) belief in Atlantis, reincarnation, magical secret societies, telekinesis, UFOs and conspiracy theories.* In the latter half of the nineteenth century these interests rapidly spread across all classes to become a staple of many eccentric societies, sectarian churches and the context of a great deal of the emergent popular-fiction industry. A prey to residual forms of atavism, the working rural poor were themselves a subject for the urban sensational press of the 1850s; one tale of witchcraft, sexual relations and abortion, for instance, showed that the poor still believed in the power of local 'wizards' who could step in when conventional doctors failed. Science and magic still complemented each other for those poor agricultural workers who were migrating from the countryside to the industrial cities or who had recently arrived.[26] In the age of progress, the inate conservatism of the rural poor was not confined to the reading of Bunyan and the family Bible, but was darker, more political, more fantastical and more complex.

These comments on the rural reading constituency suggest the need to contextualize reading habits and sometimes to consider *prima facie* evidence with reasonable scepticism. In so doing we find a complex web of habits and beliefs and that, 'however difficult and inadequate an experience, reading in the home came to be an essential element in the emergence of an independent working-class culture.'[27]

The emergence of a reading public in the latter half of the nineteenth century had, by the middle of the twentieth become a given fact. Investigator after investigator, from Wilkie Collins to George Orwell, testified to the consolidation of a mass market for literatures of the escapist kind read during leisure for mere entertainment.

---

* David Morris has coined the term techno-occultism for this phenomenon. See *The Masks of Lucifer* (London: Batsford, 1992).

Needless to say this 'new' reading public consisted solely of the lower-middle classes and large chunks of an unidentifiable but philistine nouveau suburbia.

Recent work by Joseph McAleer has confirmed the research conducted, rather informally, by the likes of Wilkie Collins and George Orwell, and McAleer has provided much new information with regard to popular publishers.[28] What is entirely missed from McAleer's account is an analysis of reading constituencies that opens up a debate about the *heterogeneous* nature of the mass reading public.

That certain sections of the lower middle and working classes could read and did so for leisure and escape, that their reading was secular and formulaic was known prior to the use of mass publishing which simply widened and deepened reading opportunities. Moreover, the reading matter and reasons for reading adopted by the 'lower' classes had penetrated middle-class and upper middle-class reading by the twentieth century and any sharp differentation between groups (something possibly visible up to the 1850s) had disappeared. Although a middle-class reader may have, and will still read other more 'literary' work, it is also likely that they will share a taste for tabloid newspapers, escapist literature and television game shows with economic and cultural groups they would not wish to mix with socially. Queenie Leavis pointed out as long ago as 1932 that there 'is no reason for supposing that novelettes are bought exclusively by the uneducated and poor' and Mills & Boon could refer to its success in the commercial lending library at Harrods just as much as to its success in the twopenny newsagent libraries of the industrial towns.[29]

Economic distance and snobbery do not change the simple facts that science fiction and detective stories appeal to all social groups and that a children's comic such as *The Beano* is read by children in both public and comprehensive schools as an adult comic such as *VIZ* is enjoyed by young white-collar male clerks from all walks of life. Fan clubs cross social boundaries. Thus, in one sense, a *mass* reading public of a homogenous nature does exist; nevertheless it is clear that within such aggregation reading consituencies provide patterns of *difference*.

Let us take two areas in which we can reconsider the reading public: literature by and for women and imperial adventure literature.

The importance of feminist thought throughout this century has been profound, as has that of feminist literary criticism which has recovered many a 'lost' or half-forgotten woman writer. Feminist literary theory has been concerned with a number of constraints put on women, firstly, but in no particular order, their oppression as writers who write against the grain, their enforced use of certain genres and styles of language in a 'patriarchal' society and lastly their subjection to pornographic and violent representation.

In order to examine these areas it is useful to turn to the production and the reading of women's literature and the literature enjoyed by women (something somewhat different). It is a truism that Shakespeare's Sister was somehow suppressed or refused a voice. There is little evidence for this (as there is little evidence for proof that Victorian men couldn't satisfy their wive's sexual needs and that they spent all their time with prostitutes or indeed that the Victorian women did not know how to reach orgasm!). It is true that certain writers changed their names or remained anonymous but the use of *noms de plume* and anonymity was often *de rigeur* for nineteenth-century writers and therefore this proves almost nothing. If Jane Austen chose anonymity so did Bulwer Lytton, who threatened to sue his publishers when they accidentally put his name in an advert for his latest novel. Jane Austen, George Eliot and even the Brontës were all recognized by F.R. Leavis as constituent authors in *The Great Tradition*; everyone knew throughout the last century who Eliot really was and that she was considered the century's greatest fiction writer. Where 'suppression' occurred it did so in the censorious atmosphere of those who feared libel, scandal or impropriety and as such women writers were treated no differently from men when dealt with by fearful publishers. It is the rare occasion which proves the rule that has as its subject the suppression of a woman's writing *because she is a woman* and the complaints of writers such as Mrs Oliphant seem merely to confirm the rule in the exceptional case.[30]*

---

* My argument is aimed at a certain dogmatic feminisn taken too often as merely reflecting a given (and never quite stated) 'reality'. Elaine Showalter asserts, for instance, that, 'the ongoing history of women's writing has been suppressed' by 'the dominant (male) group' and that (quoting Gilbert and Gubar) in the nineteenth century it was 'the antagonism of male readers' that suppressed the 'female artist'. This wilful reductionism is itself antagonistic to history and produces a creed at odds with the careful research needed to expose the complex web that produced women writers and women readers. The question of women's self-censorship and self-image is more intractable. The problem of self-perception is as much related to mere delusion as it is to any actual social circumstance and therefore should never be taken at face value – a point some critics seem to ignore.

Ouida, Mrs Henry Wood, Rhoda Broughton and Florence Barclay were all successful, independent and forceful businesswomen; James Catnach's mother continued his business when he was in prison and Geraldine Jewsbury was a highly influential publisher's reader. Mary Braddon combined magazine editing with bestselling novel writing; Madame Sarah Grand (Mrs Frances McFall) was a champion of women's rights and became mayor of Bath; Lady Emma (Caroline) Wood although dubbed too immoral was allowed on to Mudie's list, and sensationalism has done little to damage women writers from Elinor Glynn to Jackie Collins; Marie Corelli gained fame through her anonymous novel *The Silver Domino* and Ethel Lillia Voyrich made simple use of initials to gain fame with *The Gadfly*; it is true that *The Roadmender* was produced by *Margaret Fairless Barber** under the *nom de plume* 'Michael Fairless' but this was because the tale was told by a navvy; Agatha Christie is, perhaps, the most famous British novelist of our century if you exclude Barbara Cartland or Catherine Cookson.

Mrs Oliphant's complaints did not prevent her being published but from becoming financially comfortable and she herself acknowledged that perhaps she was not committed enough to her own characters to really excite the public. Finally there is the issue of anonymity which was so general and so enforced at the very lowest level of fiction that very few names either of men or women come down to us. Anonymity on the level of the middle-class novel seems never to have harmed writers of either sex and was often requested by the authors themselves; on the level of working-class fiction anonymity was a matter of common business practice and common sense, as it usually prolonged the writer's professional career.

Women writers flourished in the nineteenth century (as did women readers) and the domestic novel, family saga, detective genre, horror yarn, ghost story and children's tale as well as the more familiar romantic novel, historical drama and moral fable could not have existed without their input. Women writers were not confined to certain genres as has been suggested, but wrote across most, although the spy, adventure and western tale (with the exception of B.M. Bower) as well as science fiction tended to be male preserves.

---

* Serialized from 1900 in *The Pilot, The Roadmender* was published in book form in 1901 and was successful before the First World War. John Buchan may have used this book as inspiration for the roadmender episode in *The Thirty-Nine Steps*. Writing while convalescing, Buchan may have been given Barber's book.

Women writers flourished, as publishers catering for a mass market expanded. Whatever stereotypical images these authors are supposed to have peddled were eagerly sought by *all* women across the classes. At the very moment of their greatest patriarchal oppression (doubly so because the images were provided by other women), these readers were demanding political, health, economic and social equality. The two sides show that women were not mere dupes of circumstance but active participants in the reading process and quite able to make rational decisions despite reading the romantic 'novels' provided in women's twopenny reading. Few feminist critics notice the inherent contradiction in the fact that women were reading to *escape* the confines of their ordinary lives and that whatever propaganda their reading contained on behalf of patriarchal conformism it also offered an alternative *non-real* world where things were directed to the *control of fantasy* by women and for women.

If love and marriage were the only themes in twopenny sagas then at least they suggested happiness, harmony, equality and love, but of course they were not the only themes and death, detection, the supernatural, moneymaking, travel and the erotic were also available. The simple fact is that throughout this century women have overwhelmingly demanded stories from romance publishers that are 'moral' and ultimately conformist and where good (in the form of marriage and a family) defeats evil (the temptress, the blackguard). This may have less to do with patriarchal discourse than with an inherent need for order and harmony in complex and very unfictional lives; 'escapism had to be grounded in realism, not fantasy' and the important thing was to 'write it up in [a] homely way' not 'sensational'.[31]

A list of women writers popular in the twentieth century in Britain clearly shows the academic bias against the ordinary reading of ordinary women of all classes. This itself amounts to a massive suppression of the facts in which the enjoyments of millions of otherwise voiceless and faceless readers are denied validity because they don't participate in a struggle for linguistic or semantic liberation. Looked at in this way, *local* male or other forms of oppression can be shown to exist, but patriarchal discourse vanishes as a mere chimera of intellectualism.

This is why at least two feminist critics (we suspect middle class in origin) find women who read true crime fiction, with its violence, 'male' erotic bias and unpleasant authoritarian values incomprehensible:

Who are the actual, as opposed to the implied, readers of true-crime magazines? The British titles are not included in the National Readership Survey, but during 1984 a small survey was conducted via a questionnaire placed in all three magazines. Of the 1200 readers who responded, over 85 per cent were women and most respondents were aged between forty-four and fifty-four.

In so far as this survey accurately reflects the whole readership – and it is telling that our informant at Argus Publications said it confirmed her previous conviction that the typical reader was 'a C2DE woman aged 45+' – it seems to raise two rather puzzling questions. First, why do middle-aged women enjoy reading this kind of literature, against all the stereotypes? And secondly, given their awareness that the magazines are read mainly by women, why do the producers so consistently address their visual and verbal content to *men*? We put both these questions to the editor and to the publishers, but they were either unable or unwilling to give any opinion.[32]

In a book designed to show that men are psychologically predisposed to violence and sexual aggression ('dedicated . . . in the fight against male violence'), this point is never satisfactorily cleared up despite talk of women's fascination with 'transgression'.[33] What it does reveal is a *class* bias which needs to contextualize women's 'pleasure' in terms of patriachal discourse.

On the other hand, a great deal of transgressive male behaviour is frighteningly alien to women's experience – is directed against women, or contains misogynist elements – so that women's attraction to violent transgression cannot be unmixed with anxiety and distaste. It could be argued that true-crime literature offers a way of resolving this contradiction, or rather, a way of satisfying both sides. The woman consumer of *True Detective* can read about depraved and revolting behaviour, but in a framework which emphasizes moral condemnation and which make her appear as merely an eavesdropper on a dialogue really intended for men. This solution accommodates the desire for 'thrills' alongside the feeling that one ought not to desire them and it also allows for ambivalent feelings about the *kinds* of thrills which the magazines present.[34]

What is ignored is women's *own* pleasure in aggression, lust and violence regardless of male presence; thus moralized, working-class older women can be brought back into the sorority (of middle-class views).

Women's distaste for the oppression of pornography is also a staple of some feminist criticism. Instead, what is advocated is a female 'erotics' evident in the appearance of new popular novels under the general title 'Black Lace'. The inherent class bias of this approach is clearly seen by those creators of male pornography whom women are supposed to oppose. Headed, 'Not a made-up letter' is this recent ironic reply to feminist criticism by Stephen Bleach, publisher for Paul Raymond Publications, he says,

> It was refreshing to read about [the woman reviewer's] preference for honest 'pornography' over hypocritical 'erotica'. (I know what she's driving at, but both words have been subjected to so many different interpretations that they're all but meaningless now.) If our postbag is anything to go by, many other women share her view.
>
> Our magazines concentrate on photographs of naked women and written accounts of heterosexual sex. A good deal of the material comes from our readers, and nearly half of that comes from women – thousands of letters and photographs a year.
>
> These are certainly not coy, evasive or romantic. Most are direct, dirty and score minus 50 on the political correctness scale. The irony of this massive female response to magazines aimed at men isn't lost on us. But where else do women who unashamedly enjoy their sexuality – women who read their pornography with the lights on – have to turn?
>
> Whoever wins the intellectual argument, I suspect our female readers are having a far better time than their middle-class, middlebrow, mediocre sisters at publishing houses like Black Lace.[35]

We might conclude therefore that while women and men popular writers may have been and may continue to be constrained by genre and by formula there is nothing *inherently* repressive in this at all and the fortunes of popular authors were not and are not *merely* allied to their sexual preferences or gendered bias but to the genre they chose to, or choose to work in. Moreover, the continued and often continually useful use of *noms de plume* meant that 'male' writers of westerns and 'female' writers of romances turn out not quite as expected, while Richmal Crompton could enjoy a career happily authorially ungendered with a hero equally clearly a little boy.[36]

David Trotter has described the complex mixing of genres that went toward the writing of popular fiction at the end of the nineteenth century.[37] Yet such structural complexity seems to hide only a rather monstrous, seamless and universal discourse of repression, both of gender, class and colonial peoples. This reductionism misses the highly involved negotiation between authors and publishers, and readers, their classes, genres and ethnic origins. In an otherwise interesting discussion of the difference between American and British 'frontier' literature, Trotter points out (in a study aimed at undergraduates and from a progressively sociological perspective) of one bestseller before the First World War that it was 'unflinchingly prurient not to mention racist and sexist' despite its 'exuberant' nature.[38] The book accused was *The Dop Doctor* by Richard Dehan, an imperial romance set in the Boer War.

Trotter's judgement is, to say the least, peremptory and his enthusiastic attack on racism and sexism in the book (I fully accept the book is both) nevertheless is a moral judgement not a literary one. The problem with Trotter's attack is that it *avoids* the very issues he accuses the book of including, and he avoids either defining his terms or of saying to what degree the book is therefore guilty. Here is a classic example of critical loss of nerve (in an otherwise excellent study) in the face of an (academically) intractable popular book. What substitutes for literary sociology is moral outrage or description by accusation. One suspects that for Trotter this is a 'safe' book, being ideal as (a) a 'sympton' of sociological interest, (b) an example of racial and sexual stereotyping in the heyday of imperialism (he nevertheless offers no quoted evidence) (c) it was obviously written by a dead white European male (DWEM) and, (d) it would be unlikely to be read by students who would take Trotter at face value. What this amounts to is an abdication of the critic's responsibility to history and social context, to the reading constituency who would have purchased or borrowed the book and finally to the biographical specificity of the author. We need to begin again. To do so I will very briefly re-examine some of the issues raised by Trotter and consider some of the questions we might ask regarding the contextual evidence available. The specific problems of racism and sexism are examined more clearly in the second half of this book.

To begin at the beginning: 'Richard Dehan' was the pen name of *Miss* Clotilde Graves, a fifty-year-old woman with a bad heart who always dressed in black and ended her days in a convent. It took two years for her identity to come to light after the book was published in 1910.[39] Having already had success both in London and New York as the author of 16 plays the redoubtable Miss Graves required a *'nom de guerre'* to serve as [her] *mask* [my emphasis] when the thoughts, reflections, experiences and griefs of a lifetime . . . should be sent out into the world'.[40] And this despite the fact that William Heinemann and Sydney Pawling his assistant publisher wanted her to trade on her fame.

The Dop Doctor was a huge success both sides of the Atlantic.

> There were eighteen reprints of the first 6s edition; eight reprints of a 2s edition first issued in 1913; five of the 3s 6d edition first issued in 1918; at least eight colonial (export) editions; and various others up to 1940, making a total of thirty-seven impressions and 229,877 copies sold.[41]

Moreover, the Press were generous in their praises, seeing a book at once more complex and deep than Trotter's recent assessment, for instance,

> The *Spectator*, [commented] 'A vividly interesting novel . . . Readers who do not mind having the horrors of war laid naked before their eyes will be intensely interested by Mr. [*sic*] Dehan's book, and will be unable to read without a thrill his accounts of the adventures and escapes of the heroic defenders of the historic little town.' *Observer*: 'A great novel. The author has written a fine and moving tale, wide in its range, deep in its sympathies, full of the pain and the suffering, the courage, and truth of life.' *Daily Express*: 'Pulsatingly real – gloomy, tragic, humorous, dignified, real. The cruelty of battle, the depth of disgusting villainy, the struggles of great souls, the irony of coincidence, are all in its pages. . . . Who touches this touches a man.'[42]

However overpraised the book may have been by its pre-Second World War admirers it is revealed as a complexly 'racist' and 'sexist' work as well as much more beside of clearly a more admirable nature ('the horrors of war laid naked'). Trotter's attack on this book is a veiled attack on the *generation* who read it, and thus without care or interest taken over the question of the meaning of the Boer War and the issues raised by such a setting to the generations and classes and genders who avidly enjoyed the book (and others by 'Dehan') from 1910 to the 1940s. What Trotter's comments avoid are all the issues he needed to address, not the least of which was the gender of the author hidden as it was under a *nom de guerre*, a device used by so many others to disguise identity and cross genre borders otherwise closed.

The Dop Doctor now strikes us as inconsequential and overpraised, but unless we make some effort to understand popular literature *on its own terms* we can never come to understand anything of the continuum this book has with books more highly prized. It is essential that we understand all the determinants of a book if we are to see it both in its historical circumstances and as an enduring or ephemeral cultural artefact. The praise and interest lavished on Richard Dehan's work before 1940 is enough to require us to have some humility before the facts and to discuss less complacently the popular reading (and readership) of days gone by. What is crucially avoided by Trotter is the *specific* natures and contexts of the racisms and sexisms of *The Dop Doctor* if such exist and the nature of the 'mask' for genre authors of both sexes.

Much too has been made of the rise, late in the nineteenth century, of imperialist fiction and the wide currency it gained, especially among boys in all classes through the cheap publication of boy's own papers. The doctrine of imperialism could legitimately be seen as last-ditch attempt to replace religion as an enforcer of cultural values and certainly the muscular Christianity of duty, patriotism and honour informed writers from Sir Henry Newbolt to Rudyard Kipling, A.E.W. Mason to G(eorge) A(rthur) Henty. What emerged was religiosity or a secularized religious sense.

The supposed jingoism in the imperialist message has nevertheless to be placed in the context of the commonsense refusals of those to whom this literature was primarily addressed: the young. Working-class children could happily enjoy the pageantry and display, the street parties and Empire Day celebrations without accepting the easily decoded imperial message, a message which implied the inequality and exploitation of the very class from which such children sprang. Hence one woman recalled of her school days,

I loved poetry, and the school was assembled and they stood me on top of the headmistress's desk and I had a Union Jack draped round me. And I had to recite, 'Oh, where are you going to, all you big steamers? To fetch England's own grain up and down the great sea. I'm going to fetch you your bread and butter.' And somehow or other it stirred a bit of rebellion in me. I thought, where's my bread, where's my butter? And I think it sowed the first seeds of socialism in me, it really did.[43]

Such a love of literature but a refusal to accept its 'message' can be found in many youthful political conversion:

Now we 'ad a [teacher] . . . today you'd call 'im a communist, but looking back, he didn't tell us history out of the books. Now if you got hold of all those history books we had at the time, they was all a load of flannel, about Edward the Peacemaker, Queen Victoria and Elizabeth the First. When he did give us history the way he did give it, he did show us that they wasn't as glorious as what they made out, how we lost the American colonies and in India and places like that. He gave us a truer picture because all the books were glorifying the monarchy and I used to honestly think as a lad that there was nobody like the British. All the rest, if he was a foreigner, that was it, he was like a load of rubbish. Well, you can tell by the way they did call 'em 'Froggies' and 'Eyties' and 'Dagoes' and things like that. I mean, the only way you'd describe them was they were beneath you. But he started me on the trail, that bloke, that teacher. And later on, when I was getting on to fourteen, I started to read these historical books an' I took an interest in 'em. And I thought to myself at the time, well, what a load of rubbish we've been taught in the past.[44]

History emerges here as a type of lie or simply plain propaganda for the ruling classes (represented by teachers and 'them') but the reader is never confused into believing history is merely another form of story. As such, some history becomes a story which reinforces class control, a manipulation far more devious and brutal then mere fiction where escapism into the imperialist landscape is firmly understood as make-believe. The result is a distrust of history and an ambivalence towards fiction. Even the most overtly imperialist dogmatist needed to be aware of the necessary negotiations required to gain the reader's acceptance.

Even a cursory discussion of reading habits, reading levels and reading material reveals a highly intricate and complex set of equations. In each empirical instance the general nature of theory is tested, confirmed or rebuked, revealing the space between a 'uniform' manufactured culture and a differentiated consumption which is always personal, refuses simple historical categorization, is constantly reinvented in the 'name' of contemporaneity, either disregards or negotiates with establishment values and is finally defeated by chronological process – made ephemeral by time.[45]

6

Smart Like Us:
Culture and Kulcha

It is no coincidence that the years which witnessed the appearance of the modern corporate business were also the years which saw the fragmentation of culture and the appearance of the most acute form of the social class system. Just as the classes separated so taste was divided and redistributed among the deserving. In this new world the old categories were relentlessly broken down and replaced by professional interest groups whose powerful opinions determined market reaction. Just as surely as the older communities were moulded and reacted to the market so too came that now familiar stratification of economic groups into working-class, middle-class and upper-class *consumers* and with these came the new hierarchies of taste considered suitable for such a convenient taxonomic arrangement. Low-, middle- and high-brow tastes were born together out of economic, social and cultural desire for forms of recognizable stability in an age of inherent instability.

When money alone ruled, the cultural niceties were no longer paramount, perhaps no longer recognizable. Taste alone would make culture safe and would above all preserve civilization – for Matthew Arnold in the 1880s, as for Frank and Queenie Leavis in the twentieth century in Britain, this was the overriding obsession. The cultured person, not market forces, would now make the world civilized. But if the cultured person stood against the market place (and the very success of entrepreneurs was proof of their lack of culture) then it was a paradox that the world of literature was ultimately driven by market forces and a public whose taste for books was insatiable. To cope with this situation a whole viper's nest of reasons was paraded to justify distinctions in literary culture unknown to earlier generations. At the same time, major industrialists and corporations needed 'culture' to create the respectability which would then be recognized by the guardians of taste. Despite their pre-eminent positions as cultural arbiters both Matthew Arnold and the Leavises were essentially a self-styled 'remnant' of *amateurism* pitted against what was for them an alliance of corporate interests, professionalized literary journalism and a public taste hoodwinked by both of these former groups into accepting middle-brow literature as great art: the barbarians were not merely at the gates they were already in charge.

Two quotations give some sense of the cultural upheaval and dislocation felt by the emerging intelligentsia on both sides of the Atlantic brought about by the changes occuring in public taste in the nineteenth century.

When George Templeton Strong sat down with his diary to record his reactions to the death of Charles Dickens in 1870, he found no ready-made cultural category sufficient to sum up the novelist and was forced to deal with the kaleidoscopic, complex strands of Dickens's work and following: 'His genius was unquestionable; his art and method were often worthy of the lowest writer of serials for Sunday papers. . . . Few men since Shakespeare have enriched the language with so many phrases that are in everyone's mouth. . . . I feel Charles Dickens's death as that of a personal friend, though I never even saw him and though there was so much coarseness and flabbiness in his style of work.[1]

By 1899, William Dean Howells was one of a growing band of authors and thinkers determined to give status to the *modern* novel. In so doing it was essential to sift out those very elements that had made Dickens universally popular so few years before.

Not one great novelist, not a single one in any European language, in any country, has for the last twenty five years been a romanticistic [*sic*] novelist; while literature swarms with second-rate, third-rate romanticistic novelists. . . . If you wish to darken council by asking how it is that these inferior romanticists are still incomparably the most popular novelists, I can only whisper, in strict confidence, that by far the greatest number of people in the world, even the civilized world, are people of weak and childish imagination, pleased with gross fables, fond of prodigies, heroes, heroines, portents and improbabilities, without self-knowledge, and without the wish for it. . . . the novelist [however] has a grave duty.[2]

By 1898, the old definitions of culture hade begun to fade. No longer was culture a word associated primarily with husbandry and farming: rather now in pocket dictionaries aimed at ordinary readers, the word simply stood for refinement.

The People's Webster Pronouncing Dictionary and Spelling Guide, a pocket dictionary of 23,000 words with single-word definitions, defined 'culture' simply as 'refinement'. By 1919 *Webster's Army and Navy Dictionary* and an elementary school edition of *Webster's New Standard Dictionary* armed American servicemen and school children with precisely the same succinct definition.[3]

The concept of taste as a synonym for refined sensibility was a device inherently conservative, anti-democratic and reactionary, it served to separate and sift non-economically separable groups on lines as invisible as those of the phrenologist or spiritualist (whose own habits of mind reinforced the methods by which critics determined taste in the first place). In such a way political order in unruly and industrialized mass democracies could be maintained by other means. Such means also created vast public recreational areas, parks and gardens in city centres, municipal museums and libraries open to all, often financed from the philanthropic bequests of dying entrepreneurs. Taste was democratized and withheld all at once.

The two great literary prizes in Britain, the Whitbread and the Booker, turn on the unresolved ambiguities between the undemocratic and democratic meanings of taste. These ceremonials are both dignified recognitions of worthiness and media circuses. The very success of both these events is predicated on the happily unresolved nature of the meaning of good public taste. There is considerable negotiation in the giving of these prizes between, on the one hand, a definition of culture as educational, literary, hierarchical and somehow withheld, and on the other hand the degraded spectacle provided by the need to award the prizes on television, the journalistic discussions, the quoting of odds at bookmakers and the potential provided by Hollywood for the winning book. Any ambivalence towards such prizes is haunted by the notion that literature is simply entertainment, commodified and ephemeral like any other form of entertainment.

Yet what marks the issue of these prizes is the valorization of the contemporary. From the later nineteenth century the issue of taste was bound up not merely with an adherence to a bygone, Latinate and classical culture, refined in the present time, but also to a sensibility able to recognize the *classic contemporary* work newly created and worthy of inclusion in the pantheon. Taste became a special concern for and ability to understand the important modern work, instantly historicized into the continuities of civilized taste and behaviour. This was the province of those experimentalists whose modernism was avidly collected by patrons with considerably educated palates. They were collecting, in their taste for the avant garde, the very nature of the future. This cultural investment (also, of course, an economic speculation) was a form of refusal of the past which was apostrophized more and more as mere cliché. Even T.S. Eliot whose 'Tradition and the Individual Talent' of 1921 made a plea for historical continuity was investing in the instant modern classic, the reception of *The Waste Land* in 1922 being the validation of this principle.

Equally, F.R. Leavis, whose attempt at stabilizing literary taste around a small select group of older novelists led to endless and fruitless debate among academics, was an early advocate of James Joyce at a time when Joyce was banned in Britain. The validation of the contemporary work of literature by reference to 'tradition' and the appearance of a so-called fiction canon, creations of Eliot and Leavis respectively (Leavis based his ideas on Eliot), was the neurotic outcome of this new entity, the instantly recognizable work of art.

Rules seemed now to have replaced the work of longevity and common recognition. Once learned, these rules could be used to measure the new literary work and place it in the canon or expel it into the abyss of popular taste. In such a way, the work of literature, the new great novel, was either eternal in an instant or ephemeral and irrelevant. Taste was a weapon which had an aesthetic power beyond mere aesthetics. It crept into all areas of personal life as a marker of self-respect and integrity. For some, such as I.A. Richards, a founding father of academic literary study, taste was the equivalent of health itself.

For the critic is as closely occupied with the health of the mind as the doctor with the health of body. . . .

The most important general condition is mental health, a high state of 'vigilance'; . . . None of the effects of art is more transferable than this balance or equilibrium.[4]

Taste had a psychological resonance and was a mark of character – the trace of gentlemanly behaviour, an outlook both liberal and élitist. As such, it marked the appearance of a politics internalized in the individual, now seen as self-sufficient and self-reliant because of *inherent* good taste. In effect, the notions of taste (as cultivation) and character (as personality) were interchangeable and tautological.

The guardian of the new culture of taste and refinement were always a small minority. T.S. Eliot's *Criterion* never had more than 800 subscribers and F.R. Leavis's supposedly influential *Scrutiny* never printed above 750 copies in the 1930s.[5] By the early years of this century the battle lines had been drawn and sharp boundaries were being marked across the cultural map. Even with the beginnings of full education after 1870 in Britain, indeed precisely because of this widening of the educational franchise,

> A revolution had taken place, and George Bernard Shaw assessed it with characteristic clarity. In 1879 his novel *Immaturity* was turned down by almost every London publisher. Looking back on this event, and working out the reasons for it, he realized that a radical change had occurred in the reading public. 'The Education Act of 1871' [*sic*], he explained, 'was producing readers who had never before bought books, nor could have read them if they had'. Publishers were finding that people wanted not George Eliot nor the 'excessively literary' Bernard Shaw, but adventure stories like Stevenson's *Treasure Island* and *Dr Jekyll and Mr Hyde*. In this situation Shaw concludes, 'I, as a belated intellectual, went under completely'.[6]

It may be no coincidence that these self-styled guardians were for the most part outsiders: George Bernard Shaw, an Irish socialist and failed novelist was forced into more lucrative journalism for readers he despaired of; T.S. Eliot was an expatriot American whose (classicist and monarchist) leanings were more extreme than even the snobbery of Bloomsbury; Frank Leavis, an outsider at Cambridge who came from that very class that would produce our only woman prime minister; D.H. Lawrence, self-appointed sex guru and world wanderer, who learned his contempt for the class he hailed from through his readings of Nietzsche in the public library, a free institution created precisely to enfranchise that class, to which he could not be reconciled.

Differences between the consumers of culture were emphasized by the confusion and hostility among the arbiters of taste. In *Crome*

Yellow, Aldous Huxley caustically satirized a James Joyce-like avant-garde novelist at the same time as he aspired to become one himself:

> 'Of course', Mr Scogan groaned. 'I'll describe the plot for you. Little Percy, the hero, was never good at games, but he was always clever. He passes through the usual public school and the usual university and comes to London, where he lives among the artists. He is bowed down with melancholy thought: he carries the whole weight of the universe upon his shoulders. He writes a novel of dazzling brilliance; he dabbles delicately in Amour and disappears, at the end of the book, into the luminous Future.'
> (chapter 3)

Graham Greene in his 'entertainment' detective novel *Brighton Rock* savagely lampooned the supposed heroine who comes from the lower middle-brow readership that Greene could not reconcile himself to writing for.

> Ida turned on the gas-fire and drew the old scarlet velvet curtains to shut out the grey sky and the chimney-pots. Then she patted the divan bed into shape and drew two chairs to the table. In a glass-fronted cupboard her life stared back at her – a good life: pieces of china bought at the seaside, a photograph of Tom, an Edgar Wallace, a Netta Syrett from a second-hand stall, some sheets of music, *The Good Companions*, her mother's picture, more china, a few jointed animals made of wood and elastic, trinkets given her by this, that and the other, *Sorrell and Son*.

It should be no surprise that Greene's ambivalence over his public came from the conflict that existed between his artistic ambitions and his journalistic income gained mainly from film reviewing: 'Furthermore, the popular newspaper presented a threat, because it created an alternative culture which bypassed the intellectual and made him redundant.'[7]

By 1945, this general ambivalence among the critics and aesthetic arbitrators gave rise to a never-ending speculation over the next great work or literary movement. Critics of all hues looked feverishly around for a new cultural flourish amid the wreckage of the austerity years. Ironically, the hunt itself was a creation of journalism's appetite. In an era on the brink of even greater uncertainities concerning the role of culture and the meaning that culture had as an oppositional force strong enough to fight Americanization, popular cinema, novelettes, journalism of the 'lower sort' and finally commercial television, this was both, an ameliorative measure and an act of faith in national identity and hierarchic continuity.

> As John Lehmann recollects in *The Ample Proposition* (1966), 1945 seemed a 'time . . . of hope and confidence' with the prospect of 'a great epoch' lying ahead for the arts, promising 'a magnificent harvest', but such hopes had been quickly dashed. In *Horizon's* editorial for April 1947 Cyril Connolly vividly described the effects of the aftermath of war and Stafford Cripps's austerity programme following an economically crippling winter: 'most of us are not men or women but members of a vast seedy, overworked, over-legislated, neuter class, with our drab clothes, our ration books and murder stories, our envious, stricken, old-world apathies and resentments – a careworn people. It was self-evident to Connolly that new art could not be expected to flourish amid such drabness and privation: 'there is no deterrent to aesthetic adventure like a prolonged struggle with domestic difficulties, food shortages, cold, ill-health and money worries. Art is not a necessity but an indispensable luxury; those who produce it must be cosseted.'[8]

The new cultural enemy was not necessarily the working classes. Here was to be found a rich source of new talent and subject matter, whether it be John Braine's Joe Lampton, Shelagh Delaney's Helen and Josephine, John Osborne's Jimmy Porter, Richard Hoggart's hymn to working-class life or somewhat later the canonization of Liverpudlian working-class music. The working class were colourful, exotic and authentic. 'New Provincialism' was not a swing towards middle-brow taste, now conflated with misunderstood Leavisite attitudes, but rather an attempt to defend and recuperate the élite, hierarchical culture of pre-war modernism despite any other egalitarian or provincial bias that may have sometimes shown through.

No, the real enemy was the middle-class middlebrow vitriolically portrayed or simply ignored by writers such as Evelyn Waugh in *Brideshead Revisited* (1945), Kingsley Amis in *Lucky Jim* (1954) and John Osborne in *Look Back in Anger* (1956). Even a novelist such as Ian Fleming rarely showed interest or sympathy with the readership he aimed his novels at and who regularly took the papers that advocated purchasing or borrowing his books. This was a world of the heroic rich, the heroic poor, or the 'angry' intellectual, classless, disinherited and celebrated in Colin Wilson's *The Outsider* (1956).

Whatever vigour existed in this atmosphere was increasingly sought out and encouraged by (or recruited to) the needs of journalism, both that of the literary magazines and that of mainstream newspapers.

By the early fifties impatience with country house conventions was growing. The *Observer's* young theatre critic, Kenneth Tynan, embarked on a critical crusade against 'Loamshire' plays, and a handful of other writers began to show a similar reaction against the fiction of refined nostalgia. One of these was Angus Wilson, whose collections of short stories – *Such Darling Dodos* (1949) and *The Wrong Set* (1950) – were notable for depicting current social changes, particularly as they affected a section of the middle class, the 'nouveaux pauvres'. In his criticism Wilson began to attack the country house school and call for novelists to come to terms with the new realities of the Welfare State.[9]

Tynan's criticism was part of a wave of activities from the Third Programme's *New Soundings* (which ran from 1952 to 1953) to *First Reading* and *Encounter* edited by Stephen Spender and Irving Kristol. All went in search of elusive new talent. A war over the control of taste had begun guided by and organized around the newspaper and periodical journalist. Thus, *First Reading* encouraged,

a profound feeling that amounts almost to knowledge that a literary renaissance is about to take place, or is taking place now, in Britain. There is a great urge towards creative expression, an impatience with the verbose outpourings of sterile criticism. There is a belief that this creative drive will find new things to say; if not new things then at least old things worth saying again and important to the times in which we live.[10]

Yet such belief could also conveniently be used as a rallying cry for the *true* believers of *Encounter* to reject all those so praised. Hence Spender was able to define his journal's tastes by stating, as policy, his refusal to publish anyone praised or promoted in *First Reading*, detecting, as he did, the 'dark hand of F.R. Leavis' behind it all.[11] By the mid-1950s, 'provincial' and 'academic' were the new labels applied to fiction and poetry respectively.[12] Against these, and against the waves of popular culture, high art seemed helplessly doomed and Spender's attempts to recuperate an international, humanist avant garde out of date. For C.P. Snow the end of high modernism was to be warmly welcomed.

> On Boxing Day 1954 in the *Sunday Times* Snow applauded the 'quiet and effective counter-revolution' against the 'novel of total sensibility' and selected *Lucky Jim* as a welcome replacement for 'obsolete' works of 'mindless subjectivism' such as (almost inevitably) *Finnegans Wake*. . . . A *Spectator* article published on April Fool's Day 1955, supported the 'New Provincialism' [and the] rejection of 'Bloomsbury'.[13]

This search for the new work finally found itself a name – *the Movement* and came to the notice of a wider public during 1956 through the *Observer*, *Sunday Times* and *Evening Standard*. On the brink of political humiliation and international withdrawal the English had found a new cultural stability to restate and reinforce their identity. Taste was the recuperation of politics by other means. It was the rediscovery of a principal which led to the furious debate over C.P. Snow's 1959 lecture *The Two Cultures* – a debate into which F.R. Leavis waded axe in hand – over who should rule British culture and determine Britain's values.[14]

This was an essentially journalistic debate, even if its various advocates were primarily novelists or academics and, as such, it may be no wonder that central to the imagery of the era's most famous play, *Look Back in Anger*, is the reading and discussion of the Sunday papers, caustically dismissed but obsessively read.

> JIMMY: Why do I do this every Sunday? Even the book reviews seem to be the same as last week's. Different books – same reviews.
> . . .
> I've just read three whole columns on the English Novel. Half of it's in French. Do the Sunday papers make you feel ignorant?
> CLIFF: Not 'arf.
> JIMMY: Well, you *are* ignorant. You're just a peasant.
>
> (Act. 1)

Further irony is added when one realizes that these debates about the *rejection* of middle-brow liberalistic conformism were conducted in the name of independence of thought through publications determined by the policies of corporate publishing interests.

[*Encounter*] appeared in October 1953, to be followed by the launch of the *London Magazine* in February 1954. Only now did it appear that English letters might recover from the epidemic of closures which had hit literary magazines in the late forties. The revival of the London literary scene was in fact being financed from two very unlikely sources – Daily Mirror Newspapers Ltd., whose chairman, Cecil King, sponsored the *London Magazine* as a 'useful piece of do-gooding' at the suggestion of Rosamond Lehmann (and appointed her brother John as editor), and the CIA, which funded *Encounter* under the cover of the 'Congress for Cultural Freedom'.[15]*

Middle-browism and middle-class taste generally became the victims of all the protagonists in the struggle for the high ground of culture during the 1950s but this was simply symptomatic of a much older struggle, stretching back across the previous century for the control of print itself – the parallel coming to being of modern taste and corporate control. The fear of corporatism, consumerism, middle-browism and a mass reading public has driven twentieth-century cultural hierarchists. A selection of views across the century confirms a growing mania, amounting to a neurotic drive, for a separation compelled by fear of cultural debasement and defilement. It is always a battle to the death.

In America the distaste for philistinism has extended from Thorstein Veblen's *The Theory of the Leisure Class* published as early as 1899 through to the work of Allan Bloom whose 1988 attack on the 1960s, *The Closing of the American Mind*, itself became a middle-brow bestseller and to Harold Bloom's *The Western Canon* (1995).[16] The 'death' of literature debate which to Allan Bloom signalled the end of refined and civilized values in a liberal (but not liberated) culture, was joined during the 1980s by E. Donald Hirsch Jr, Roger Kimball and William Bennett.

The death of the old literature in the grand sense, Shelley's unacknowledged legislation of the world, Arnold's timeless best

---

* Although they seemed unable to determine editional policy or curb intellectual independence.

that has been thought and written, Eliot's unchanging monuments of the European mind, from the rock drawings in Lascaux to *The Magic Mountain*, has seemed to people who matured intellectually in the ancien regime of high culture nothing less than the setting of the sun of the human imagination in the evening-lands of Western civilization.[17]

Even Robert Hughes, expatriot Australian domiciled in the United States and quite capable of logically and sensibly debunking both P.C. rejectionism and neoconservative canonical revisionism, cannot resist a swipe at that cultural *bête noir*, television.

> Those who complain about the Canon think it creates readers who will never read anything else.
>
> If only! What they don't want to admit, at least not publicly, is that most American students don't read much anyway and quite a few, left to their own devices, would not read at all.
>
> Their moronic national babysitter, the television set, took care of that. In 1991, the majority of American households (60 per cent, the same as in Spain) did not buy one single book. Before long, Americans will think of the time when people sat at home and read books for their own sake, discursively and sometimes even aloud to one another, as a lost era – the way we now see rural quilting-bees in the 1870s. No American university can *assume* that its first-year students are literate in a more than technical sense. Perhaps they never could. But they certainly can't now. It is hard to exaggerate the narrowness of reference, the indifference to reading, the ... cultural shallowness of many young products of American TV culture, even the privileged ones.[18]

However, in the latter half of the twentieth century more books are being produced than ever before. For some critics this was itself proof that 'real' or serious reading was in terminal decline. Statistics quoted by Alvin Kernan give some idea of the growth of print in an age supposedly inimical to it.

> When the impact of television first began to be felt, 11,022 books were published in the United States. In 1970, when the impact of the computer began to reach major proportions, the number of books had risen to 36,071. In 1979, after almost thirty years of television and ten years of major computer use, 45,182 books

were published in the United States. Book publishing revenues in the United States in 1950 were less than $500 million; in 1970 they were more than $2.9 billion; in 1980, more than $7.0 billion. In new forms of computer printouts and desktop publishing, microfilm and microfiche, laser disks storing millions of words, computer databases containing masses of information in readable form, as well as in magazines, newspapers, and conventional books, the flood of print continues and grows.[19]

Yet, for guardians of culture this increase in reading material was of necessity simply the production of more corporate consumables merely dressed up as literature. One such social commentator, Herbert I. Schiller, argues that the publishing industry and the very idea of literacy (as the mark of a humanistic mentality) are opposed. For Schiller, literacy as defined a self-expression and self-emancipation is being underminded by a new and powerful culture industry.

Another feature (mostly ignored) of the modern cultural industries is their deeply structured and pervasive ideological character. The heavy public consumption of cultural products and services and the contexts in which most of them are provided represent a daily, if not hourly, diet of systemic values, spooned out to whichever public happens to be engaged. 'The typical film from which investors anticipate a profit', writes film analyst Thomas Guback, 'may be art or non-art, but it is always a commodity.' The same can be said for Broadway musical comedies, best-selling novels, and top-of-the-chart records. They are commodities and ideological products, embodying the rules and values of the market system that produced them. Multi-million-dollar investments in film, theater, or publishing can be relied upon to contain systemic thinking. In the late twentieth century, those few spaces that have escaped incorporation into the market are being subjected to continuous pressure and, often, frontal attack.[20]

Such capitalistic totalitarianism is Orwell's *1984* nightmare written for a mass consumer public and Schiller's opposition can trace its heritage as much to the Thoreau of *Walden* as it can to the work of Theodor Adorno, Leo Lowenthal or Noam Chomsky.

The result of this corporatism is the fascism of a market organized to produce more but with less variety: to frame things and

experience in the language of *Newspeak*. For Paul Fussell this amounts
to 'the dumbing of America', in which culture most books are not
read but shown, consumed or worn as labels; the corporate book is
the new literature of corporate humanity, to be rewarded with
corporate prizes and reworked into other more lucrative corporate
activities (e.g. film and television).

> [N]ow BIG BAD books – those immense, everlasting weighty
> novels that middle-class people like to be seen toting around –
> are specifically the commodities that keep numerous publishers
> from foundering, and only one per season, if it catches on, will be
> enough to do the trick.
>   For years the industry has puzzled over the question of why
> people acquire these wordy, overstuffed, great big thick novels
> promising a protracted read lasting from September ('the fall list')
> until June or July. The best answer: if you read only one book a
> year, and you're proud of it, you want that one *to look like a book*
> – thick, hardbound, serious, one to be seen with on bus, train, or
> plane, or on the street, and one so heavily advertised and well
> known that your owning a copy will proclaim your solid location
> in the main line of consumers.
>   . . . the expensive hardbound is not always the most important
> commodity being sold: the subsidiary rights (first and second
> serial, movie, stage, audiocassette, TV, T-shirt etc.) often bring in
> more money. Novelist and scriptwriter Larry McMurtry has had
> the wit to notice that 'it is really reductive to call what we have
> now a 'publishing industry', when it is a media complex, in which
> promotability, not literary merit, is the *sine qua non*.[21]

Culture in Britain, was and is, according to its own guardians, in
little better state than in the USA and considerably worse *because* of
the USA! Given the thoughts of these American commentators it is
therefore doubly ironic that both George Orwell and Richard
Hoggart blamed Americanization for the lowering of cultural standards in Britain. Here is Hoggart attacking the new consumerism.

> Perhaps even more symptomatic of the general trend is the read-
> ing of juke-box boys, of those who spend their evening listening
> in harshly lighted milk-bars to the 'nickelodeons'. . . . [M]ost of
> the customers are boys aged between 15 and 20, with drape-suits,
> picture ties, and an American slouch. . . . [M]any of the customers

– their clothes, their hair-styles, their facial expressions all indicate – are living to a large extent in a myth-world compounded of a few simple elements which they take to be those of American life.

They form a depressing group. . . .

The hedonistic but passive barbarian who rides in a fifty-horse-power bus for threepence, to see a five-million dollar film for one-and-eightpence, is not simply a social oddity; he is a portent.[22]

Better public transport, easy access to libraries and those milk bars were all to blame for the philistinism of the young. For contrasting yet complementary views of youth one only has to compare Anthony Burgess's pessimistic *A Clockwork Orange* (1962) with Colin MacInnes's optimistic *Absolute Beginners* (1959). Notwithstanding, it was not youngsters who were the real enemies of taste – after all the doors of the citadel could be closed against them and, to be fair to Hoggart, youth was not beyond intelligent, educational redemption.

The real enemy, as Queenie Leavis, the other partner in that formidable Leavisian double-act pointed out during the 1930s was 'middle-brow' literature masquerading as high-brow art – this was the really fraudulent activity and she attacked it with a vengeance. Her target was Dorothy L. Sayers in a review printed in *Scrutiny* of *Gaudy Night* and *Busman's Holiday*.[23]

For Q.D. Leavis, Dorothy Sayers's books were not just bad, they were BAD, to use Paul Fussell's terminology: exhibiting 'elements of the pretentious, the overwrought, or the fraudulent' but mistaken by those *who should know better* for the authentic product.[24]

This odd conviction that she is in a different class from Edgar Wallace or Ethel M. Dell apparently depends on four factors in these novels. They have an appearance of literariness; they profess to treat profound emotions and to be concerned with values; they generally or incidentally affect to deal in large issues and general problems (e.g. *Gaudy Night*, in so far as it is anything but a bundle of best-selling old clothes, is supposed to answer the question whether academic life produces abnormality in women); and they appear to give an inside view of some modes of life that share the appeal of the unknown for many readers, particularly the life of the older universities.

Literature gets heavily drawn upon in Miss Sayers's writings,

and her attitude to it is revealing. She displays knowingness about
literature without any sensitiveness to it or any feeling for quality
– i.e. she has an academic literary taste over and above having no
general taste at all.[25]

How revealing that the academics themselves were the barbarians,
middle-brow, semi-literates whose learned opinion merely sanctioned popular taste; how revealing that Sayers should have worked
in advertising; how revealing that academia was, after all, merely
another branch of business. 'In fact the more one investigates the
academic world the more striking appears its resemblance to the
business world.'[26]

For Mrs Leavis's husband in another *Scrutiny* article, entitled 'The
Literary Racket', things could not be expected to be otherwise.

But social pressure and the pressure of the Advertising Manager
are, after all, symptoms rather than causes. The radical fact is the
advance of civilization. The supply of literature has become an
industry subject to the same conditions as the supply of any other
commodity. For many firms publishing is a business like the
manufacture of 50s [shillings] suits, and the methods of Big Business are accordingly adopted. The market is raked for authors –
for potential profit-makers – the wares are boosted by the usual
commercial methods. The gigantic advance in output that makes
good reviewing more than ever necessary has been its destruction – by asphyxiation in various forms.[27]

In the 1980s, fate led avant-garde British and America academics
to roundly and widely condemn the exclusive, canonical, Eurocentric
attitudes of the Leavisites and New Critics who, for purposes of
vilification, they rounded up together. Now, of all things, the
Leavises were the barbarians, so it is hardly surprising that the
reforms in education brought about by the Conservative govern-
ments of the 1980s were themselves understood by many liberal
and left critics as the return of a virus formed around Leavisism.
The government itself and the Secretaries of State for Education
were now the targets of accusations of barbarism and while the
government's policies (specifically over testing) may have been
confused this hardly excused the reaction of left-centre liberal English professors who signed their names to an equally confused letter to the *Times Higher Education Supplement* and which took as its
central concern the 'appropriation' of Shakespeare.

As University Professors of English, we view with dismay the Government's proposed reforms to the teaching of English in schools.

Like all academics, we expect sound grammar and spelling from our students; but the Government's doctrinaire preoccupation with these skills betrays a disastrously reductive, mechanistic understanding of English studies.

Similarly, its evident hostility to regional and working-class forms of speech in the classroom betrays a prejudice which has little or no intellectual basis, and which is seriously harmful to the well-being and self-esteem of many children.

We are all committed to the study of Shakespeare; but to make such *study compulsory* for 14-year-olds, as the minister intends, is to risk permanently alienating a large number of children from the pleasurable understanding of classical literary works.[28]

[italics mine]

The letter left unquestioned the relationship between Shakespeare and popular working-class forms of expression. What might these be?

The continuing centrality accorded Shakespeare on stage, in print and as a cultural and educational marker even in the 1990s is indicative of the more general trend towards culture's modern hierarchical nature and the necessary readjustments that accompanied that progress. In England, theatrical regulation prevented Shakespeare's plays from being seen in full by popular audiences who watched abbreviated versions heightened by the musical accompaniments and interludes that allowed 'unlicensed' theatres to pretend that Shakespeare was merely a display of rhetoric during an evening otherwise given over to a concert. In America, Shakespeare had little status on the East Coast and didn't start to become regularly played until the 1840s.

And yet, there is ample evidence to show that alongside Shakespeare's canonization there remained a thriving popular theatre for Shakespeare played quite possibly nearer to the playwright's intentions. In England there is evidence of a knowledge of Hamlet in melodramas such as *The Factory Lad* (1832) a play written by John Walker who wrote short plays for the popular theatre between 1825 and 1834, and in America by Louisa Hamblin's 1839 play of Robert

Montgomery Bird's novel *Nick of the Woods* (1837) in which there is an opening speech reminiscent of *Julius Caesar*.[29]

Of importance here is the shadowy presence of Shakespeare in these two popular melodramas which both echo his more extravagant character devices. Shakespeare then, had a clear presence in the popular theatre both in his own right and as an influence on plays where audiences may not have recognized his presence. Moreover, as academics like Harriett Hawkins have clearly demonstrated his language rhythms endure in films like *Snow White*, songs such as Michael Jackson's *Thriller* and even jazz lyrics, while his work has been continuously updated through Broadway shows, films and television plots. Hawkins convincingly demonstrates that Shakespeare first became a standard in the America mid-west and frontier not on the East Coast.

> It came from strolling players who followed the flatboats floating down the Allegheny and rode into the rowdier pioneer towns springing up around and across the Appalachians. . . . But where did these vagabonds get their knowledge of Shakespeare? The real infusion of Shakespeare's art into the American literary tradition began around 1835, when a schoolteacher named William Holmes McGuffey published two school readers designed to introduce children in rural schools to the best models of their own language.[30]

Ironically the pioneers who measured their lives through Bunyan, the Bible and Shakespeare first encountered him in a school book.

> They were bought in job lots and used as basic English textbooks in the very elementary schools of the empire of the Mississippi and the South. In the sixth edition there were 138 selections from over a hundred authors, and Shakespeare was the preferred author of choice with nine extracts. Time and time again the memoirs of pioneers across three thousand miles are studded with saws and instances from the Bible, *Pilgrim's Progress*, and Shakespeare. Children in log huts who could only imagine New York or London and who, unlike the divines of New England, had never heard of Rousseau or Goethe, could – unlike the divines of New England – yet quote Hamlet and recite the Fall of Wolsey. For the distribution of the McGuffey readers stopped short of New England. Everywhere else, the readers sold, at the last count, something like 200 million copies.[31]

It is not only the hierarchists of culture like Allan Bloom who misunderstand the role of Shakespeare in Anglo-American culture but also his opponents who fail to recognize that Shakespeare resonates in popular culture too and that there is no reason to fear the imposition of required reading if that required reading belongs to both ends of the cultural divide and signifies in a multiplicity of ways: imposition is not control, regulations are often honoured in the breach.

Lawrence W. Levine, in his excellent book *Highbrow, Lowbrow* has shown how it was the battle over the ownership of 'Shakespeare' that constituted the centre of the culture wars and that it was this battle that accelerated the cultural divide that marked the nineteenth century in America.

In 1992, as the letter to the *Times Higher Education Supplement* proved, the ownership of Shakespeare was again in dispute in both Britain and the United States . . . *plus ça change*. The end of the Cold War, the fall of the Soviet bloc and the re-emergence of liberalism all suggest that the question of cultural values had not gone away, nor would it.

We have seen the considerable attention and continued fascination born of horror that popular culture and by implication mass-democratic modern society (both industrial and urban) continued to exert over 'disenfranchised' intellectuals. Often this attention was dismissive, sometimes it has been downright hysterical. For one critic even middle-brow prize-winning authors, can be 'gutter writers' providing 'pathetic garbage under disguise',

> Middlebrowism becomes truly offensive only when it veers into glaring pretentiousness, or takes on certain characteristics of gutter culture, a sinister phenomenon which is of extreme interest, but which has no connection with literature. It must be mentioned here only because it is beginning to take over middlebrow territory, which (as we have seen) does have literary features. . . . Reviewers of the *Time Out* sort, and others, are beginning to fail to be able to distinguish between this kind of material and the seriously intended.[32]

thus 'D.M. Thomas's *The White Hotel*, one of the few successes of this sort to be treated as having literary quality, reads as though it

were the desperate plagiarism of a professional masturbator'.[33] Even
sympathetic commentators finally baulk at the *exuberant popularity
of mass art*. For Raymond Williams, fearful of the future at the end
of his life (in thoughts echoed better by Robert Hughes), television
was still the opium of the masses.[34]

Against such a tide of professional distaste there have been those
who have defended popular fiction (in its middle-brow/low-brow
and pulp incarnations) but in many cases this has been tempered
with disclaimers in order to placate those who feel anyone interested in popular culture (and therefore contemporary life) is a pathological case. Lawrence Levine, in a work I have already cited as
exemplary in showing the merely historical (rather than theoretically valid) divide that occurred in nineteenth-century culture is
still unable to avoid an apology to the unknown and, by implication, sceptical reader. He tells us, that '[his] own interest is not in
attacking the notion of cultural hierarchy per se' at the very moment he proves cultural hierarchy to be aesthetically unjustified
except by the ad hoc historical development of defensive rules.[35]
Peter Keating in an otherwise groundbreaking analysis of late nineteenth-century fiction, its consumption and formal development is
unable to make real sense of the popular forms that came into being
from the 1880s onwards.

> The imagery of exploration was clearly as important to the ro-
> mance as to the realistic novel and social documentary, and here
> also it functioned on both a literal and a metaphorical level, though
> its emphasis was totally different. The realist, the journalist and
> the sociologist employed exploration imagery to dramatise present
> social conditions, to draw the reader's attention to neglected ar-
> eas of contemporary life. In contrast, the writer of romance em-
> ployed the same imagery in order to escape from the present, or,
> if he had a point to make of direct contemporary relevance, to set
> up a process of extrapolation that the reader was expected to
> follow through. Of the four major kinds of late Victorian romance
> examined here – historical, scientific, supernatural, detective –
> only the writer of detective fiction shared the social explorers'
> preoccupation with present time and conditions. The other three
> were interested in the present only in so far as it could be placed
> within the huge vistas of space and time of which it was, if truly
> understood, merely an insignificant speck. In the process, they
> divided among themselves not merely types of fiction, but time

as well. The historical novelist took as his special province the whole of time past; the writer of science fiction took the whole of time future; while the writer of the supernatural and occult embraced or ignored both time future and time past in his exploration of states of consciousness which were beyond any concept of time available to human understanding. . . . Day-dream and adult play really had taken over.[36]

Thus popular fiction becomes again *simple* escapism designed to a formula: commercial and therefore of only historical interest. Geoffrey O'Brien in his semi-serious exploration of the 'Lurid years of Paperbacks' (to quote the book's subtitle) suggests:

The paperbacks were a microcosm of American fantasies about the real world. They took the ordinary streets, the dives, the tenements, the cheap hotels, and invested them with mystery – with poetry even – turning them into the stuff of mythology. Shamelessly exploitative, they made their points with a maximum of directness. No trace of subtlety was permitted to cloud the violent and erotic visions that were their essence, and that very lack of subtlety lifted them out of this world. The people they depicted seemed to exist in some impossibly energetic super-America parallel to the one we know. . . . They are, then, little monuments, frozen moments in the history of a culture.[37]

And yet O'Brien is also capable of seeing such escapism and parallelism as pointing to deep and disturbing social concerns, usually ignored or half realized in more respectable fiction.

The Thirties pulp imagery of secret societies bent on world domination, mad sadistic scientists, and bloody avengers is plainly fantastic, but by the late Forties these images are taken as utterly real, just as the rocket ships of *Flash Gordon* and *Buck Rogers* become actual cigar-shaped phenomena seen in the sky. . . . The Thirties pulp hero in mask and cape, battling the Purple Menace or the Green Menace, has by 1947 become a down-to-earth Mike Hammer battling the Red Menace.

In such an atmosphere, the pulp imagination can rise to new heights of glory. An L. Ron Hubbard can move from second-rate science fiction to the founding of a worldwide 'religion'. A hack thriller writer like Howard Hunt can end up acting out his fantasies as national policy at the Bay of Pigs and the Watergate.[38]

If such books are a neglected popular art form they are ultimately only *symptomatic* of historical change and social divergence. The vitality of these popular forms then becomes frigidified in a historical moment backdated and bankrupt if still amusing, a view substantially repeated by others.

> The essays . . . seek instead to weave together the text, the genre and the specific history of the period. And all these essays create specifically different 'histories' in order to answer the question why those books were a popular 'good read' in their own day.[39]

John G. Cawelti, as long ago as 1979, pointed out why academia should study popular arts forms as *art* but his argument was tautological at best and was itself unable to resolve the relationship between historical instance and aesthetic continuity. Here the patterns appear to be familial prior to their becoming cultural.

> Older children and adults continue to find a special delight in familiar stories, though in place of the child's pleasure in the identical tale, they substitute an interest in certain types of stories which have highly predictable structures that guarantee the fulfillment of conventional expectations: the detective story, the western, the romance, the spy story, and many other such types. For many persons such formulaic types make up by far the greater portion of the experience of literature. Even scholars and critics professionally dedicated to the serious study of artistic masterpieces often spend their off-hours following a detective's ritual pursuit of a murderer or watching one of television's spy teams carry through its dangerous mission. . . . In fact, they are examples of what some scholars have called archetypes or patterns that appeal in many different cultures.[40]

If 'older children and adults' are also sometimes 'scholars and critics' then a study of popular forms becomes a deep regressive psychotherapy in which the archetypes of popular literature take on a mythic deep structural form. For the critic of literature, a recognition of this mythic power is also a recognition of artistic value but only if the value is *formulaic*. Such an argument affirms in an ironic way the repeatable pattern so often attacked as debased by other critics, but it salvages popular forms only if they become eternal, deep, unconscious and historically continuous – in other words another version of serious literature. For Cawelti, historical continuity requires a mythic or 'archetypal' substratum more folk than pop, more Jung than Freud.

However, Cawelti's thorough treatment of such formulas, in the western, romance, detective story etc., did attempt 'to illustrate how the changing story patterns through which this mythology is dramatised relate to cultural changes'.[41] Nevertheless, Cawelti is stuck with the problem of relating myth to history. How can popular fiction be essentially modern and mythic? Thus it is that times change but the mythology remains timeless – taken up and 'dramatized' anew in each suceeding generation. History and the cultures that sustain it are, in the final analysis, simply gratuitously ephemeral expression of the archetypes behind popular fiction. The result of Cawelti's formal specificity is ultimately metaphysical vacuity.

Cawelti followed such British studies as Colin Watson's *Snobbery with Violence* and E.S. Turner's *Boys will be Boys* neither of which was aimed at an academic audience but both of which revealed a whole universe of attitudes and consumption in which detective fiction, thrillers, penny dreadfuls and boys-own adventures were once enjoyed but which has now passed.[42] Pieces for nostalgia only. It is these types of book however that bridge the gap between scholarly investigations and affectionate, often uncritical, but usually highly knowledgeable works by and for aficionados by writers such as Ron Goulart in the USA, Peter Haining in Britain and even such books as Stephen King's *Dance Macabre*, an intelligent narrative of King's own chosen genre.[43]

Leslie A. Fiedler in a book about contemporary mass entertainment leads an attack on the cultural mandarins which recognizes the aggressively 'defensive' attitude of the defenders of cultural standards (including Marx) but which at the same time is unable to see what makes popular art intrinsically different from highbrow creation and *indifferent* to highbrow demands. Thus,

What [he will] be discussing are the kinds of songs and stories which have tended, since the invention of moveable type, to be 'ghettoized', which is to say, excluded from classes in 'literature' and endured only as long as they clearly know their own place.[44]

And of one of the great nineteenth-century popular authors Eugene Sue:

But if Sue was falsified in his own self-consciousness by the theor-
izing of the *Phalange*, in the consciousness of his contemporaries
and ours, he was even more drastically falsified by Marx who
taught us first to regard him, and all like him, as purveyors of
junk, panderers to the misled masses.[45]

Yet his next thoughts suggest an overly literal view, itself paranoid,
about the meaning of popular forms:

> Clearly, what we consider 'serious novels' or 'art novels': works,
> say, by Henry James or Marcel Proust, Thomas Mann or James
> Joyce, are indistinguishable, *before the critical act*, from 'best-
> sellers' or 'popular novels' by Jacqueline Susann or John D.
> MacDonald, Conan Doyle or Bram Stoker. Despite peripheral
> attempts to sort them out before the fact by invidious binding or
> labelling, by and large, they are bound in the same boards and
> paper; edited, printed, distributed, advertised and peddled in quite
> the same way.[46]

It is not *after the fact* that the critical act becomes important but
throughout production and prior to any production in a complex
relationship between art and the many processes and factors in its
making and consumption. The aesthetic question is always a critical one and always *dynamic* – there can be no 'fact' to follow.

C.W.E. Bigsby, who edited the volume in which Fiedler appears,
reveals the ambiguity in the interested critic's attitude to popular
art forms. Again, we have an attack on the cultural hierarchists, in
this case, Matthew Arnold, Oswald Spengler, Ortega y Gasset, Karl
Jasper and F.R. Leavis, but this is itself followed by:

> But just as Spengler had seen the city, with its aggregated masses,
> as providing only a parody of community, so the communal
> modes suggested by the media are, perhaps, more apparent than
> real. Far from creating a global village with shared values ex-
> pressed in a common visual and verbal symbolisation, the city-
> world of today and the media with which it addresses itself may
> be seen as creating only the imagery and *not* [my italics] the
> substance of communication. Thus the film is the first mass art in
> which people are gathered together in communal buildings in
> which the communal element is unimportant. Television, simi-
> larly, groups the family in the posture of group contact only to

interdict the contact which that configuration implies. Symbol without content. When the teenager plugs the transistor into his ear, he necessarily unplugs from those around him; the juke box, in order to function, must make conversation ineffective. Progressively, society falls back on visual images, distrusts language, fills the air with Muzak to avoid silence, and plumbs the individual psyche in preference to chancing a human relationship which implies an avoidable vulnerability.[47]

Such comments, compounded by others, such as the commonplace that 'post-literate popular culture is very much a product of the machine age' and examples drawn almost exclusively from 'legitimate' forms show that Bigsby is unsure what should be said about popular forms and that any form of culture which utilizes electronics (television, transistor radios and juke boxes) is quite beyond his 'pre-electronic' understanding.[48] On the one hand he can point out (if rather weakly),

Yet the potential for social subversion which popular culture also clearly possesses (as in the comic book, pornography, the lyrics of acid-rock), explains the difficulty in defining a phenomenon which has been seen both as the cause and effect of social dislocation and the embodiment of a liberated democratic spirit.[49]

and on the other hand he can state (perhaps his deeper opinion) that,

The commonplaces of Hollywood, Broadway, the cartoon, the comic book, the Western, the detective story, are all concerned with offering assurance that things are under control, that ambiguity will be resolved, that violence is assimilable, that disorder will resolve into order, that sexuality is not anarchic, that death is not real, that injustice is a temporary state, that rebellion is a predictable phase which will be subsumed eventually in a necessary corporate stability.
Art and literature, on the other hand are rooted in a fundamental dissonance between appearance and reality, indeed express a basic conviction that reality is indefinable.[50]

This ambiguity is more pronounced elsewhere. In an extraordinarily old-fashioned and well-meaning text-book which seeks to celebrate

and define popular literary style (published as late as 1990) Walter
Nash, without a hint of irony can tell us that,

> Here in the airport lounge, how becalmed our voyagers are, all
> spellbound and dreambound! . . . We are all characters in enjoy-
> able bad books, it seems. We are in the right place for Popular
> Fiction . . . to keep us happy and hypnotized in our confinement.[51]

The message ultimately is the same as Bigsby however,

> Pop fiction does have its merits, and they are by no means neg-
> ligible. . . . Our deeper allegiance, nevertheless, is to a very special
> kind of 'merit', which we detect in the capacity of a book to illum-
> inate our own experience, to enlarge our perceptions of human
> nature and conduct, and, without overt moralizing to establish
> and confirm in us the knowledge of a morality. The lessons of
> 'serious' literature are not quickly learned.[52]

By the late 1980s the study of popular fiction became theorized
within the new post-structuralisms and thus began a short and
profitless war over the canon and literary hierarchy, élitism in the
academy etc., in which mass culture became the site of a political
struggle for the ownership of English letters as we saw earlier in
the debate over Shakespeare in British schools. The result was that
'newer' texts from outside the so-called 'canon' were admitted, *but*
only if they displayed proof of 'contradictions'. Thus studies of
Barbara Cartland novels concentrated on 'highlighting',

> a contradiction in the narrative, between the intended 'message'
> which focuses on the role of a woman as a transcendent, spiritual
> being, and the actual process of narration which concentrates on
> the more mundane reality of 'love and marriage'. The main nar-
> rative threatens to undermine the romantic message by highlight-
> ing the historical 'necessities' which lead women to pursue men
> and to turn love into an 'economically rational career'.[53]

Inevitably, such contradictions show up what plain common sense
knew, namely,

> although Cartland's novels can be interpreted in a manner which
> renders them potentially subversive of the author's overt inten-
> tions, that does not mean that they generate an alternative view
> of female identity.[54]

Such approaches tell us only that Cartland is neither politically correct nor an academic. Cartland's work is criticized for what it is *not*, while ignoring what its own *voice* speaks and why such a voice is so successful – surely not because the poor women who *like* Cartland are all fools? Cartland's agenda, which in its belief in *seduction* is curiously close to some contemporary theory, does not fit well with a left-liberal feminist agenda. Ultimately, this approach does little to explain Cartland's texts or their specific cultural position – it is in fact a value judgement disguised as analysis. Popular women's fiction is only good *if* it is both feminist and subversive; a question of taste rather than history. Thus for one contemporary editor, in an otherwise well argued book, a contributor to a volume of women's writing, 'shows how [Jean] Rhys constructs a feminist anticolonialism. The novel subverts colonialism, the appropriation of what is different, other; it subverts colonial romance, and turns over then refertilizes the psychologically and socio-politically rich romantic fictional soil of *Jane Eyre*.'[55]

How curious that for Cawelti the fiction of the mass market deals in deep mythic constructions available only to formalists and anthropologists of contemporary life while to a latter-day feminist the only good popular fiction (admittedly middle-brow) is one that overturns mythic structures – thus it becomes self-consciously high, self-reflexive, subversive and radical (that is, feminist canonical). Not surprising then that some critics had to make 'feminist interventions' into SF (in order to produce remainder fodder which was good politics and bad art). In each case popular art required correction and academic therapy. Thus, popular fiction is lost amid the real row over academic Newspeak. One grovelling apology will suffice for a range of critics who are involved with the popular arts for reasons which suggest they are using this material as an *excuse* in the war over 'gender' definitions and control.

Following on from this, it is not the intention that the contributions by male writers to this collection should be seen as 'men doing feminist work'. Such a strategy is a contradiction in terms and one which frequently registers that characteristic masculine practice of appropriation and even in its more bizarre manifestations the most extraordinary arrogance of 'setting women right', 'correcting' the 'errors' of feminism. Rather, the objective is to begin to frame, describe and unearth the notion of 'men as readers' as a *project* rather than as the usual, unquestioned normative procedure. Clearly, this raises questions about self, sexuality and identity within specific social and historical formations. It should also be agreed that the readings and arguments set forth here are inflected by our generation (we are in the main of that generation who entered secondary and higher education in the 1960s) and by our ethnicity (all of the contributors are white English or American women and men).[56]

For some, such absurdities were left aside to be replaced by others so that,

> Those who read or scrutinize Dickens as a novelist secure within the canon (if not 'the great tradition'), and ignore his simultaneous appearance on TV at Sunday tea-time, are substituting a previously freeze-dried version of the past for the dynamics of historical process. A properly *historical* reading of Dickens, or any other writer, has to recognize these seismic shifts – movements which make any Richter-like measurement of 'popular' and 'classic' fiction futile or partisan.[57]

Setting aside the foolish snipe at F.R. Leavis who did *not* include Dickens in the canon and specifically made him a special case of great popular writing, we are confronted with the suggestion that Dickens is a 'text' (i.e. a nexus) rather than a mere text and that we can no longer see Dickens as a historical figure in an actual location – after all what does the writer mean when we cannot 'ignore his simultaneous appearance on TV', simultaneous with what? In all, this type of writing suggests, all protestations to the contrary, that these writers actually do not *like* popular fiction or art (so different from George Orwell or Richard Hoggart for example) and are far happier in the land of middlebrowism. Liking popular fiction and the popular arts is (as any fan knows) to create a hierarchy of taste and a popular set of canonical rules – an aesthetic of the popular which is at one and the same time a social negotiation – a *success*, not, in short, a failure of portrayal or of genre subversion or of not having politically correct views. Indeed, few writers will take the popular arts for what they are on their own terms. This is a shame, as only *The Modern Review* seemed willing to take on popular culture in a serious way. Cosmo Landesman, one of the *Review's* founders, pointed out in 1993,

The cultural studies movement wasn't really interested in popular culture in itself – for them it was means to a radical end. Never mind the merits of this or that film, what mattered was waging the war against the oppressive Eurocentric culture of Dead White Males. The movement enjoyed a monopoly on the subject of popular culture, until the appearance of *The Modern Review* in 1991. Under the banner of 'Low Culture for Highbrows', *The Modern Review* rejected the cultural studies notion that popular culture was only worth studying if it served a radical cause.[58]*

It may come as no surprise to the reader to find that the *Review* is essentially anarchic-entrepreneurial, overtly capitalistic-Thatcherite and at the same time peculiarly traditionalistic and conservative. When it came to it, only certain elements of the Right could take popular culture for what it was and is.

---

* Almost as these words were written *The Modern Review* closed due to falling circulation figures (below 10 000 readers) and an extremely public disagreement between the editor Toby Young and the owner, Julie Burchill. The failure of the enterprise is, however, equally indicative of the collapse of the category distinctions that I discuss in Chapter 12.

7

Living in Technicolor: The Rules of Pulp

Can there be an aesthetic of pulp? For those who would defend high culture the notion of an aesthetic of pulp would simply be a misuse of the term; for those who would defend low culture there would be an avoidance of the question as not relevant. Caught between antagonism and embarrassed approval it remains to create an aesthetic of pulp which acknowledges both social force and artistic taste. We have descended through highbrow culture to middlebrow culture but pulp is a rejection of both, a messy, sprawling, indefinite phenomenon with a vitality that is both exciting and terrifying.

Pulp may be popular (as the academic uses the term popular culture) but often it is not; it may deal in the commonplaces and stereotypes of everyday life, but again often it may not. Always pulp will be allied to the commercial but not necessarily determined purely by it. Thus, while *Star Trek* is popular culture, *Star Trek* novels and products are pulp and kitsch respectively, existing just as much as lifestyle as literature. *Betty Page in Bondage* was pulp but hardly popular, while *Coming of Age in Samoa* became pulp in the 1960s through its consumption by sexually curious teenagers, as did the life story of April Ashley, one of Britain's first sex-change cases which was designed as pulp, and *Lady Chatterley's Lover* which was not. Edward, Baron Russell of Liverpool's *Scourge of the Swastika* (1956), the horrendous retelling of Nazi war crimes, was read by many at the time of its publication in paperback with the same salacious interest as *Those about to Die* (1958), written about the excesses of the Roman Circus and produced by freak expert Daniel P. Mannix. And between both of these books stands Garry Hogg's *Cannibalism and Human Sacrifice* (1958), the opening line of which invites a salacious reading, thus, 'man is a carnivorous animal: he eats flesh'.

Popular canonic fiction can also fall into the illicit, both knowing and refusing to know what it is doing. Here, for instance, is Rider Haggard:

There, not more than forty or fifty miles from us, glittering like silver in the early rays of the morning sun, soared Sheba's Breasts; . . . I am impotent even at its memory. . . . Their bases swell gently from the plain, looking at that distance perfectly round and smooth; and upon the top of each is a vast hillock covered with snow, exactly corresponding to the nipple on the female breast.

(*King Solomon's Mines*, chapter 6)

'Impotent' indeed if the fetishized object of desire is a little lower on the female anatomy.

'She burned,' he went on in a meditative voice, 'even to the feet, but the feet I came back and saved, cutting the charred bone from them.' . . . he drew something forth which was caked in dust that he shook on to the floor. It was covered with the remains of a rotting rag, which he undid, and revealed to my astonished gaze a beautifully shaped and almost white woman's foot. . . . Poor little foot!

(*She*, chapter 9)

It is the last comment 'poor little foot' – so spuriously pious, so gloriously knowing, that disguises and yet makes the preceding passage into pulp and does not merely leave it as popular. Pulp too is what this comment by Stan Lee (creator of Spiderman) becomes by a slip of the tongue when refering to Rider Haggard.

I think people love things that are bigger than life, that are filled with fantasy, as long as they're done in such a way that they seem to be believable . . . H. Rider Haggard's *She, King Solomon's Mines*, movies [*sic*] like that.[1]

Pulp is what refuses respectability by its very craving for the respectable. Pulp is the illicit dressed up as the respectable, but it is not disguised, nor does it hide its true nature from the consumer. Thus it becomes a type of coded play: a seduction agreed in advance by both sides but *unspoken* by either. Pulp pleasure is illicit pleasure. Such pleasure comes from reading for the *wrong* reasons and knowing it. Pulp does not want to be respectable, it wants to pretend to be respectable – it is, to use a pulp-generated metaphor, transvestite in its enjoyments. Then pulp is not to be defended, nor

is it to be made more available for serious study at the academy –
pulp never went to school and hates the academy. Academic respect kills pulp with kindness. Pulp does not wish to be part of the
canon – what does it care for the canon except to plunder and
pastiche it (as the contemporary 'serious' artist now plunders and
pastiches pulp). Here pulp has its own language and rhythm which
only becomes pidgin when assimilated into or compared with 'respectable' language. It is essential for pulp to remain pulp and for
it to retain its *unassimilable* nature, thereby preserving the *frisson* of
its secret passion enacted among fans, coteries, cults and followings
– the secret handshakes of the initiated. What canonical work or
author ever aroused such inexplicable passion in the ordinary consumer except when it became a *lifestyle* lived beyond the actual
literature – a subculture for readers? Isn't this passion for the details of geographical location, personality and anecdote exactly a
pulp transformation in the followers of the Brontës or D.H. Lawrence? What difference is there here between academic and amateur? Literature lived as lifestyle is pulp. Pulp needs no defence,
indeed it has no defence in its refusal to be determined by cultural
rules.

Such as pulp is, it is always illicit, rarely controllable, maybe
actually illegal but only sometimes subversive. Some writers in their
exploration of working-class popular entertainment and its reor-
ganization by market and hierarchic social forces are keen to point
out that while church music, variety theatre and English football
were all *reorganized* by forces *opposed* to the spontaneous entertainment of the urban working class, nevertheless resistance was and is
a constant theme of ordinary life. Thus for these writers the thriving streetlife of the early nineteenth century was subverted and
indeed destroyed by capitalist manipulation. What was lost, it is
argued, was at least a subculture of artistry and skills in popular
recreation.[2]

Such an analysis, with its populist Marxist argument, seems naive and redundant. The dichotomy of worker and capitalist rarely
exists in such a simple form when looking at the question of cultural participation.[3] The working class embraced professional soccer and reworked their response to the game in a vital and usually
positive (and often rebellious and violent) manner. In other words
they were not manipulated. Rather an accommodation was reached
which came from negotiations both spoken and unspoken, allowing new rituals, social activities and traditional factors to play their

part. Pulp culture, like working-class culture, is a negotiation which is neither unthinking, nor spontaneously naive, but thought through at a level which seeks to gain everything from hierarchic culture while yielding as little as possible. The logic of pulp is not necessarily the logic of educated society nor may it even be the logic of working-class resistance. Sometimes it will revel in an unresolvable and irresolute illogicality – the knowing and not saying of pulp as *form*.

A word needs to be said about this accommodation between capitalistic producer and ordinary consumer. It is far too simplistic to argue that each time a woman reads a magazine advocating heterosexual marriage, or a Barbara Cartland novel, a rubber fetishist goes and buys a favourite magazine or a teenager buys a Batman comic that they are all equally vulnerable, equally exploited, equally duped. To patronize every reader of Harold Robbins and Jackie Collins is to grossly misjudge and diminish the subject.

Curiously, both hardline Marxist commentators and cultural élitists (sometimes one and the same) often seem blind to this fact and the fact of the essentially unpredictable nature not just of the market but of those who make the market work – authors, publishers and readers (consumers and producers). John G. Cawelti stated categorically in 1979:

> One cannot write a successful adventure story about a social character type that the culture cannot conceive in heroic terms; this is why we have so few adventure stories about plumbers, janitors, or streetsweepers.[4]

And Walter Nash, as late as 1990 and against the evidence of commercial and technological history, could echo 'can we imagine a romantic tale in which the leading man is an obese plumber?[5] It hardly needs pointing out that two such fat, ugly plumbers, Italians from New York, incarnated as Super Mario Brothers have adventures and save romantic princesses. Popular culture is not without its own sense of irony.

Vance Packard had this to say on the market and the forces that dominate it in his bestselling populist work of the 1950s *The Hidden Persuaders*. He pointed out that,

> In the early fifties, with over-production threatening on many fronts, a fundamental shift occurred in the preoccupation of people

in executive suites. Production now became a relatively secondary concern. Executive planners changed from being maker-
minded to market-minded. The president of the National Sales
Executives in fact exclaimed: 'Capitalism is dead – consumerism
is King!'[6]

Yet consumerism seemed the result of manipulative, totalitarian
psychological warfare:

> As early as 1951 [experts were] exhorting ad agencies to recog-
> nize themselves for what they actually were – 'one of the most
> advanced laboratories in psychology'. [They] said the successful
> ad agency 'manipulates human motivations and desires and de-
> velops a need for goods with which the public has at one time
> been unfamiliar – perhaps even undesirous of purchasing'. The
> following year *Advertising Agency* carried an ad man's statement
> that psychology not only holds promise for understanding peo-
> ple but 'ultimately for controlling their behaviour'.[7]

The consumer was king only if the consumer was a fool! The paradox escaped all but a very few. If the end result was the creation of
the age of the 'image' then what that image came to represent was
the negotiation necessary to create a market and commercial success.[8] Commercial success, i.e. the ownership and successful exploitation of the means of distribution (rather than production), through
networks and marketing, was no guarantee of controlling consumers only of controlling sales.

The simple fact was that Packard was witnessing the fragmentation of capitalism (euphemistically now called consumerism)
where *no* predictive methods could adequately foretell, organize or
manipulate groups of purchasers. The desire to manipulate public
opinion and thus purchasing by creative packaging was never so
strong as to programme anarchic choice out of ordinary people.
Indeed, there is no simple correlation between the desired directed
meanings of the ownership of production in the mass arts and any
equivalence to their consumption.

This can be shown through a consideration of the comic book
industry in the United States: an activity bound to the commercial
world but *consumed* privately, illicitly and sometimes subversively.

The comic strip is as old as the twentieth century, now a venerable age, and comic books themselves have been with us for over

half a century, gaining a respectability nowadays that was neither expected nor desired. This special art form, which until recently was recognized only by its antithesis to both art and form, is the product of a creativity at once industrial and commercial as well as aesthetic. The world of comic books is no less related to that of advertising and Hollywood than it is to the more 'legitimate' realm of literary publishing. Indeed, it is only recently that comic-book producers have seen themselves as working within mainstream publishing and have found acceptance, through the appearance of graphic novels, within that world.

Comic book production is a hybrid activity: an *industrial* artistic activity which has created an imaginative and imaginary space for itself out of the popular cultural forms of American urban, commercial life. From this world emerge two of the greatest iconic figures of the century: Batman and Superman, and with these the evolution of a pantheon of villains including Lex Luthor and the psychotic presiding genius known as Joker. These creatures belong to a universe uniquely its own.

The external pressures on the industry that brought 'the Comic Code' into existence in the 1950s have, in the 1990s, given way to internal pressures within an industry bifurcating into both children's publishing and adult publishing and which has once again – but this time not innocently – to confront the adult themes of violence, sexuality and obsession. The comic-book medium has now reached a level of sophistication that combines Hollywood effects at pocket-money prices; even graphic novels printed on good quality papers and handsomely bound sell at a reasonable price. The world of the pop art collector and the museum curator has finally come together with the world of the pulp fan and the fanzine. The last few years have made respectable the realm of commercial artefacts, throwaway ephemera and popular consumables: the postmodern age is the age of popular art become high art, commercial comics transformed into icons for a literate and visually and semiologically sophisticated audience.

Yet, as comic books have gained respect, their artists have discovered their own artistic roots before the 'rules' were learned and codified, before practice became mechanical and conservative. The medium is still dominated by the genre of the superhero and supervillain – a titanic and never-ending struggle, not just between good and evil but between authority and anarchy, between a benevolent authoritarianism and a demonic and chaotic outer cosmos where temporal life is constantly upset, inverted and demolished. Comic books are about irruption and control and, as comics gain a kind of reverence, these themes paradoxically reoccur in more extreme and pathological form.

Dark heroes, little differentiated from villains in their obsessions, stalk work read by serious and approving adult, literate collectors. *The Killing Joke* transformed old Batman material into a shocking remodelling of classic and conservative Batman themes. The highly controlled and aesthetically exacting artwork released the violence and horror within the psyche obsessed with crime. Batman meets Joker in the Asylum at last. This 'shocking' irreverence again returns comic-book literature to its rightful place: a truly popular culture, anarchic and gaudy, mythic and protean, anonymous and 'naive'. Such violence in adult comics may again herald certain innocencies.

The current acclaim heaped upon 'star' artists may be little more than a retrograde step. Only time will tell. What is of consequence is that comic-book artists' work is no longer available to 'great' artists to rework for museums. Thus, Roy Lichtenstein's 1960s reworking of comic themes for the purpose of producing great art has been displaced by comic book artists' work *itself* being recognized as art in its own right. Such art is, however, already commercial, industrial and 'anonymous'. For art collectors of comics, the question is one of style not content. In the world of comics, authenticity in artistic creation is gained by reworking those themes, costumes and scenarios first thought out by others, often as long as 50 years ago. Batman, Superman, Green Lantern or Spiderman are reworked and remoulded generationally by an industry that is both conservative and recuperative about its commercial properties. Both Batman and Superman are commercial properties, before or perhaps because they are cultural and artistic icons. In this the comic-book artist is an 'anonymous' craftsman despite any individual wealth or fame – superheroes will continue without him and (if his creatures do not revert to him by copyright) they will be drawn and narrated by others. That Batman and Superman were the property of their companies was the saving grace and the personal disaster of their creators.

Pre-eminent among our modern icons stand Monroe and Batman, both in their own ways a focus for the differing and multiple messages of modernity. In either case – the one screen goddess, the other comic-book graphics – the image is infinitely reworkable, renewable, commercial and consumable. The image is convertible (through franchising of goods and through other media) and open to historical accretions (malleable to an age and a demand, in which such demands are added without removing other older dimensions which themselves signify as 'nostalgia'). Consequently, the image of Batman becomes not just that of a character but a resource for modern cultural messages – a place for an inexhaustible supply of meanings. Such reworking of meaning links the world of the superhero and the world of Batman specifically to the conditions governing urban, *contemporary* myth. Batman as image, and as an accretion of tales and meanings, has passed into modern consciousness: violent mean-streets detective in the 1940s; cold war conservative in the 1950s; camp satiric figure of the 1960s and brooding, psychotic authoritarian of the 1980s and 1990s. Yet always there is the urban modernist landscape, the metropolitan alienation and disturbance of Gotham City aka New York – iconic city of the modern imagination.

In this respect Bruce Wayne belongs to another universe in his rural mansion, where he is sequestered with his butler and his smoking jacket – image of a 1920s and 1930s hero who began his activities in public school and ended them as a gentleman adventurer and amateur detective. Bruce Wayne was outdated as a character at his inception – already the adolescent literature (sub-British in origin) from which he took his cue preferred the world of criminality and urban chaos to the world of gentleman-millionaires. But Richie Rich went native: not Tarzan but the Batman – a dark vampiric figure driven by his strange and insatiable appetite for consuming crime. Batman is a heroic figure from capitalism's evolution, a New Dealer born out of the Depression into a Death Wish vigilante.

The obsessional appetite of Batman gives rise to the *doppelgänger*, the Joker: the true 'objective correlative' for Batman's impulse to punish. We recognize in Batman and Joker the anarchic impulse of capitalism, an entrepreneurial spirit removed from the laws of time, space and 'reality'.

The poisoned chemical-loaded water that turned Joker's hair green and his lips red and his face white is the original ecological disaster from which the spirit of demonic appetite could be released: a true creature of the urban, industrial, western world. The demons of appetite grapple on the rooftops of Manhattan, and middle-class propriety and sobriety find themselves threatened and protected by authoritarian mania and anarchic psychosis. Such figures pass into our consciousness without our necessarily having read or even seen much actual comic-book work – the images are ubiquitous.

It was the ubiquity of these images that frightened the cultural guardians in the 1940s just as previously cultural guardians had been frightened in the 1840s by the rise of popular (that is, uncontrolled) literature. At once, it seemed, comic books had established themselves as legitimate news-stand magazines *and* also become illegitimate cultural products – subversive *because* commercially successful. As a new medium, comic books were becoming more violent, erotic and horrific, money spinning 'non conformity', 'perversions' and brand loyalty. By the late 1940s, comic-book covers sported lurid and violent scenes. On the cover of *Crime Does Not Pay* for May 1943, a half-dead man is being thrown into an apartment incinerator as the police burst in with tommy guns. The artist writer and publisher was Charles Biro.[9] *True Crime Comics*, created by artist and writer Jack Cole, was by 1947 already producing stories with titles such as 'Murder, Morphine and Me' which aficionado Ron Goulart has called 'sexy, fevered and violent in the extreme'.[10]

At the same time, that is from the 1940s onwards, there had begun a noisy wave of protest against comic culture from alarmed cultural guardians.

In May of 1940, for example, an editorial in the *Chicago Daily News* labeled comic books a 'national disgrace'. Written by Sterling North, the piece was not a critique but a call to arms. Charged North, 'Badly drawn, badly written and badly printed – a strain on young eyes and young nervous systems – the effect of these pulp-paper nightmares is that of a violent stimulant. Their crude blacks and reds spoil the child's natural sense of color; their hypodermic injection of sex and murder make the child impatient with better, though quieter, stories. Unless we want a coming generation even more ferocious than the present one, parents and teachers throughout America must band together to break the "comic magazine." ' North's recommended cure for this blight was good books. 'There is nothing dull about *Westward Ho or Treasure Island*,' he declared optimistically. North concluded, 'The shame lies largely with parents who don't know and don't care what their children are reading. It lies with unimaginative teachers who force stupid twaddle down eager young throats, and, of course, it lies with the completely immoral publishers of the comic'

– guilty of a cultural slaughter of the innocents. But the antidote to the "comic" magazine poison can be found in any library or good book store. The parent who does not acquire that antidote for his child is guilty of criminal negligence.[11]

PTAs, teachers organizations and library associations added their voice to what became by the middle 1950s a McCarthyite witch-hunt for moral criminals, subversives, deviates and crypto-fascist-communists. By 1948, radio shows were airing programmes such as 'What's wrong with the Comics?' and in the same year the Association for the Advancement of Psychotherapy held a symposium on the 'Psychotherapy of Comic Books'.[12]

The speaker whose voice emerged most clearly from that 1948 symposium was Dr Frederic Wertham, a senior psychiatrist from the New York Department of Hospitals. Features and newspaper articles with titles such as 'What Parents don't know about Comic Books' from *The Ladies Home Journal* of 1953 kept Wertham's name before the public until in 1954 he published *Seduction of the Innocent* in which he,

connected comic books with every kind of social and moral perversion imaginable including sadism, drug abuse, theft, murder and rape. Some of his allegations burst at the seams with evil: 'Homosexual childhood prostitution, especially in boys, is often connected with stealing and with violence. For all these activities children are softened up by comic books'. While focusing on the crime and horror comics, Wertham had a special distaste for superheroes.

'What is the social meaning of these supermen, superwomen, super-lovers, superboys, supergirls, super-ducks, super-mice, super-magicians, super-safe crackers? How did Nietzsche get into the nursery? . . . Superheroes undermine respect for the law and hard working, decent citizens'.[13]

In an attempt to defend their now overly visible industry, publishers formed first into the Association of Comics Magazine Publishers and then appointed an attorney to head their lobby. Henry Schultz, however, was not able to fend off a Senate Subcommittee hearing in which, just as with the later 'Lady Chatterley' trial in England, there was the usual level of foolishness displayed by the authorities. The results however went contrary to the spirit of that later 'trial'. In order to stave off regulation and backruptcy, the comic publishers reformed as the Comics Magazine Association of America and instituted their own Hays Code under the Comics Code Authority.[14] From now on comics would carry a code-approved seal indicating that the work was wholesome, entertaining and educational.

The Comics Code, in its comprehensiveness and in its authoritarian attitudinizing proved to be, and remains, a classic guide to the nature of pulp: the mirror image and antidote to pulp's Technicolor dreaming. Among such rules as those which banned attacks on religious or ethnic ('racial') groups and required women to be portrayed 'realistically' and 'without exaggeration of any physical qualities', rules apparently sane and reasonable, were a far larger group which demanded certain 'general standards' which would tend towards 'good taste' 'decency' and good grammar. Thus, for example,

- Illicit sex relations are neither to be hinted at or [*sic*] portrayed. Violent love scenes as well as sexual abnormalities are unacceptable.
- Respect for parents, the moral code, and for honorable behavior shall be fostered. A sympathetic understanding of the problems of love is not a license for morbid distortion.
- The treatment of love-romance stories shall emphasize the value of the home and the sanctity of marriage.
- Passion or romantic interest shall never be treated in such a way as to stimulate the lower and baser emotions.
- Seduction and rape shall never be shown or suggested.
- Sex perversion or any inference to same is strictly forbidden.

Anti-authoritarian ideas, represented exclusively as 'criminal' acts were also to be banned from now on, hence,

- Policemen, judges, government officials and respected institutions shall never be presented in such a way as to create disrespect for established authority.

Moreover, if erotic tales were to be curbed so too were their accompanying genres, crime . . .

- Crimes shall never be presented in such a way as to create sympathy for the criminal, to promote distrust of the forces of law and justice, or to inspire others with a desire to imitate criminals.

• If crime is depicted it shall be as a sordid and unpleasant activity.

• Criminals shall not be presented so as to be rendered glamorous or to occupy a position which creates a desire for emulation.

• In every instance good shall triumph over evil and the criminal punished for his misdeeds.

• Scenes of excessive violence shall be prohibited. Scenes of brutal torture, excessive and unnecessary knife and gun play, physical agony, gory and gruesome crime shall be eliminated.

and horror . . . .

• No comic magazine shall use the word horror or terror in its title.

• All scenes of horror, excessive bloodshed, gory or gruesome crimes, depravity, lust, sadism, masochism shall not be permitted.

• All lurid, unsavory, gruesome illustrations shall be eliminated.

• Scenes dealing with, or instruments associated with walking dead, torture, vampires and vampirism, ghouls, cannibalism and werewolfism are prohibited.

In all cases, either of sex, violence or horror, the reader was to have the reinforcing message of moral condemnation, the very language used subject to control and manipulation: made safe, made wholesome.

• Profanity, obscenity, smut, vulgarity, or words or symbols which have acquired undesirable meanings are forbidden.

• Although slang and colloquialisms are acceptable, excessive use should be discouraged.

Moreover, this was *intended* to be an intrusion into the privacy of the consumer and, if advertising was required to tell the truth, it would only do so wholesomely, avoiding the very issues (salacious, vulgar) that urgently exercised the minds of adolescent readers.

• Advertisement of medical, health, or toiletry products of questionable nature are to be rejected.

In the seeds of such benevolent authoritariarism, the tendrils of political correctness begin to flex.

William Gaines, who had been a flourishing publisher prior to the Senate Hearings and whose testimony was much remembered, initially refused to join the new Association. Blackballed, he ironically salvaged his career by founding MAD Magazine with Harvey Kurtzman, a satirical refusal as well as an ironic testimony to the leftover paranoia of 1940s America and the Cold War mania of the early 1950s.

When all is said and done, satire may be seen merely as revenge after the fact. For many Americans forced out of their jobs in publishing and journalism, Britain must have appeared a liberal haven. Yet Britain was also suffering a wave of official hysterics in the form of book prosecutions aimed at closing down the pulp paperback trade that had grown up by the end of the Second World War. Unlike America, the attack tended to be piecemeal and undirected. Unfortunately its effects were nevertheless largely the same.

The most important prosecution was that brought against the publishers and printers of the 'Hank Janson' novels and the subsequent trial of Stephen (Steve) Frances, Janson's creator. Janson was the creation of the shortage of American pulp crime fiction during and after the war and the ability of small author/producers to cash in on trends or, as in this case, gaps in the market: by 'mid 1953 over eight million copies (of Janson novels) had been sold in five years'.[15] This huge success was based on a mixture of violence and erotica, a disregard for pre-war values and a fascination with 'modern' concerns which were Americanized, youthful and consumerist as well as inimical to rigid class boundaries. It was also based on the opposite of all these categories: a literature aimed at a 'working class' or a 'proletarianized' readership craving imaginary freedoms in a more authoritarian Britain now defined by its welfare state, national military service, continued rationing, utility and deepening austerity. Janson looked forward to the sixties while alleviating the fifties. Whatever the case, 'Janson' was a huge success, and seemed, with its values and cover art, an attack on conformist establishment values, the sort of book that Raymond Hoggart later vilified in *The Uses of Literacy*.[16]

Steve Frances wrote as Janson, the books based on fake autobiographical details. Indeed, Frances had never even been to America, rather getting his ideas from Hollywood gangster movies, novels, guides and *Inside America*.[17] Furthermore, when interviewed on David Farson's television programme *Success Story*, Frances chose to heighten the Janson character by wearing a mask! By the late 1940s and early 1950s, Frances was successful enough to live modestly in Spain, and like Edgar Wallace and Barbara Cartland made use of a dictaphone and secretaries to create his stories. Frances also used other names: Ace Capelli; Johnny Greco; Steve Markham; Tex Ryland; Link Shelton; Max Clinten.[18] Finally, perhaps exhausted with watching over every aspect of his one-man business, Frances sold the rights to the name Janson to publisher Reginald Carter in 1952.[19]

Increasingly under the notice of the Director of Public Prosecutions, Carter was himself brought to trial for publishing obscene material, having been previously raided by Scotland Yard. Seven Janson novels were brought as evidence.[20] Opening on 14 January 1954 at the Guildhall, the trial paved the way for the successful prosecution of other publishing houses and was only halted by the more famous Lady Chatterley trial in 1960. In the eyes of the prosecution it did not matter if it was Hank Janson or D.H. Lawrence in the dock – both became equal in the face of prosecution and censorship. Even the concept of 'intention' to corrupt and deprave was dubiously dropped in the first trial so keenly was a successful conviction sought. Badgered by the prosecution the defendants were finally found guilty by a jury little inclined to persecute them. Summing up, Recorder Gerald Dodson made it clear that it was modernity itself that was on trial.

> No doubt you are quite aware that you are being asked to slide, to let yourselves slide into the degeneracy of modern times as depicted in these books which have been produced on behalf of the defence. . . . contributing to the general slide downwards of this type of modern literature.[21]

Mervyn Griffiths-Jones who led the prosecution was to reappear some years later when he unsuccessfully prosecuted *Lady Chatterley's Lover*: ironically, respectable Penguin were the publishers. Times were indeed changing.

The sentence in the spring of 1954 ruined the publisher and the printer and an appeal was quashed.[22] Yet this was not the end of the story. Having returned to Britain, Stephen Frances was arrested for authoring obscene books. Frances defended himself with the equivocation so typical of this period. He claimed the books had been 'written' by Geoffrey Pardoe (probably a pseudonym for his secretary who took dictation and therefore had actually *typed* the books!).[23] By 1954, Janson was selling more copies than ever and even the NAAFI was proved to have purchased the books for national servicemen.[24] In 1955, The Horror Comics Bill was brought before Parliament and by the late 1950s it was clear that a new ruling on obscenity was needed. The Obscene Publications Act of 1959 attempted to fulfil that requirement.

The results of this continued assault by the establishment coupled with overproduction, undercapitalization and a national printers' strike finally destroyed the success of the 'mushroom' publishers and their pulp production, but one cannot help thinking that what actually occurred was the suppression of a whole class of literature and a whole class of reader and, perhaps, readers *from* a certain class. Modernity was indeed under siege. Much later these episodes of actual British book-burning and suppression were little documented and almost forgotten. Even a recent book recording the trial of *Lady Chatterley's Lover* which was edited by H. Montgomery Hyde and has an introduction by him blatantly ignores the immediate post-war cultural determinants of the prosecution and the trials for obscenity which led up to Penguin finding themselves in the dock of the Old Bailey. Instead, Hyde chooses to document 'worthy' books irresponsibly prosecuted.

> During the thirty years following the case of *The Well of Loneliness*, several prosecutions for obscenity in England aroused public interest. They included *Sleeveless Errand*, a novel by Norah James in 1929 (condemned); Count Potocki de Montalk's poems in 1932 (condemned); *Boy*, a novel by James Hanley in 1934 (condemned); *Bessie Cotter*, a novel by Wallace Smith in 1935 (condemned); *The Sexual Impulse*, a medical manual of sex instruction for lay readers in 1935 (condemned); *Love Without Fear*, a similar work by Dr Eustace Chesser in 1942 (acquitted); also five prosecutions of novels in 1954 – *The Image and the Search*, by Walter Baxter (formally acquitted after the jury had twice disagreed); *September in Quinze*, by Vivian Connell (condemned); *The Man in Control*, by Charles McGraw (acquitted); *Julia* by Nargo Bland (condemned); and *The Philanderer* by Stanley Kauffman (acquitted). In all these cases except the second, where the poems were not printed, the publishers were also convicted. Several classics were also ordered to be destroyed, such as the *Satyricon* of Petronius and the *Decameron* of Boccaccio.[25]

What collectively is forgotten is the far greater attempted suppression of popular reading before the 1960s.

Equivocation seemed the only defence on both sides of the Atlantic as the following dialogue, reminiscent of Stephen Frances's statement, suggests. This time it is John O'Connor of Bantam Books introducing evidence to the 1952 House Select Committee on Current Pornographic Materials. When questioned by Edward Rees of Kansas, the hearing turns into a trial.

MR. O'CONNOR. Let's see. I have read *Don't Touch Me* [a then-controversial novel by MacKinlay Kantor], and perhaps that is a good one for your purpose.

MR. REES. You say that is a good one?

MR. O'CONNOR. I thought it might be a good one.

MR. BURTON. For our purpose.

MR. REES. What do you say about it? Is it good for the public?

MR. O'CONNOR. Am I being questioned now on the contents of the book?

MR. REES. Yes. You said it was good for us, and I am asking you.

MR. O'CONNOR. I sensed from what I read of the earlier hearings, that the committee is searching for books which, in its opinion, tend toward the pornographic side, but that does not by any means mean that I agree with the committee.

MR. REES. What I want to know is, do you approve that book for reading?

MR. O'CONNOR. I can't answer the question, that question, 'yes' or 'no,' because that is a question –

MR. REES. Do you think it is a good book for the public to read?

MR. O'CONNOR. I do; yes.

MR. REES. And you approve that sort of stuff?

MR. O'CONNOR. May I expand my answer?

MR. REES. Well, I just asked you if you said that is good; that is the end of it. It is either good or bad.

MR. O'CONNOR. I believe, if this book is not pornographic, if it is not pornographic –

MR. REES. Do you think the material is good, the reading of it is good?[26]

The inconclusive nature of this 'trial' by other means led, as in Britain, to a clean-up campaign by the industry. Malevolently attacked in America and lamentably also repeatedly attacked in Britain, paperbacks seemed to their persecutors to represent modern life – their suppression the reinstatement of an old-fashioned moral order.

> Some of the most offensive infractions of the moral code were found to be contained in the low-cost, paper-bound publications known as 'pocket-size books.' . . . The so-called pocket-size books, which originally started out as cheap reprints of standard works, have largely degenerated into media for the dissemination of artful appeals to sensuality, immorality, filth, perversion, and degeneracy. The exaltation of passion above principle and the identification of lust with love are so prevalent that the casual reader of such 'literature' might easily conclude that all married persons are habitually adulterous and all teen-agers completely devoid of any sex inhibitions.[27]

In none of this, of course, could any one, prosecutors and prosecuted alike, quite put their finger on what was so subversive. At its best, it was simply an unstated threat of something decayed and of changing times. Hierarchized moral authority, vested in an established oligarchy, could just as easily be supported as questioned by this material. Perhaps what pulp highlighted was an unspoken fragility in the system in which collectivism, either of the right or of the left was now under threat from a protean literature at once individualistic, erotic, violent, consumerist and youthful – like the urban environment in which it flourished. Such literature was a direct consequence of modern American urban history, but it was never founded on a political programme. Rather it was illicit by being made illicit, ironically and supposedly subversive of the very values that allowed it to succeed and which provided its usually conformist readership with the values and attitudes we label 'American'. In Britain, perhaps 'modern' was a code word for American, as some years before New York had, for Henry James, been synonymous with Jewish values.[28]

The impulse to ban, seize and burn books during the 1950s as well as the parallel hounding of publishers, printers and authors, was in the first instance a moral crusade. Yet this moral crusade, conducted to protect the public good and mobilized through the use of legislation almost a hundred years old was also a 'political' campaign waged by other means. The origination for such an impulse is graphically demonstrated by a prosecution in the 1850s brought against Robert Martin, a minor pornographer who brought out a penny weekly entitled *Paul Pry* during 1856. The journal itself provided a veneer of morality for a large dose of harmless prurience, including letters to the editor asking sexual questions and anecdotes about London's sexual haunts. His tales included the adventures of one Rt. Hon. Filthy Lucre which came to the notice of the authorities and led to Martin's prosecution for immorality (then classed as a misdemeanour). The comments of Lord Campbell, Lord Chief Justice of England, suggest a growing authoritarism and intolerance.

His Honour, after reading the account of the Rt. Hon. Filthy Lucre's gallantries, expressed 'astonishment and horror', particularly at the low price at which it was sold. Hitherto, he said, there had been some check to these publications, arising from the high price which was extracted for them. . . . But to sell them for one penny was a state of things which his Lordship, with great feeling, pronounced a disgrace to the country. It was no excuse, he said, that the defendant had also sold the *Household Words* and other publications of most interesting moral, instructive and beautiful character, for which the country was indebted to Mr. Charles Dickens. The jury agreed that these cheap publications had 'a far greater tendency to demoralize' than more costly ones.[29]

Here is the key to the suppression of pulp material – its inexpensive nature and ready availability. Economic liberty equalled moral laxity – at least, it seemed, for the lower orders – while expensive pornography was presumably less likely to corrupt those with a classical education (that is, the upper class). It was indeed the rich 'wot got the pleasure'.

The issue did not rest there. Lord Campbell then presented a bill to Parliament in order to strengthen the current law on obscenity. Violently opposed for attacking civil liberty, it remained for Campbell's successor, Lord Chief Justice Cockburn, in 1868 to pronounce (again during a judgment on a Robert Martin publication) that the test must be the 'tendency' to 'deprave and corrupt'.[30] The die was cast both sides of the Atlantic which led to so much mischief in the 1950s and the necessary equivocation of authors such as Stephen Frances and publishers such as John O'Connor. At least in part, the suppression of pulp was motivated by economic and class concerns (covertly political) which were simultaneously moral and ethical attitudes. One should not forget that many respectable ordinary people would have seen such prosecutions as a triumph of common sense and civil decency.

Having come thus far in our argument it should be possible to talk of the aesthetic of trash without the nature of this amalgamation (trash *and* art) becoming a contradiction in terms and without those same terms simply recreating it as the inversion (perversion) of serious art. Of course, trash art is always connected to serious art by those who would judge one by the other – like high art, trash is itself and always reflects its 'other'.

In this equation one need only reverse terms: art is serious and permanent, trash is ephemeral and light; art reveals and trash conceals; art is a new reality and trash is an old reality repackaged; art is unique and authentic while trash is formulaic and mechanical; art is history and trash is nostalgia; art is truth but trash is lies; art emancipates as surely as trash incarcerates. Such an equation will always put trash art down, and it will always be *correct* for the simple reason that the terms of the equation were written by those to whom it falls to 'defend' serious art. I do not wish to challenge those terms, determined as they usually are by those ethical considerations (masquerading as aesthetical) of interest groups whose standpoints are irreducibly there to defend an interest. The canon is a necessary and logical (though not *natural*) determinant of modern cultural and hierarchical social division: it defines as it excludes. Trash art and pulp visions get their definition through exclusion and thus gain the strength primarily to be what they are and not something other.

Trash art, loved to destruction and always one step ahead of its analysis will, of necessity, always incorporate a *hierarchy* of pulp values, the creation of fans, each of whom knows what comes where and in what order of acceptableness. A pulp aesthetic then emerges. Aesthetic and commercial, pulp speaks its own language and has its own grammar, both of which must be learnt. Thus will be created cults, fans, aficionados, desperadoes and addicts, fanzines and conventions – lives determined by reference to potent fictions with genres as organizing principles for people's lives. Pulp knows its audience and that audience determines its life, which is purely ephemeral, the product of mass production and cheap materials, and because ephemeral eventually carefully collected and preserved (usually by those in search of a substitute for their own lost past). Thus does commercial entertainment end as personal destiny. Speaking a secret language of desires unfulfilled, pulp is truly a type of embarrassing perversity negotiated between producers and consumers – a guarantee of order and yet anarchically sub-cultural.

To destroy the canon by opening it up to trash (now, of course horribly respectable) would simply be to remove one set of criteria of judgement for another, this time a hierarchy of reading practices (theory) as rigid as the previous pattern. One way or another, legitimation would be imposed on the actual anarchy of printed material. Thus in one guise or another, trash would merely play the canonic game and the fantasy escapism of pulp become simply a secondary reality parallel to that of an established avant garde; another reality in which common sense and madness are partners. As the benchmark by which high culture knows itself in its reflection, pulp remains gloriously bad taste. Pulp is an ethical division in society made into an aesthetic question of culture.

Trash art is the ever illicit enjoyment of contemporaneity. It is a refusal *without* consequence, a resistance which is also an accommodation. In this way it differs from subversive literature, which is resistant *with* consequences, although unintended consequences may be imposed upon pulp by others. Pulp celebrates the *now*, the industrial and the metropolitan in history: nature and human progress are rewritten in these terms. Pulp is the eternalized moment of the now lived irrationally in the overtly sentimental, nostalgic, sensational, erotic, romantic, violent and fantastic. Without an encumbering *authenticity*, trash art is liberated into a space of pure effect and style. But if pulp escapes authenticity altogether (and therefore bourgeois realism) it does not fall into the anti-humanism of avant-gardism. Pulp is not a pursuit of structure for its own sake (although pulp has many structures). Whereas for the modernist, structure was meaning (not just a carrier for it), for pulp, meaning precedes structure in the conditions needed to tell a story or create a character. If avant-gardism is determined by the subordinate clause, pulp is determined by the single imperative clause: it is a case of being versus doing as determinant of character and culture – the psychological against the social. And the peopling of this narrative, preceding and defining it is already determined by a framework of author/reader networks: doctors and nurses, space travellers and aliens, criminals and detectives, cowboys and Indians, super-heroes and supervillains.

All these characters had emerged or were developing as fictional figures when the intellectual avant garde tacitly agreed that psychology and sociology (and therefore alienation, immobility and impotence) were the determining factors in the making of the metropolitan ego. Popular genres and their fictional inhabitants however, consistently denied the onslaught of the psychological and the social. Nevertheless, they were not merely recuperations of older, heroic ideas of the self but rather contemporary attempts to locate the self in character and determine character by *action*. The choice of hero and heroine was played out in the professional and techno-logical spaces of new careers and, in the case of cowboys or space travel, current frontiers of knowledge.

Because read and understood by millions, these narratives act for us as fictional realms of social possibility. If Anglo-American avant-gardism was about self, then pulp, even or especially in its extrem-ist forms (superheroes, etc.) was about *society* and the constraints on action. Yet it must be firmly stated that pulp is always deterministically individualist and personal in its interpretation of social action. In the act of portraying social factors, pulp converts these factors into traits of *character* lived in the public sphere as acts. Indeed, popular fiction emphasizes personality within a structure different from that of much avant-garde art. It emphasizes episodic narrative (good for serialization), teleological and purposive move-ment (the unveiling of secrets and the unmasking of villains), out-ward appearance and the avoidance of psychology and an elevation of character over plot. All this is provided within a bland (or height-ened) accessible language which reinforces the values of society. While many 'serious' novels written in this manner emphasize sci-ence, social determinism, class confrontation and sexual warfare, the less serious convert these issues into personalized battles: the spy novel, cowboy novelette, romantic love story and detective novel predominate – in a phrase, works of fantasy which reduce or re-make the social into the personal.[31]

Urban, 'proletarian' and fantastical, pulp is also loud, brash, sexy, violent, passionate and unlikely. Protean in its forms, although constrained by a limited number of scenarios and plots, it is both predictable (on the level of genre) and unpredictable (on the level of manipulation of reader expectation). Creating its own reader patterns and stealing from any cultural area to form new channels of communication, pulp is happiest when it traverses the media and uses each medium as an infinitely transferable resource.

Pulp is the first to give content to new media: film, radio, televi-sion. These then give back to pulp its vibrancy and life. Pulp is not one medium but a *transferable condition* of the medium's content and structure. Disrespectful of boundaries, pulp as form is anarchic, capitalistic, market-led: its characteristic heroes and heroines are individualists – larger than society or outside of social constraint, their fate demonically personal. Nevertheless, these characters are always fated (chosen) to be superheros, or else fall in love, by forces greater than themselves – if a man's gotta do what a man's gotta do, if creatures from a dying planet choose earth to conquer, if the boy from the back street becomes a mobster, then it is fortune makes it so. The circumstances of constraint are at once also the circumstances and possibilities of anarchic individualism. In this paradox, pulp content is both individualistic and socially decided. For those producing pulp, their task will be aesthetic *and* industrial, determined by a commercial context. For readers, their act will be a communal, conformist activity and a *private*, escapist, secret passion (like making love or going to the cinema). Thus pulp acts to confirm control in the realm of the imagination and escapes from such control by use of the same mechanism.

Pulp is an infinite attempt to put back the 'lost' security of the 'I' of self in its battle with time. Thus it becomes, unexpectedly a nostalgia for self. But now this self is only recoverable in its weird reflection as gangster, alien, superhero or cop. In pulp, we recognize ourselves as strangers: contradictions of escapism and conformism, banality made strange. Through such a formulation (that is, the banal made strange) we can relate pulp art to the folkloristic urban legends collected under such titles as 'The Hook', 'The Phantom Hitchhiker' or 'Poodle in the Oven'.[32] Such semi-oral tales circulate among adolescents and adults in all metropolitan areas. While many of these tales can be traced into the last century, *none* can really be shown to exist outside a modern, industrial, urbanized and technologized environment. These are truly tales of the city and of the automobile, and they express erotic, demonic and violent fantasies surrounding our relationship with cars, ovens and microwaves, fast food, modern hairstyles, drug addiction, canned drinks, television, telephones and sexual freedom. Clearly such tales make the banal strange and turn the technological into the magical: all are *parables of the contemporary* (they are never related as just legends), continuously updated to conform to present conditions, feeding off new consumer goods and mass interests. In this way they obviously relate to the governing principles of pulp art, but while pulp and urban legends (sophisticated oral anecdotes of the 'stranger than fiction' type) have common ground, the former is not merely myth for modern mentalities. Rather, urban legends are parallel, non-literary excursions into the pulp arena, secondarily using pulp material within a pulp context Such an explanation allows us to see how readers and audiences situate their identities both communally and individually within such forms of reworked banality – the ordinary as the weird and the weird as determinant of a self both outside social constraint (in the world of anecdotal demonic phenomena) and accepting of social constraint (the reinforcing of a collective metropolitan imagination). Such is the folklore of the literate and the intelligent.

Thus pulp may be, and will probably be, the central formation process of an individual's cultural and personal aspirations – freedom, power, love, success, security, happy endings; abandoned and also authoritarian, paranoid and traditionalistic. Such displacements make pulp fully aware of what it is formally and technically but also tell of what it cannot be and cannot know (need not know), of itself and its social and historical place. Craving respectability through such illegitimate means may leave pulp sometimes illegal or subversive but it will always leave it *illicit*.

And what of Betty Page left 'in bondage' at the beginning of this chapter, that other Marilyn, the dark one? These are my Betty pages dedicated to another history and another glamour.

After one early broken marriage Norma Jean became Marilyn Monroe and married a baseball star and a world renowned playwright; after an early broken marriage, Betty Page moved to New York and found Irving Klaw, small-time pin-up photographer and cheesecake pornographer; Marilyn starred in *Bus Stop* and *The Misfits*, Betty starred in *Teaserama* and magazines such as *Eyeful*. Marilyn – Monroe – icon and goddess, died the mistress of a president, Betty Page simply vanished after a *Playboy* centrefold one day in 1957. RIP Monroe, long live Betty.

Betty Page is the raven-haired double, the illicit *Doppelgänger*; in her oversize, badly fitted bondage gear she appears a cut-price Marilyn whose own couture was body-clinging, sprayed on, sequins and all. But Betty is no cut-price Marilyn, rather she is the respectable girl who acts out the disreputable with her body-to-die-for and her sham innocence, her wide eyes and kinky accessories: harem-girl, Tarzan-girl, girl-next-door. For a time Betty Page was a teacher of English; the theory of pulp is written on her body, she takes it with her, displays it in the curves of her stomach and the rise of her breasts. Here is the nice-naughty girl, whose body is the icon of pulp, pulp in action – pulp consciousness. There is no theory of pulp from *within*. Betty Page is that theory lived as action – herself the Queen of Trash and the Muse of this book.[33]

Part II
Ars Gratia Artis

8

The Ripper Writing:
A Cream of a Nightmare Dream

Jack of Hearts, Jack O'Lantern, Jack the Giant-Killer, Jack the Lad, Jack Sheppard and Springheeled Jack; 'Jack', a common name that represents ubiquity: the nomenclature of the ordinary. In the late nineteenth century as for us in the late twentieth there was only one Jack – *the Ripper*; of the famous nineteenth-century criminals this one alone has endured into legend. Of Charlie Peace, Neill Cream or Israel Lipski little is remembered; of other famous murders only the victim is recalled: Maria Marten offering herself to melodrama and Fanny Adams to a coarse joke. Jack survives, but not merely because he was not caught.

This chapter is an attempt to consider the determinants and the progress of the Ripper legend as both text and history and to consider the constellation of historico-psychological notions that have gathered around the name of the Ripper.

Jack, it seems, timed his murders at a correct psychological moment, for almost immediately, not least for their ferocity, his deeds became the stuff of legend. He instantly became both a particular and a general threat, a focus for numerous related fears among metropolitan dwellers across Europe and America. One newspaper late in 1888 declared,

> The Whitechapel murderer, having been arrested all over the metropolis and in several provincial towns, is now putting in an appearance in various foreign countries, and also in the United States of America. . . . [he is] a Russian with a religious mania . . . murdering Magdalens in order that their souls may go to heaven, or [on New York advice] . . . [He is] a butcher, whose mind is affected by changes of the moon.
>
> (*The Times*, 3 Dec 1888)

Already, only one month after the murders had ceased, Jack has an international 'appeal'. His ubiquitous nature allows him appearances on both sides of the Atlantic and he is claimed by or accused of being a variety of nationalities. The article is already in light-hearted mood and Jack has taken on the serio-comic aspects of Sweeney Todd, himself a type of 'butcher'. Not only may he be both a Russian religious and sexual fanatic, but he may also be a New Yorker under biblical delusions (which the paper places under the 'Ezekiel Theory'). The Russian is not merely a religious fanatic but also a 'nihilist' and a member of a 'secret society' – Russia (the paper tells its readers) being notorious for secret societies. Thus, Jack becomes the focal point for an attack on foreigners (in particular Russians) and especially foreigners who are bent on undermining society in secret via covertly ritualized murder.

This mixture of grim charnel humour, political and religious fear, xenophobia and sexual innuendo (those journalistic 'Magdalens') partook of the atmosphere during the murders. At one end of the spectrum *Punch* (13 October 1888) dedicated a doggerel verse to the Ripper around a cartoon of Jack as a Mephistopheles bill-posting London with his latest exploits. This lampoon of the recent 'penny-dreadfuls' and 'Ripperana' was matched more seriously by the upsurge of anti-foreign agitation fanned by phantom messages (supposedly by the Ripper) accusing 'the Juwes', and by the Assistant Metropolitan Police Commissioner's claim that 'in stating that he [Jack] was a Polish Jew [he was] merely stating a definitely established fact' (which nearly started a pogrom in the East End).

On 13 February 1894 the *Sun*, a sensationalist newspaper, began printing a piece of popular investigative journalism about the 'real' Ripper, traced by 'WK', one of the staff reporters, to Broadmoor, 'a living tomb of a lunatic asylum' (17 February 1894) where the 'greatest murder mystery of the nineteenth century' was about to be solved by Jack the Ripper's 'confession'. This further accretion to the legend attempted to locate Jack in the world of 'debased' humanity in Broadmoor where inmates (and especially Jack) showed no moral awareness of the import of their deeds. In linking his home life to 'Camden Town' and his criminal insanity to Broadmoor the paper ably accused middle-class prudery of responsibility for Jack's upbringing. Nevertheless, the paper absolved that same class from blame by accepting that, in contrast to Jack, the paper's readers obviously possessed moral awareness. Curiosity was thus legitimized by a veneer of morality.

Unlike the clippings of the 1880s, this series put together insanity and the middle class. The murders were already thought of as the work of a depraved doctor. Nevertheless, the linking of 'the greatest murder mystery' and a 'living tomb' put together mysteriousness and living death in a way guaranteed *not* to reveal the killer's identity and guaranteed to increase sales of the *Sun* for the duration of the series. Moreover, the paper could congratulate itself and its readers on tracking down the perpetrator without undoing the 'edge' of fear they wished to create – for, as the paper clearly stated, this lunatic had *escaped* in order to kill. So horrible was he, so morally unaware, that armed guards stood about his bed. Jack's ubiquity is therefore reinforced by his unnamed status (he is identified only by initials) and by the hints of his origins and his ability to vanish from the lunatic asylum at will if not guarded. The lunatic asylum was represented by the paper as a type of purgatorial doom from which the 'living dead' returned to reap vengeance on the twilight world of the living (twilight, precisely because the victims were prostitutes). One mysterious world preys on another. Indeed, by returning from Broadmoor the journalist literally returns from the dead to tell his tale.

Medical and criminological science are used in this series to reinforce secrecy and threat; commercialism dictates the possibility of other (and) endless articles on the Ripper.

However, even during the season of the killings in the autumn of 1888, papers quickly realized the value of Jack's exploits, conducting their own post-mortems and reporting coroner's verdicts at length. *The Times*, for instance, ran articles in its *Weekly Edition* from September 1888 to November 1888. On 28 September 1888 it gave a full page to the social background of Spitalfields and the poverty endured there by Annie Chapman, the Ripper's first victim. *The Times* was quick to guess the direction in which police might look. They thought a post-mortem surgeon's assistant might be the culprit because of 'his' specialized knowledge of the uterus, which was removed from the victim's body.

The Times further noted the curious circumstance of an American surgeon who wished to include real uteri with a journal he was mailing to clients! Could this bizarre surgeon, whose name was not known, have prompted the killer to get 'a uterus for the £20 reward?' asked the paper. In a later issue, next to the report of other Ripper murders (26 October 1888), a clergyman protested in a long letter at the condemnation of the destitute by the middle classes, at their hypocrisy over prostitution and at their ignorance of the conditions prevailing in the East End. He concluded that this had 'blotted the pages of our Christianity'.

The freakish, of which the nineteenth century was inordinately fond, found itself beside the missionary, which in its guise as Mayhew, Engels or Booth consistently restated the ordinariness of the 'freak' (the destitute, the prostitute, the opium addict, the derelict). 'Body snatching' (and the notion of a uterus as a 'free gift' with a new journal) then weirdly allies itself with murder for greed (the reward offered of £20) and murder as the act of the desperately destitute. Jack becomes the focus for the bizarre in the ordinary misery of everyday life in the metropolitan slums. Jack the murderer becomes Jack *the missionary* who focused on problems other investigators were unable to bring to such a wide audience. Murder allowed for social reform. The newspapers, by keeping Jack the centre of attention, ironically kept the slum problems central too.

After reports covering three months by *The Times* and *The Times Weekly Edition*, the newspaper concluded that 'the murderer seems to have vanished, leaving no trace of his identity . . . with even greater mystery' (*The Times*, 10 November 1888). Jack the Ripper, given his *nom de guerre* by Fleet Street, was the first major figure to offer himself to, and to become, a creation of journalism. By the 1880s newspapers commanded audiences large enough to make Jack a major figure of international interest rather than a local folktale figure for the East End of London.[1] The power of journalism and the crowded warrens of the central city of the Empire together provided ground for the dissemination of the legend, a legend based upon both fear *and* curiosity – a terrible ambivalence. The possibilities for the dissemination of *rumour* could never be more fortuitous, and letters from 'Jack' fed interest and added to the atmosphere of uncertainty.

Indeed, Jack's letters themselves may have been the work of an entrepreneurial journalist providing 'copy' for himself. These letters, conveying a black humour and a certain 'bravado' (*Stratford Express*, 7 May 1965), may be read not merely as the realization of the power (for the first time) of the mass media but, whether authentic or fake, yet another accretion to the fictionalizing of the Ripper and the self-advertising and self-confidence of an entrepreneurial murderer (acquiring kudos by self-advertisement).

These letters convey a music-hall atmosphere and a self-important theatricality through which the Ripper's letters create an imaginary persona for the perpetrator. Addressed to 'the Old Boss', and signed (at least once) 'from Hell', Jack goes into his music-hall act for the bewildered audience – appalled, amazed (and applauding) the virtuoso performance. 'He' tells us that

> I was goin' to hopperate again close to your ospitle – just as i was goin to drop my nife along at er bloomin throte them curses of coppers spoilt the game but i guess i will be on the job soon and will send you another bitt of innerd.

In another letter he finds the search for his identity a source of amusement: 'They say I am a doctor now. Ha! Ha!'

Each letter becomes a performance put on by an actor assuming a part. The letter-writing gives a self-importance to the writer and a grandeur and status which is uncompromised by capture and identification. Hence, this letter activity becomes, for the legend at least, as important as the deeds themselves just as Davy Crockett or P.T. Barnum were to make legends of their own lives by writing their 'autobiographies' and adventures.

The Ripper letters are a form of *true life confession* heightened to the level of a fiction which embraces a 'cockney' persona, a sense of black humour, a melodramatic villain ('them curses of coppers') and a ghoul (sending 'innerds'), and mixes it with a sense of the dramatic and a feeling for a rhetorical climax. In these letters life and popular theatre come together to act upon the popular imagination. The Ripper (now possibly many 'Rippers' all reporting their acts) autographs his work as a famous artist (death as creativity) – anonymous and yet totally well known. Here, confession only adds to confusion (even Neill Cream claimed to be the Ripper). Jack's letter 'from Hell' concludes 'catch me when you can', adding a sense of challenge and a stronger sense of a 'hint' to the frustration of authority in its quest for an actual identity to the murderer.[2]

By the time of these letters Jack has ceased to be one killer but has become a multiplicity of performing personas for the popular imagination. The possibility of copycat crimes (although finally dismissed from at least two other 'torso' cases) lent to Jack the amorphous ability to inhabit more than one physical body (a point which I shall develop later).

Consequently, for the late nineteenth century, the Ripper became a type of 'folk' character whose exploits spilled into the twentieth century via cinema, theatre and fiction. In our own century the

Ripper has been tracked and traced by numerous writers after a positive identity. Writers have named a Russian doctor called Konovalov (Donald McCormick), the Duke of Clarence (Thomas Stowell), William Gull (Stephen Knight), Montague Druitt (Daniel Farson) and J.K. Stephen (Michael Harrison) as possible candidates. Each, in his turn, has been refuted – the 'royal theory' being denied by Walter Sickert's son Joseph, who dismissed it as a hoax that he had played on an over-receptive author. The 'debate' heats up every few years with new flushes of theory and further refutations, while works such as Stephen Knight's *Jack the Ripper: The Final Solution* added to the growing heap of books searching for scandal in suburbia or in the freemasons, in highest government or the royal family.[3] Knight, himself a journalist, stated in the *East London Advertiser* (7 December 1973) that 'the evil presence of Jack the Ripper still seems to haunt . . . the imagination of crime investigators', and he noted that in the 1970s letters were still arriving from people claiming knowledge of or claiming actually to be 'the Ripper'. In the twentieth century Jack has become the centre of a conspiracy debate. Indeed, so vast is the volume of literature to date that Alexander Kelly was able to write an article for *The Assistant Librarian* about his compilation of a bibliography of 'Ripperana and Ripperature'.[4]

The Ripper literature however is far from confined to the work of amateur sleuths (and they are a study in themselves) but extends to both fiction and film. Such fictionalization began almost immediately in 1889 with J.F. Brewer's *The Curse upon Mitre Square* and has continued in a steady stream of writers including Frank Wedekind (1895), Marie Belloc-Lowndes (1911), Robert Bloch (1943) and many others, and the Ripper has also made appearances in science fiction and fantasy tales, has been a staple of thriller movies and has appeared in opera (Alban Berg's *Lulu*) and pop music (a single by 'Lord Sutch').[5] As Kim Newman points out 'The Ripper' is a type of *given* of a certain landscape – a required designation or focus for a number of traits.[6] Jack the Ripper is a name for both a necessary fiction and a fact missing its history. Here fiction and history meet and mutate so that the Ripper can be searched for by 'historians' of crime at the very same moment that he can appear in a Batman comic. Separable from his origins, the Ripper is a strange historicized fiction, a designation for a type of murderer and his scenario (for the game is to give 'Jack' his real name and collapse fiction into biography), while also being a structural necessity for a type of fictional genre: the author of the 'Dear Boss' letter, etc. The Ripper is never quite the same person as the slayer of several prostitutes.

> Whereas popular heroes . . . usually have their origins in a particu-
> lar work or body of fiction, they break free from the originating
> textual conditions of their existence to achieve a semi-independ-
> ent existence, functioning as an established point of cultural ref-
> erence that is capable of working – of producing meanings – even
> for those who are not directly familiar with the original texts in
> which they first made their appearance.[7]

This dual movement and reciprocity can be seen clearly in the parallel claims made on the Ripper by the latest 'biographer' and by the artists and scriptwriters of Batman. As has been said of Adolf Hitler, that other bogy man of our own century, the figure overshadows the circumstances and as with Hitler so the Ripper acts as 'a dark mirror held up to Mankind'.[8] It was indeed the appearance and exposure of the Hitler diaries that were uppermost in researchers' minds when the 'Diary' of the Ripper was itself published in 1993.[9] Apart from the simple matter of authentication, the 'Hitler' and 'Ripper' diaries are curious mirror images: the Hitler diaries represent a scandal of celebrity while the Ripper diaries represent a scandal in the ordinary; the Hitler diaries were needed as proof of innocence (of the persecution of the Jews and of war-mongering) while the Ripper diaries were needed as proof of guilt (of a psychcopathic personality); both sets of diaries purported to be major documents authenticating the narrative and nature of historical process. Whatever the two sets of documents actually represent they both attempt to put a *face* and fix a character on to two historical figures whose evil actions are at once ambivalently symbolic and legendary and yet specific and located. This ambivalence seems irreconcilable with the nature of the facts of either case as the facts are themselves transmogrified into symbolic co-ordinates for the transmission of the two legends; in this way authentication acts as a means of refictionalizing the subjects under scrutiny. Each stage is simply more authentic (less fictional) than the last in a chain of never-ending speculation.

In chasing the identity of the Ripper and in placing his person-ality upon numerous more or less well-known historical characters (the latest being James Maybrick) investigators acknowledge the bizarre silence at the heart of the tale, a place where history has closed in upon itself and refused its *fact*. History becomes an abyss antagonistic to its own determinants and played upon by conspiracy in the fiction of the secret of Jack's identity. Scanning the grim, grainy, obscure picture taken of Mary Kelly's eviscerated body as if in search of clues we become dabblers in the oracular and the occult. In her photo the Ripper steps out of Victorian history to become the *epitome* of Victorian history, its embodiment and spokesman.

It is hardly surprising that Jack the Ripper has passed so easily into the world of fiction. Jack's most recent incarnation has been in the pages of DC Comics' *Gotham by Gaslight* as the opponent of Batman himself.[10] Dedicated to 'Elsa Lanchester, the Bride of Frankenstein' and with an Introduction by Robert Bloch, Jack the Ripper travels across the Atlantic to Gotham City for his final showdown. The comic treats Batman with the same seriousness as the Ripper and Bruce Wayne's own biography is rewritten and reauthenticated during the story (indeed is integral to the Ripper's identity). In such a context, Batman is as 'real' as the Ripper and using a 'what if' scenario he is placed not in 1940s or 1950s America but back in time – the 1880s. Who else would the greatest comic crime fighter confront in a steam-driven Gotham but the Ripper, only worthy opponent of the Bat. (Just as Sherlock Holmes had been pitted against the Ripper in the film *The Seven Per Cent Solution*.) Both Batman and Jack the Ripper become designationary loci for a scene and a moment. As such, Batman is every bit as real as the Ripper, inhabiting a location every bit as real and as distant as the foggy streets of London. New York/Gotham City or Victorian London, Jack the Ripper and Batman are the locations and the inhabitants of a certain modernity. As Robert Bloch points out (writing as the Ripper), 'Batman? Yes I know the name'.[11] Batman's authenticity (*the* Batman as he has now become) and the status of his myth are reaffirmed in our ability to accept the migration of his character into a historical past. That Jack the Ripper awaits him is confirmation of his status, that there is parallel publication of Ripperological works and comic books only heightens the reciprocity between the production methods of two different yet dependant forms of publishing.

As Geoffrey Fletcher in the *Daily Telegraph* (9 October 1974) commented, 'hence it is that Jack belongs not only to the criminologist, but also to folklore'.

The first part of this chapter dealt with the rapid dissemination of the Ripper legend and its endurance in popular publishing. I now wish to turn to the constellation of possibilities around which this publishing industry revolved and upon which the legend was built.

It is obvious that any legend requires a small and possibly spectacular fact to unleash a great deal of 'fiction'. Before turning to the legend as a type of 'fictional' genre it is necessary to consider the Ripper legend as revolving around (a) a series of bizarre and ferocious crimes, (b) an impotent and mocked authority (the Criminal Investigation Department being left totally in the dark and being criticized from Windsor), (c) a mysterious and unapprehended felon, and (d) the power of fiction and the use of the human sciences.[12]

The murders of autumn 1888 allowed for the appearance of a new urban dweller, a dweller on the limits of society and yet fully integrated into it – the homicidal maniac, *the psychopathic killer*. Unlike de Sade, the psychopath is always *in disguise*; his intentions and his secret actions are on another plain from his social responsibilities. Consequently, the psychopath delineates that absolute psychological and mental 'deterioration' that Kraepelin had considered as a form of dementia praecox and that was not defined as schizophrenia until 1911. The Ripper, however, was seen as split not merely in personality but in *morality* as well. The case of the psychopath is a case not of deterioration of mental power but of a demonic engulfing of the egotistic soul by a monstrous and sensuous will. Here the psychopath unites theology and science, unites the lowest and the highest impulses in his society. The psychopath is ill and yet suffers only from an overwhelming need to impose his will on his surroundings. The psychopath 'lets go' only in order to secrete his lost personality more fully in those daylight hours of responsibility. The demonic had not yet lost its force in the 1880s, reinforced as it was by scientific research.

In order to explore the paradox of the psychopath more fully we can turn to the popular fiction of the 1880s. Robert Louis Stevenson's *Dr Jekyll and Mr Hyde* was published in 1886, two years before 'Jack' made his own spectacular appearance.

Stevenson's story deals specifically with split personality – split between the sensual and the socially and morally responsible. Jekyll is the epitome of middle-class propriety, living in a street described as having houses with 'freshly painted shutters well polished brasses and general cleanliness', while Hyde is a monstrous and 'ape-like' maniac who lives amid the sexual depravity of Soho: 'that dismal quarter of Soho seen under these changing glimpses, with its muddy ways, and slatternly passengers, and its lamps, which had never been extinguished or had been kindled afresh to combat this mournful reinvasion of darkness, seemed, in the lawyer's eyes, like a district of some city in a nightmare'.

This duality of personality and class (the more working-class the more depraved) is considerably complicated by Stevenson's own mixing of Darwinism and pseudo-science. Degeneracy for Stevenson (as for Edgar Allan Poe in 'The Murders in the Rue Morgue') is a decline into an animal state – the noble savage has become the sex-crazed ape. However, this motif (repeated by Rider Haggard in *She*) is interrupted by a 'psychological' study of Jekyll from whose dark side Hyde is generated. Jekyll has always been aware of his dual nature:

> Hence it came about that I concealed my pleasures; and . . . I stood already committed to a profound duplicity of life . . . that made me what I was and, with even a deeper trench than in the majority of men, severed in me those provinces of good and ill which divide and compound man's dual nature. In this case, I was driven to reflect deeply and inveterately on that hard law of life which lies at the root of religion, and is one of the most plentiful springs of distress. Though so profound a double-dealer, I was in no sense a hypocrite; both sides of me were in dead earnest; I was no more myself when I laid aside restraint and plunged in shame, than when I laboured, in the eye of day, at the furtherance of knowledge or the relief of sorrow and suffering. And it chanced that the direction of my scientific studies . . . led wholly towards the mystic and the transcendental.

Indeed, it is Jekyll's very aspirations toward the ideal that have caused his degeneracy. Such a duality makes Jekyll tell his friend that 'if [he is] the chief of sinners [he is] the chief of sufferers too'.

Highlighted here is not schizophrenia as illness but Jekyll's schizoid nature as showing signs of *moral* degeneracy. Mental decay is seen as a consequence of original sin lurking in the hearts of all men of whatever class – the more denied (by the respectable) the more virulent its final outburst. Stevenson makes this quite plain in his description of Hyde's manic progress during the opening narrative. He lets his narrator tell us that 'then came the horrible part of the thing; for the man trampled calmly over the child's body and left her screaming on the ground. It sounds nothing to hear, but it was hellish to see. It wasn't like a man; it was like some damned Juggernaut'.

Hyde becomes an abominable *it*, a desecration of the sanity of the human causing revulsion even in the doctor who witnesses the deed. Equally this combines with fear at the bizarre and freakish appearance of the culprit: 'There is something wrong with his appearance; something displeasing, something downright detestable. I never saw [a man] I so disliked, and yet I scarce know why. He must be deformed somewhere; he gives a strong feeling of deformity'. Hyde combines animality and the terror of the 'troglodytic' with fear of evil, for he has 'a kind of black sneering coolness ... really like Satan'.

This mixture of the animal and the devilish comes from the perverse idealism of Jekyll, a scientist and pillar of society who is bent on unlocking *his own* potential for experiencing the limits of perception through the power of his own will. His science is therefore put to the cause of metaphysical speculation. He tells us that, 'it chanced that the direction of his scientific studies ... led wholly toward the mystic and transcendental'. Here, then, the scientist manipulates the soul in order to reorganize the nature of the body, for, in destroying the 'fortress of identity' Jekyll employs science as if it were magic: 'man is not truly one, but truly two'.

Stevenson's short story became a massive popular hit when published. In it he summed up the pseudo-science of the popular imagination as well as the confused state of the emergent psychological sciences which were 'treating' schizophrenic patients. The psychopath (Mr Hyde is such through his maniacal killing for killing's sake and the enjoyment he gains) crosses the border of scientific discourse and acts as its limit, beyond the rational explanations of form and natural function. Instead, the psychopath takes us beyond science and before it into theology, into the analysis of *sin*.

In picking upon this duality, Stevenson made repeated statements about the nature of evil and its relationship with insanity. He tells us,

The pleasures which I made haste to seek in my disguise were, as I have said, undignified; I would scarce use a harder term. But in the hands of Edward Hyde they soon began to turn towards the monstrous. When I would come back from these excursions, I was often plunged into a kind of wonder at my vicarious depravity. This familiar that I called out of my own soul, and sent forth alone to do his good pleasure, was a being inherently malign and villainous; his every act and thought centred on self. . . . The situation was apart from ordinary laws, and insidiously relaxed the grasp of conscience. It was Hyde, after all, and Hyde alone, that was guilty. Jekyll was no worse; he woke again to his good qualities seemingly unimpaired; he would even make haste, where it was possible, to undo the evil done by Hyde. And thus his conscience slumbered.

Here the 'monstrous' connects with meta-laws that organize consciousness but cannot escape from it, for *will* (according to Jekyll's philosophy) and the drive to power dominate the consciousness of mankind. According to Stevenson, from the socially responsible, the morally restrained and the intellectually ideal come anarchy, moral degeneracy and perversity dominated by a Calvinistic notion of predestined sin.

As with Jekyll and Hyde so Jack the Ripper too was seen as an inhuman, if not non-human, monster who combined possible middle-class respectability (a doctor or a surgeon) with lower-working-class savagery (an immigrant, 'Leather-Apron', a mad butcher). The Ripper united both classes inasmuch as he was excluded by his acts from both (just as were his victims). The Ripper was both a technician (a post-mortem surgeon, a doctor, a butcher) and an insane lunatic (incapable of finesse). He was supposedly at once able to focus his aggression in anatomical detail and yet unable to curb its force. Thus, the forensic nature of the Ripper's 'work' (his 'job') provided a focal point for popular fears and prejudices against those professions dealing in the limits of the 'decent' (psychologists, doctors, post-mortem surgeons, forensic experts). The Ripper's supposed anatomical expertise suggested all sorts of horrible possibilities about the life of the 'expert' and the specialist. His ability with a knife united him to the very professionals paid to track him down!

Like Hyde, he was the *alter ego* of the police force and the letters clearly demonstrate him showing off his expertise to them and the vigilante forces operating in Whitechapel. Later his dual nature as criminal and enforcer-of-law became explicit when reports of his deerstalker gave one attribute to the occupier of 221b Baker Street, whose business was forensic science, whose other real-life model was a surgeon and whose friend was a doctor.

Thus the Ripper was not merely a murderer but the catalyst for a series of psychological and social reactions. He combined the supposed popular idea of the expert as well as the darker side of the madman, lunatic, animal degenerate. As a median point between middle-class respectability and a debased Darwinian proletariat, the Ripper became the invisible man; like Jekyll he might well have said that 'for him in his impenetrable mantle, the safety was complete. Think of it – he did not exist!' The Ripper's letters acknowledge the pretence of cockney patois while pointing directly toward a middle-class author – but the author of what: a letter or the murders? The Ripper is both murderer and social 'reformer', both scientist and magician.

In the previous section of this chapter we have seen that the combination of popular prejudice and fiction produced a character and a rationale for the Ripper *qua* murderer *and* respectable member of society. His split nature (if such it was or presumably had to be) was completed by a hypocrisy concerning the very people he killed (the 'Magdalens'). For these people were themselves invisible, acting as a certain outlet *and* limit to urban society. The psychopath and the prostitute were two ends of a society that refused to acknowledge their presence. Invisibly, they provided their services on the edge of the rational, morally degenerate as both supposedly were.

Yet Jack the Ripper's threat is one that spills back into 'ordinary' society and threatens that society. In the period when the legend of 'the Ripper' begins, the psychopath becomes an urban reality but as a character-type is not quite part of a mental spectrum and yet is not fully freed from being a theological problem either. Jack combines notions of evil, insanity and moral justice at the moment when the nineteenth century saw itself as the century of progress, enlightenment and escape from 'moral' prejudice. The Ripper's name denotes a certain consequent frontier for the human sciences at this time.

At the culminating point of the human sciences came the science of legitimized 'murder'. James Berry, the public executioner at the time of the 'Ripper' murders, wrote his autobiography in the 1890s and in it we see combined Jack's role as breaker *and* upholder of the law and of natural justice.[13] Berry, who became an abolitionist (he decapitated one of his clients because of an incorrect 'drop'), viewed his work as 'a job like any other'[14] and H. Snowden Ward in his appraisal called Berry 'tender-hearted'.[15] This businesslike and tender-hearted man carried out public executions and gave his rope to Madame Tussaud's. His contribution to the human sciences was to calculate the proportion of rope needed relative to body weight, in order to cause death without mutilation of the victim. He also endeavoured to 'understand' the mind of a murderer, whom, unlike the general public, he viewed as neither a 'fiend' nor a 'monster'.[16] He commented that he hoped he could 'advise his readers to consider that a murderer has as much right to judge the state as the state has to judge him',[17] which is an oddly radical comment for the ultimate enforcer of the state's law! Indeed, Berry saw quite clearly the anomaly of his position.[18] Hence he becomes both killer and killed, both culprit and revenger, both state appointee and state victim. Within Berry's own person these ambiguities were traced.

James Berry and Jack the Ripper are joined by the technology of death. This unites and yet ultimately separates their purposes, for Berry participates in the oddly humanitarian enterprise that Michel Foucault sees as a movement from torture to the timetable in dealing with miscreants. Berry, working in secret, takes on the onus of the executioner's task as a duty as well as a job. His book portrays a deep ambivalence as well as pride in work well done. The business of death puts professionalism at a premium. Berry's expertise is, however, the expertise of an almost defunct craftsman, for, although hanging remained for another eighty years, its power was severely limited and its function debilitated by secrecy and humanitarian concern. The acknowledged schizoid nature of the executioner begins to crack open in James Berry and his autobiography in his constant justifications and special pleading. The Ripper takes pride in his particular executions, for Jack belongs to another *older* tradition of execution.

Michel Foucault, quoting eighteenth-century sources, gives the grisly details of the form of public execution then required in France:

> The executioner, who had an iron bludgeon of the kind used in slaughter houses, delivered a blow with all his might on the temple of the wretch, who fell dead: the *mortis exactor*, who had a large knife, then cut his throat, which spattered him with blood; it was horrible sight to see; he severed the sinews near the two heels, and then opened up the belly from which he drew the heart, liver, spleen and lungs, which he stuck on an iron hook,

and cut and dissected into pieces, which he then stuck on the other hooks as he cut them, as one does with an animal.[19]

We may compare this to Jack's own 'private' (but very public) methods. His last victim, 'Mary Kelly ... was lying on her back on a bed, where she had been placed after the murderer cut her throat ... he set to work mutilating the body, which was stabbed, slashed, skinned, gutted and ripped apart. Her nose and breast were cut off; her entrails were extracted: some were removed.'[20]

In the eighteenth century executions became a ritual in which the 'main character was the people, whose ... presence was required for the performance'.[21] By Jack's time public execution was long since over, but Jack took on the symbolic weight of a 'higher' justice operating beyond the arm of the law, exposing and cutting out the cancer of sexual commerce. His role was acknowledged in his instant fame and his ferocity in his attack on the condemned: the prostitute class. It appears that Jack represented the return of a social memory of the proximity of death (by violence, cholera, starvation) now distanced by the work of social and medical reformers.

In that latter half of the industrialized nineteenth century ceremonies about the integration of death had long ceased to be necessary. In a sense the body had gained utility value but lost its 'sacred' humanness (its 'mystery' that early Christians feared). Jack represents the unconscious of that society – a repression not yet exorcized; he forcibly reminded society (unable to speak of bodies without blushing) of the crudest function of that mass of organs. Jack clearly unites ideas about the mortification of the flesh and the technology that manipulates the body (the human sciences: biology, psychology, forensic science, medicine). One end of the spectrum acknowledges desire for and the power of the flesh while the other denies both and reduces the body to a mass of functions and utilities: an automaton. The body hence becomes ironically 'sacred' (as an object in religious devotion to be escaped *from*) and yet also machinic.

Yet the savagery of Jack's attacks suggests more. As the attacks became more savage, so the mutilation of the victim became more complete. Finally it took pathologists six hours to piece together the empty shell of Mary Kelly scattered around the room in which she died. For Jack this final attack meant more than an attempt to punish womankind for its sins and its tempting flesh. Here the body is emptied, turned into a shell into which the murderer could plunge his knife and hands. The emptying assumes the form of an attempt to 'go beyond' the boundaries of flesh in a 'new' and horrific way. This violence demolishes and liquefies the body, which flows away and takes with it its ego boundaries. The body is opened, penetrated, dissected, made totally possessable.

As the bodily boundaries vanish we are reminded of the search for the auguries at Rome, a desperate search for a stable and knowable destiny. As the uterus determines the growing foetus, so the 'innerds' of the female body offer themselves for decoding. But what do they signify? Nothing, or more properly, an absence, for the place of origin is missing. The quest carried out by the probing knife reveals only a mess of tangled 'innerds'. Jack's attack signifies a going beyond toward an otherness that is totally non-human. The object and the possessor mesh into one critical quest.

What did Jack search for? Inside the body, finally opened, the culprit used the technique of a manic autopsy in order to find the non-body: the beyond and yet absolute of his own existence – his soul perhaps? In finding this origin Jack may have been able to find his own significance unhindered by the body which forced him to kill. For Jack as for his public, these killings, graphically illustrated and documented in the popular press, may have signified, as they still may do, the final frenzied acknowledgement of the coming of the age of materialism.

The body of the 'Magdalen' signifies the absence of purity and the presence of sin; but what does each weigh – what atomic weight can be assigned to the soul? Can the significance of the Ripper's violence, which has fascinated readers and researchers for so long, be explained in this way – that his quest was for a lost and discarded origin and that his method was a repressed and supposedly outdated one? The object of Jack's killing is not to take on the power of 'the other' but to bypass 'the other' altogether in order to confront otherness itself.

This may be borne out perhaps in the nature and morbid (perhaps healthy?) interest of generations of readers. Jack's killing partakes of a deep sub-stratum of cultural knowledge, a cultural awareness of the nature of sacrifice. If this appears far-fetched we can turn to René Girard's *Violence and the Sacred*, an anthropological work which appeared in 1972.[22]

First, though, let me briefly recapitulate the ideas outlined above. I have drawn attention to the dual nature of the popular notion of alienation – both demonic and machinic, with its consequent ambiguities over the relationship of victim to killer: social pillar and social pariah. At this juncture the psychotic killer, a product of urban life at the end of the nineteenth century, appears as both mentally defective and metaphysically gifted – both cancer and purgative. I have further suggested the possibilities and limits of Jack's 'quest' and the disturbance to identity that that caused. To further this inquiry let us now return to Girard's work on sacrifice.

Girard tells us that initially 'the sacrificial act assumes two opposing aspects, appearing at times a sacred obligation . . . at others a sort of criminal activity'. He notes the 'ambivalent' nature of sacrifice but says this does not fully account for its 'value'.[23] In his view, 'sacrifice contains an element of mystery',[24] and it is this mystery that he wishes to penetrate. Quoting Joseph de Maistre, he adds, 'the sacrificial animals were always those most prized for their gentleness, most innocent creatures, whose habits . . . brought them most closely into harmony with man'.[25] Indeed, we are told that 'sacrificial victims are almost always animals'.[26]

Here then we see that Jack the Ripper and James Berry share both a criminal and a 'sacred' (legitimized by the state) obligation. Berry acknowledged the ambivalence in his role. Moreover, in both cases, secrecy adds an air of mystery to the proceedings. The 'Magdalens' fit the role of sacrificial 'animals' through their own ambiguous position: both gentle, and aggressive in selling their wares; innocent and sexually aware; *and* in harmony with 'man' while in competition with and engaged in commercial transactions with him.

We may go further, for Girard points out that the very lowest (slaves) and the very highest (sacrificial kings) are the ends of the sacrifice spectrum.[27] But he concludes that 'in many cultures women are never, or rarely, selected as sacrificial victims',[28] because of the feuds this would cause between husbands and children and the class that claims them. However, these points can be easily met, for prostitutes are both 'animals' and 'Magdalens'; both subhuman and sacred. Moreover, in the culture of which we speak these women are precisely those that were forced (therefore to the popular mentality *chose*) to break all their ties with husbands, children, class. They became the sacrificial victims for that culture, without ties or kinsfolk to gain revenge on their behalf. At one end of our spectrum Jack does nothing illegitimate – but his act is illegal for he kills outside the *context* of the sacrificial system (long since forgotten, of course, in the nineteenth century). His act is both sacred and lunatic, bestial and totally 'sane'.

Moreover, Jack's acts of sacrifice/murder appeal to a deeply archaic level of human response – a response long since channelled
elsewhere into 'humane' destruction for sane offenders and lunatic
asylums for 'morally degenerate' offenders. In the 1880s these two
conditions partook of a peculiar mixture of demonic ability and
psychological disintegration neither properly disentangled from the
other in either the popular imagination, literature or the human
sciences.

Yet we must go deeper to fathom the legendary power of Jack
(for structuralist approaches consider the action of legend and myth
in too formalistic a way). We have seen the specific historico-
psychological aspects of the Ripper's enduring fame. But we must
return to Girard for our final formulation of his power over our
imaginations.

Girard considers sacrifice an attempt by society to 'deflect upon
a relatively indifferent victim . . . the violence that would otherwise
be vented on its own members, the people it most desires to protect'.[29] Consequently 'the sacrifice serves to protect the entire community from its own violence.'[30]

Let us return to *Dr Jekyll and Mr Hyde*. Jekyll *generates* from *his
own* personality the characteristics of the psychopath. His dual nature
partakes not of a ghostly *Doppelgänger* but of aspects from *within*
himself. His violence is a hatred of his own class and its expectation
of restraint and decorum – its understanding of order. Girard comments on the Bible story of Cain and Abel that 'Cain's "jealousy" of
his brother is only another term for his own characteristic trait: his
lack of sacrificial outlet'.[31] Right at the beginning of *Dr Jekyll and Mr
Hyde* we are introduced to Mr Utterson the lawyer, the ultimate
figure of respectability, who 'was austere with himself' and who
says of himself, 'I incline to Cain's heresy.' As with Jekyll, it is more
than a psychological problem; it is 'deeper'. Like Jack, Jekyll crosses
a profound border, a border that disturbed 'anthropologists' and
theologians alike in the nineteenth century.[32]

Thus we see the truly ritualistic and 'psychological' nexus of Jack's
violence, for his work dissolves boundaries, acts as a gaping maw
into which perception of order and rightness are sucked. Jack's
name as well as his deeds and the deeds in his name disturb our
order, trangress boundaries, translate legitimacy into illegitimacy
and the sacred into the bestial and translate them back again. For
Jack there is no 'other', only a gaping hole within self that is beyond
reconciliation with laws of man or God.

Jack, like any legendary figure, represents this effectively because he steps out of historical circumstance and into the imagination of the future. As such, like King Arthur or Robin Hood or Count Dracula, he is the undead. Jack, however, bypasses the criminal underworld, for he does not belong to it. He is outside that underworld, which is itself defined within the comprehension of the living (the non-animal). Jack is demon/animal and therefore totally other, therefore unrecognizable (invisible), therefore the perfect criminal. He disturbs the human only to reinforce it. Indeed, this monstrosity embeds himself in the imagination of each generation that needs his presence. For that reason alone there is a smile on the face of the Ripper.

The historical details of the Whitechapel Murders are nothing less than the facets of a scenario for a script about modernity itself. Reworked in fiction and film as well as the focus for true crime books (of the solve-it-yourself variety), the Ripper's deeds are ever reworked to remain forever contemporary, and thus curiously emphasized by layers of nostalgia. The Ripper's script has violence, eroticism, sentimentality and the supernatural: a text to live out the sensationalism of the modern.[33]

9

West is East:
Nayland Smith's Sinophobia
and Sax Rohmer's Bank Balance

It is commonplace nowadays to note the inherent racism of English fiction at the beginning of the twentieth century. Sapper, Dornford Yates, John Buchan, Edgar Wallace and many others are targeted as the promulgators of a fearsome and totally irrational hatred of all things foreign. For them the Black, the Chinese, the Argentinian, the Levantine and the Jew become sinister 'niggers', 'chinks', 'dagos', 'greasy levantines' and 'oily Jews'. The race hatred of these authors employs a feverish conjunctivity, with oily Jews who are both capitalists and 'bolsheviks', or Chinese who are mandarin warlords and opium den keepers in Limehouse. Moreover, when not acting themselves these essentially cowardly folk employ peculiarly simian dacoits or things of a polyglot and nauseous origin.

That such feverish racism could become so popular and that the overt racism carried along in that popularity was so rarely noticed by the consumers of such hatred needs some explaining. Although such disgust at foreign things was general and central to much fiction of the time it was also used in a gratuitous and quite unnecessary way to 'fill-in' when the action dulled. Such targeting of minority races is important not merely because we nowadays consider it loathsome, but because it was the result of the imaginative processes of creativity and life-enhancement claimed by novel writers. Furthermore, it was not the result of racial contact, but of an unknowing racial quarantine, and where not of quarantine of double-think. John Buchan often had despicable Jews in his work while openly supporting the ideals of Zionism and admiring its advocates. The question, therefore, remains to be answered as to why there is such race hatred and why such unconscious acceptance of its message?

The novelist Sax Rohmer was one such pedlar of racial hatred and it is especially toward an understanding of his work and its own particular and peculiar racial resonances that this chapter is dedicated. D.J. Enright in his introduction to the reissued *The Mystery of Dr Fu Manchu* tells us:

Arthur Henry (later Sarsfield) Ward was born in 1886 [actually, 1883], of Irish parents living in Birmingham. He worked very briefly as a bank clerk in Threadneedle Street, and then as a journalist. At 20 he had two stories accepted, at last, by *Pearson's Magazine and Chamber's Journal*, and adopted the pen-name Sax Rohmer, later explaining that 'sax' was Saxon for 'blade' and 'rohmer' meant 'roamer'. Some years afterwards (so the story goes) he and his young wife consulted a ouija board as to how he could best make a living. 'C-H-I-N-A-M-A-N' came the enigmatic answer. Before long, and after ghosting an autobiography by the comedian Little Tich, Rohmer wrote his first story about the Chinaman Dr Fu-Manchu (the hyphen was dropped after the third novel). *The Mystery of Dr Fu Manchu* (1913) and subsequent books sold in their millions, notably in the 1920s and 30s, were translated into many languages, and adapted for radio, television and comic strips.[1]

And this great success, we are told was due to the fact that '[he] made [his] name on Fu Manchu because [he knew] nothing about the Chinese!'[2]

It is worth lingering over Fu Manchu's cultural origins. Born in the decade of the publication of *Dr Jekyll and Mr Hyde*, just prior to the first Sherlock Holmes tale and only five years away from the doings of Jack the Ripper, Arthur Henry Ward was to spend his childhood as one of the urban lower middle class who fed off the new popular scandal press which had come into existence during the 1880s and 1890s. Surrounded by growing class dissension the new journalism would particularize the threat posed by unions and by the labour movement as one by particularly wicked individuals whose conspiratorial natures threatened the very peace of the people on behalf of whom they fought. Thus a paradoxical situation arose in which people instinctively took the news from newspaper moghuls whose entrepreneurial interests were inherently opposed to the collective interests of their lower-middle-class and working-class readership. The reader's desire for a conservative stability in their own lives contrasted with the emergent moneyed working and lower-middle class to which they themselves belonged bent willy nilly on rising to middle-class sobriety. Hence, individual desire for a stable status quo was threatened by the class movement of those very individuals.

To cope with such changes, which seemed inexplicable in class terms and deeply disturbing in personal terms, the readership of the new journalism and of the popular thriller were treated to externalized threats that could 'easily' be accommodated to the new serried front parlours of the numerous lower-middle-class suburbs which went sprawling out into the countryside around urban centres and which were serviced by the suburban railway lines; on every platform a W.H. Smith bookstand and in every third-class compartment a thriller to equal those read, perhaps, in the first-class carriages. Moreover, the new enforcedly *leisured* mobility of the train service could be put to use by the publishing fraternity, and in so doing the taxonomic and conservative dimension of the suburban stopping train could unite the various carriage classes in their daily rehearsal of the class system.

Having been a journalist who serviced this commuter trade, Arthur Ward then wrote thrillers for the same audience. This commuter mentality which, combined with a mentality used to standardization and repetition, allowed the work of Sax Rohmer to translate easily into the technological world of the radio and cinema. The repetitiveness of the form of the Fu Manchu tales was part of the internalized need of people whose daily routine was itself *formally* repetitive, the expected *escapism* of the tales being a blind for the formula repetition of the genre's conformity to stock patterns which were easily reproduced and duplicated. Hence, even though the diabolical doctor's methods are amusingly antiquated they are reproduced on an exotic production line of indivisible thrills.

But the biggest chink in Fu Manchu's armour consists in his peculiarly elaborate and roundabout techniques of assassination and his use of highly eccentric accomplices. They include, a scorpion attracted by the perfume in which a preliminary letter to the victim has been soaked, an army of zombies (*The Island of Dr Fu Manchu*, 1941, set in the Caribbean), a lethal gas, the device of pulling people out of windows with a silken cord once they have been drawn there by a strange cry ('the Call of Siva'), and a hollow can containing a live adder. Fu Manchu speaks of his 'partiality for dumb allies': among them, a cat whose claws are coated with deadly poison, a hamadryad, black spiders, an insect which crosses a tsetse fly with a plague flea, a venomous giant centipede from Burma, an Abyssinian sacred baboon, mice who run around with tiny bells attached to their tails and thus frighten people to death, and ('the most ravenous in the world') Cantonese rats.[3]

This exoticism of content, therefore, was used exclusively to reinforce the mundane and ordinary through the episodic repetitive form of the tales. Readers escaped only to look up from their book in half relieved fear: seeing their pipe racks; wearing their slippers. This desire for a type of conformity can be seen in Ward's choice of a *nom de plume*. In a period hell-bent on recovering a Celtic past Ward denied his Irish ethnic origins by choosing a supposedly exotic name. 'Sax' might mean blade but it sounds like Saxon, that is, a *true* Englishman. Sax Rohmer, with its hint of danger (Rohmer–Roamer–Rover – a man of mystery) nevertheless also tells of a straightforward need to be *within* a community of interest. Such a community required an outsider to threaten it in order to bring mutual antagonisms to the surface the more easily to dissipate them harmlessly in anti-outsider and anti-foreign hatred.

By all accounts Sax Rohmer, as author and as Arthur Ward, happily married family man, had found his particular niche. He had 'the good fortune to have been born to authorship at just the right moment to reap the benefit of cheap printing, big-scale serialization . . . and the direct marketing and wide distribution made possible by the growth of the railways.'[4]

He also started writing at the moment when 'Literature had joined the list of human products that the industrial revolution brought within the field of organized exploitation. It had become a commodity.'[5] Moreover, he wrote for and, despite wealth, belonged to a class that:

> nursed no hopes of climbing into the seats of power, but their contentment always was tinged with the fear of falling. They prayed for a three-fold stability: the stability of the country in relation to the rest of the world, political stability – the continued prevalence of those rules of behaviour which they had been brought up to revere.[6]

So why was it that such a man wrote novels whose only message, according to Colin Watson in *Snobbery with Violence*, was 'one of

racial hatred'?[7] And why is it that 'So vehement and repetitive were
Sax Rohmer's references to Asiatic plotting against "white" civilization that they cannot be explained simply as the frills of melodramatic narration. The man clearly was possessed by some sort of
private dread'?[8]

To answer these questions we must turn to the novels themselves. Ward, as Sax Rohmer, was one of many lesser authors who
owed a debt of gratitude to Conan Doyle for the basic relationship
at the centre of their narratives. Petrie, with his love of authorship,
is a straight copy of Watson (even to his MD), although his knowledge of psychology only runs to pseudo-expert pronouncements on
Fu Manchu's mentality which he diagnoses as 'symptomatic of dangerous mania' (*The Return of Dr Fu Manchu*, chapter 13). Yet the
relationship between Petrie, Nayland Smith and the narrative itself
borders on a pastiche of Conan Doyle. It is a reified 'commodity'
solidified around certain stock characters.

> I had jumped to my feet, for a tall, lean man, with his square-cut,
> clean-shaven face sun-baked to the hue of coffee, entered and
> extended both hands with a cry:
>   'Good old Petrie! Didn't expect me, I'll swear!'
>   It was Nayland Smith – whom I had thought to be in Burma! . . .
>   'Mysterious enough for you?' he laughed, and glanced at my
> unfinished MS. 'A story, eh? From which I gather that the district
> is beastly healthy – what, Petrie? Well, I can put some material in
> your way that, if sheer uncanny mystery is a marketable com-
> modity . . .'
>   (*The Mystery of Dr Fu Manchu*, chapter 1)

Yet with all his old-boy exuberance Nayland Smith is no Sherlock
Holmes. He is unable to prevent the diabolical machinations of his
foe Fu Manchu, rarely solves a crime, never gets his man and is
forever being helped out of horrible cliff-hanger situations by the
mysterious slave-girl Kâramanèh. Withal, that his authority is maintained at a laughable level of magnitude.

> 'My name is Nayland Smith,' he said rapidly – 'Burmese Com-
> missioner.' He snatched a letter from his pocket and thrust it
> into the hands of the bewildered man. 'Read that. It is signed
> by another Commissioner – the Commissioner of Police.' With

amazement written all over him, the other obeyed. 'You see,' continued my friend, tersely – 'it is *carte blanche*, I wish to commandeer your car, sir, on a matter of life and death!'

(*The Return of Dr Fu Manchu*, chapter 2)

It is by now not an authority based on ability, but simply on class lines made invisible by a false textual authority centred on commanding (and upper-middle-class *sporting*) individuality. 'It was an insect, full six inches long. . . . These things I realized in one breathless instant; in the next – Smith had dashed the thing's poisonous life out with one straight, *true blow of the golf club*' (*The Mystery of Dr Fu Manchu*, chapter 3; my italics). Nevertheless, within the tales individuality is defeated at every turn by circumstances dictated by deadly commodities – gas, orchids, centipedes, trap-doors and booby-trapped boxes.

Unlike Sherlock Holmes, Nayland Smith is a roving representative of the West, acting on behalf of the 'interests of the entire white race' (*The Mystery of Dr Fu Manchu*, chapter 1). But now that representation is paralysed and inescapably doomed merely to holding back the floodtide of the *invisible* 'Yellow Peril' (*The Mystery of Dr Fu Manchu*, chapter 6), a peril only ever present in its representatives. The character of Nayland Smith is one caught between his own designated role as the representative of Western white culture (the 'golf club') and his war with the never-to-be-pinned-down Si Fan, a secret organization, in a secret place in China, plotting unspecified horrors against the West. In this way Nayland Smith becomes just another victim of the repetitive machinations of the dread Chinese doctor and his dacoits, thus representing not Western action but a more deadly form of fictional inertia bogged down, as Nayland Smith is, in the formal standardizations of Rohmer's own plotting. For, despite Rohmer's extravagant episodic style, which was a consequence of serialization, his work lacks the usual sequential and teleological narrative technique of most novels.

Quite different from Sherlock Holmes, Nayland Smith is never greater than the sum total of Rohmer's bit-part tales. Ultimately, of course, he is dispensable, for he is merely an oppositional usher of Fu Manchu himself.

Dr Petrie, who bubbles with repressed, and often not so repressed, hysteria throughout is the real conduit to the heart of each tale. His exotic obsession with Kâramanèh, the slave of Fu Manchu, allows for innumerable escapes from impossible corners (paradoxically, the male reader's mundane existence) and an exotic and erotic awareness that brings Edwardian latent obsessions with middle-eastern women to the fore.

> Kâramanèh was a closed book to my shortsighted Western eyes. But the body of Kâramanèh was exquisite; her beauty of a kind that was a key to the most extravagant rhapsodies of Eastern poets. Her eyes held a challenge wholly Oriental in its appeal; her lips, even in repose, were a taunt. And, herein, East is West and West is East.
>
> *(The Mystery of Dr Fu Manchu*, chapter 27)

However, Kâramanèh is no liberated woman, despite her deadly ability with a gun. She is a triple victim: of slavery, of Petrie's daydreams and of Western erotic sadism: ' "Throw me into prison, kill me if you like, for what I have done!" . . . She twisted around so that the white skin was but inches removed from me. . . . I clenched my teeth. Insane thoughts flooded my mind. For that creamy skin was red with the marks of the lash!' (*The Return of Dr Fu Manchu*, chapter 5). Indeed, the extreme of this attitude occurs when Nayland Smith tells Petrie that he should 'seize her by the hair, drag her to some cellar, hurl her down, and stand over her with a whip' (*The Mystery of Dr Fu Manchu*, chapter 12).

Petrie, a victim of his own worst wet-dream-girl nightmares is, however, the direct line to Dr Fu Manchu, who mistakenly considers him his equal in scientific knowledge. Thus, Petrie's overt upholding of Western racism is joined *textually* to the Chinese menace. Indeed, the most vehement racial invective comes not from Nayland Smith but from Petrie's own overly imaginative pen.

> I found myself bound along Whitechapel Road. . . .
>
> Jewish hawkers, many of them in their shirtsleeves, acclaimed the rarity of the bargains which they had to offer; and, allowing for the difference of costume, these tireless Israelites, heedless of climactic conditions, sweating at their mongery, might well have stood, not in a squalid London thoroughfare, but in an equally squalid market street of the Orient. . . .
>
> Poles, Russians, Serbs, Roumanians, Jews of Hungary, and Italians of Whitechapel mingled in the throng. Near East and Far East rubbed shoulders. Pidgin English contested with Yiddish for

the ownership of some tawdry article offered by an auctioneer whose nationality defied conjecture. . . .

North, South, East, and West mingled their cries. . . . Sometimes a yellow face showed close to one of the streaming windows; sometimes a black-eyed, pallid face, but never a face wholly sane and healthy. This was an underworld where squalor and vice went hand in hand through the beautiless streets, a melting-pot of the world's outcasts; this was the shadowland, which last night had swallowed up Nayland Smith.

(*The Return of Dr Fu Manchu*, chapter 11)

Clearly divided into West End and East End, London became the microcosmic battlefield of Imperial neuroses. In 1913 (yet already in the 1880s when Ward was born) London *was* the Empire for fictionalists, in novels and in journalism – the East End became the Dark Continent, not Africa but South East Asia, an inscrutable land beyond the comprehension of the white race of the West End. But what was most important was that the West End was *also* inscrutable to Rohmer's readers in their suburban solitude. Nayland Smith might belong to a clubland to which few could aspire, but his *real* battlefield was *suburban* London – 'the quiet suburban avenue' at the heart of his readers' domestic world (*The Return of Dr Fu Manchu*, chapter 8). Such suburban danger was constantly repeated and follows Conan Doyle's own interest in dangers lurking in the newly built villas of South London's Upper Norwood (Rohmer lived in Herne Hill, South London) and North London's Finchley. 'You ought to see his house in Finchley. A low, squat place. . . . Damp as a swamp; smells like a jungle. . . . The rest of the house is half a menagerie and half a circus. He has a Bedouin groom, a Chinese body-servant, and heaven only knows what other strange people!' (*The Mystery of Dr Fu Manchu*, chapters 10 and 11). Wapping, Shadwell and the 'notorious' Ratcliffe Highway (*The Return of Dr Fu Manchu*, chapter 10) crawled out to the suburbs and mysteriously called charabanc loads of suburban dwellers on trips to Limehouse in search of non-existent opium dens and sinister aristocratic cocaine addicts (see Sir Crichton Davey in *The Mystery of Dr Fu Manchu*, chapter 1).

But if these Sunday afternoon trippers came in search of the titillation of having pointed out to them the 'real' life origins of dubious opium dens such as 'John Ki's [junky] Joy Shop' (*The Hand of Fu Manchu*, chapter 5) or Shen Yan's (*The Mystery of Dr Fu Manchu*,

chapter 6), which in all probability were no more than the dwellings of poor seamen, then what greater thrill than to imagine that
each pig-tailed Lascar was a potential enemy, each malignant look
(of hatred or contempt at the gawping tourists) was the disguised
Dr Fu Manchu himself. These gawping tourists in their own land,
in their own city, the heart of Empire, were not Sinophobes bent on
holding back the waves of alien ships' workers but idly curious
Sunday afternoon tourists whose ignorance fed Sax Rohmer's bank
balance. And nowhere was that bank balance better served than
with the invention of Rohmer's great monster, for like all thriller
writers Rohmer knew that the real centre of such a genre was a
monumental villain against whom the ordinary decent folk pitted
their limited wits.

Rohmer's descriptions of Dr Fu Manchu are highly instructive.

This man . . . is, unquestionably, the most malign and formidable
personality existing in the known world today. He is a linguist
who speaks with almost equal facility in any of the civilized languages, and in most of the barbaric. He is an adept in all the arts
and sciences which a great university could teach him. He also is
an adept in certain obscure arts and sciences which no university
of today can teach. He has the brains of any three men of genius.
Petrie, he is a mental giant. . . .

Imagine a person, tall, lean and feline, high shouldered, with a
brow like Shakespeare and a face like Satan, a close-shaven skull,
and long, magnetic eyes of the true cat-green. Invest him with all
the cruel cunning of an entire Eastern race, accumulated in one
giant intellect, with all the resources of science past and present,
with all the resources, if you will, of a wealthy government –
which, however, already has denied all knowledge of his existence. Imagine that awful being, and you have a mental picture of
Dr Fu Manchu, the yellow peril incarnate in one man. . . .

Of his face, as it looked out at me over the dirty table, I despair
of writing convincingly. It was that of an archangel of evil, and
it was wholly dominated by the most uncanny eyes that ever
reflected a human soul, for they were narrow and long, very
slightly oblique, and a brilliant green. But their unique horror lay
in a certain filminess (it made me think of the *membrana nicitans*
in a bird) which, obscuring them as I threw awide the door,
seemed to lift as I actually passed the threshold, revealing the
eyes in all their brilliant viridescence.

(*The Mystery of Dr Fu Manchu*, chapters 2 and 6)

Set within a jewel of purple prose and hyperbolical nonsense, Dr Fu Manchu rises upon the stage of world villany the most complete of terrors. Rohmer repeated the description, like an intoned ritual, in book after book. But if Dr Fu Manchu is the *beyond* of all imagination he is also, paradoxically, within the cognizance of the 'partly' literate public who clammered for more of him – he signified for that public who knew Shakespeare stood for genius (although his plays may have been unread) and that Satan was a genius (or more properly Milton's Satan was a genius, as we may consider Arthur Ward's literary knowledge would have found this Satan simply by association with Milton).

But, if Fu Manchu's origins are directly and commonplacedly English literary, then from whence the Chinese connection? In this it is noteworthy that Rohmer said that '[he] made [his] name on Fu Manchu because [he knew] nothing about the Chinese!' and that he found his 'Chinaman' through the use of a 'ouija board'. If, for the moment, we dismiss the ouija board comment as hokum then the Chinese connection still needs to be made. So where did the dread doctor originate from? One origin may be the mysterious Chinese Tong boss 'Mr King', who Rohmer tried to find during a series of journalistic forays into Limehouse in 1911.[9]

Yet, if one looks for a possible original model for Dr Fu Manchu one need look no further than the famous music hall 'Chinese' magician Chung Ling Soo. Chung Ling Soo was in reality William Ellsworth Robinson, a New Yorker born in 1861. Formerly an illusion builder he was invited, in imitation of the original real Chinese magician Chung Ling Soo, to perform at the Paris *Folies Bergère*. Changing his stage name to Hop Sing Loo, Robinson finally decided to plagiarize the name Chung Ling Soo. By skilful publicity, Robinson, the fake Chung Ling Soo, was able to oust the real Chung Ling Soo and take his place. The authentic and original Chinese magician was now irrevocably replaced by a white man in costume who had shaved off his Victorian moustache and donned a Mandarin costume and pigtail. Indeed, Robinson's whole life was a way of

acknowledging the greatest illusion he ever performed, namely the skilful way in which he lived up to the identity of his *alter ego* from the moment he shaved his head to don his first pigtail on 17 May 1900.

A master of the art of mime, Soo never spoke on stage, even though he often gave marathon performances of two hours duration. Off-stage in public he would continue to wear his Chinese make-up and spoke only 'Chinese', accommodating reporters through the 'interpretations' of his stage manager, Frank Kametaro. In 1908 he did allow the first edition of the *Liverpool Theatrical News* to publish a story regarding his true identity, mainly as a ploy to clear his name from any accusations that might be levelled against a member of the race that had committed the atrocities of the Boxer Rebellion. The story went unnoticed. The public did not want to know, probably dismissing it all as a hoax. In the eyes of the public Soo continued to live up to his publicity as 'A Gift from the Gods to Mortals on Earth to Amuse and Mystify', while in retrospect Robinson sedately earned his title as the all-time Emperor of inscrutability.[10]

This vivid and extraordinary performer was almost certainly one major influence on the character of Dr Fu Manchu. Indeed, the bullet-catching trick that in 1918 led to Soo's death may account for at least one episode in which Fu Manchu is 'fatally' wounded only to recover for the next adventure.

Given that Sax Rohmer's wife was a music-hall juggler, given he wrote sketches and theatrical songs, given his friendship with George Robey and given his ghosting of the autobiography of Little Tich we can surmise that he may well have been personally acquainted with Chung Ling Soo.[11] If not, at least he would have been familiar with the latter's role as a performer. The message of the ouija board may well simply have been the auto suggestion of a man who had recently visited the music hall and seen a 'Chinaman' perform.

We have seen the coincidence between various forms of 'popular' culture and the commodification of fictional 'types'. In this respect two forms of commodification, that of fiction and that of 'the Orient', allowed for a marketable package that could be sold in the same interchangeable way. Hence, Rohmer's writing career which happily embraced commercial fiction also allowed for the selling of exotic perfumes, the end result of a number of unsuccessful manufacturing ventures. Commercial fiction and perfume were both merely manufacturing ventures.

Rohmer's perfume, called 'Honan' was put in an exotic bamboo-clad package and fixed with a silk tassel.[12] Rohmer's company had a workforce of 12–14 Chinese headed by a manager, Ah Sin.[13] Barker's Department Store in Kensington was the outlet and:

The long-suffering Ah Sin was now called upon to become an actor. He had to be the 'real, live Chinaman', since he was the only one of the native employees who could speak English. They decked him out in a gorgeous national costume (hired from a theatrical outfitters) complete with a false pigtail. Pigtails had gone out with the Dowager Express – Sax was aware of that – but the shoppers would expect him to have one, so they included it.[14]

That a Chinese was required to pretend to be a 'Chinaman' suggests not merely a travesty, but an obvious ambivalence in the English mind over the oriental type. Sax Rohmer himself was aware of this ambivalence in his own psychological and emotional ties to Limehouse. Many years after the appearance of the first Fu Manchu story Rohmer wrote,

> Nowadays . . . I like to think that a Chinese and a Chinaman are not the same thing. When I began writing, 'Chinaman' was no more than the accepted term for a native of China. The fact that it has since taken on a derogatory meaning is due mostly to the behaviour of those Chinamen who lived in such places as Limehouse.[15]

However, the last line, in its slippage from Chinese to 'Chinamen', used as a synonym for *criminal*, exposes Rohmer's vagueness as well as his racism.

We may say now that Fu Manchu and that from which he sprang, the stock pantomime Chinaman, were ideal vehicles for the packaging of thrills but yet here they also represent a disturbance in the simple commodification of formula thriller fiction. This doubling back upon a stock and marketable object ('formula' fiction) does not merely gives a greater longevity to characters caught in a nostalgic byway of cultural history, but also adds a *frisson* of doubt over the stability of the very notion of a marketable object itself (in this case 'the thriller'). Fu Manchu represents a monstrousness in the heart of a technologically 'secure' world – he represents a diabolical disturbance which allows for the intrusion of a 'reality' that is metaphysical and denies the outward appearance of material things. As a scientist from the Orient, Fu Manchu is so advanced that he is more a magician ('the occult student and the man of science' [*The Mystery of Dr Fu Manchu*, chapter 24]). Indeed, in one episode he even resurrects the dead.

In this, Fu Manchu is the focal point for a *disturbance within things*. He becomes the occult representative of a lost world of supernatural causality which underpins and yet confronts ordinary life. This can clearly be seen in the episode in which Nayland Smith and Petrie visit Kegan Von Roon ('orientalist and psychic investigator') in chapter 22 of *The Return of Dr Fu Manchu*. Craigmore Hall, Van Roon's house, is clearly borrowed in its setting from *The Hound of the Baskervilles*. It is both ancient and evil. Moreover, Van Roon who appears 'American' (that is, ultra modern!) is, in fact, a Chinese (therefore, an ancient) agent of Fu Manchu! The house, with its incredibly ancient lineage, its association with Glastonbury, with magic and with Madame Blavatsky, is an apparent denial of the modern and a confirmation of the fearful otherness of things.

It is a veritable wonderland, almost as interesting in its way, as the caves and jungles of Hindustan depicted by Madame Blavatsky.... The tower itself is of unknown origin, though probably Phoenician, and the house traditionally sheltered Dr. Macleod, the necromancer.... it is quite possible to see the ruins of Glastonbury Abbey from here; and Glastonbury Abbey, as you may know, is closely bound up with the history of alchemy. It was in the ruins of Glastonbury Abbey that the adept Kelly, companion of Dr Dee, discovered, in the reign of Elizabeth, the famous caskets of St Dunstan, containing the two tinctures.

(The Return of Dr Fu Manchu, chapter 22)

Fu Manchu himself is even denied material presence at the end of *The Mystery of Dr Fu Manchu* when a theory of supernatural and demonic origin is ascribed to him, 'there is a superstition in some parts of China according to which, under certain peculiar conditions ... an evil spirit of incredible age may enter into the body of a new-born infant' (*The Mystery of Dr Fu Manchu*, chapter 27).

In Rohmer's world the materiality of presence is a peculiarly haphazard affair, neither objects nor people conforming to the known laws of physics or human biology. This may partly be explained by Rohmer's own life-long interests in Egyptology (Petrie was named after the Egyptologist Flinders Petrie), orientalism and the occult.

During the nascence of Dr Fu Manchu, Rohmer completed *The Romance of Sorcery* (1913), joined the Order of the Golden Dawn, met Aleister Crowley and dabbled in occultism. His wife was psychic and he seemed to attract metaphysical phenomena. Recurrent dreams haunted him as did hallucinatory dreams. In one such dream an exotic oriental dancer materialized in his bedroom. This materialization, which Rohmer considered a *real* visit from another plane of existence, may have been the original for Kâramanèh. Indeed, Petrie often finds himself unable to distinguish between waking and sleeping states.

Here, perhaps, lies one of the secrets of Fu Manchu's power to fascinate. The Sinophobic message of Rohmer's books is underpinned by three theories: the notion of a conspiracy which is based upon a corporate, international secret society acting out of Limehouse, the notion of a parallel supernatural plane of existence and the notion of eternal recurrence.

The modern world, represented by Nayland Smith, is a world essentially haunted by an international mafia with supernatural powers; powers which at once uphold and disestabilize reality and whose presence is material yet invisible.

Rohmer, who was a lapsed Catholic and whose fanatical Catholic mother died an insane alcoholic, wrote thrillers at whose core is a repressed noumenal immanence. It is an immanence that is profoundly disturbing and distressing; it is satanic and fascinating – the commodification of desire: the supernaturalization of the capitalist enterprise.

Such a complex set of motival forces run through Rohmer's books. Audiences were thrilled because Rohmer offered, through a 'Chinaman' *another* history and *another* plane of meaning. Modern life was absurd, Fu Manchu was absurd, but only if one failed to see that the laws of creation were other than those of modern materialism. The commodity danced to laws which upheld and yet denied the very functions of the commodity as commodity/object. Consequently, it is not the 'Chinaman' who is other in these tales, but Englishness itself, the suburban world of Sax Rohmer's adoring readers.

10

This Revolting Graveyard of the Universe: The Horror Fiction of H.P. Lovecraft

The twentieth century has had two major sources of inspiration for the horrific imagination. The first is Hollywood, where modern cinematographic technology has been used to reproduce the Romantic Gothic worlds of Mary Shelley's *Frankenstein*, Gaston Le Roux's *Phantom of the Opera* and Bram Stoker's *Dracula*. The work of Universal and other studios' horror movies have been widely distributed and are well known, appearing nowadays regularly on television. The second major influence is the work of Howard Phillips Lovecraft, a pulp-fiction writer whose short life ended before the Second World War. Where the studios were motivated by publicity and commercialism, Lovecraft was motivated by horror of publicity and by a disgust with commercial enterprise. Lovecraft remains, fifty years after his death, an enigmatic writer and a strange and stranded personality. He wrote 'popular fiction' which never was and still is not popular; he considered himself a man of letters who wrote exclusively for pulp magazines; he instinctively felt that he was a gentleman but was actually the son of a commercial salesman; and he was a writer in the early twentieth century who owed nothing to the work of James, Eliot, Pound or Lawrence. His output was small, consisting of two novellas (one published after his death) and some short stories, many of which were completed by others after his death. In many ways Lovecraft has been an influence on film makers (especially Roger Corman) and on other writers (Robert Bloch, Ray Bradbury, Colin Wilson, Ramsay Campbell and Stephen King), but Lovecraft himself remains locked away – a cult interest for fantasy fanatics (who are rare) and academics or intellectuals (who are rarer).

Who was H.P. Lovecraft and what did he do? He was born on 20 August 1890 in Providence, Rhode Island.[1] We are told that:

Lovecraft was of predominantly British stock on both sides of his family. His father was the son of an Englishman who had lost his fortune and emigrated from Devonshire to New York in 1847 and married a girl of British descent – an Allgood from Northumberland, descended from a former British officer who remained in the United States after what Lovecraft himself, ardent Anglophile that he was, would term 'the disastrous Revolution'. On his mother's side, Lovecraft was, in his own words, 'a complete New-England Yankee, coming from Phillipses, Places, & Rathbones'.[2]

In 1898, his father, named after the hero Winfield Scott, died of a serious and lingering illness. Lovecraft was eight. For some time his father had been a paretic, muscularly paralysed and mentally incompetent. Winfield Scott Lovecraft died insane, perhaps from untreated syphilis, but, before he did, he and his small son spent time together on the father's occasional visits from the hospital to which he had been sent.[3] After his father's death, Lovecraft was brought up in the exclusive home company of the Lovecraft women – mother, aunts and grandmother.

After his father's death Lovecraft began to suffer from terrifying nightly disturbances and nightmares, which lasted until his own death in 1937. In order to deal with these unresolved nightmares Lovecraft wrote them into his letters or adapted them into short stories. Although he hated Freud's concepts, which he considered paltry and inconsequential, his attempts at fiction and at verse can be seen to be a prolonged working-through of his unsatisfactory relationship with his father – a man whose insanity was accompanied by periods of hallucination.[4] One of Lovecraft's later pantheon of 'gods', the terrifying and imbecile Nyarlathotep, may owe his origin, many years later, to the period of the elder Lovecraft's madness, for everything leads 'me on even unto those grinning caverns of earth's centre where Nyarlathotep, the mad faceless god, howls blindly in the darkness to the piping of two amorphous idiot flute players' ('The Rats in the Wall'). Indeed, this imbecile god is *the* impulse of the universe:

And through this revolting graveyard of the universe the muffled, maddening beating of drums, and thin, monotonous whine of blasphemous flutes from inconceivable, unlighted chambers beyond Time; the detestable pounding and piping whereunto dance slowly, awkwardly, and absurdly the gigantic, tenebrous ultimate gods – the blind, voiceless, mindless gargoyles whose soul is Nyarlathotep.[5]

But this terrifying and significantly 'faceless' entity was not always a god, for Lovecraft transformed dream material of another kind, a kind much closer to the commercial traveller that was his father:

Nyarlathotep is a nightmare – an actual phantasm of my own, with the first paragraph written *before I fully awaked*. I had been feeling execrably of late – whole weeks have passed without relief from head-ache. . . . I had never heard the name NYARLATHOTEP before, but seemed to understand the allusion. Nyarlathotep was a kind of itinerant showman or lecturer who held forth in publick [*sic*] halls and aroused wide spread fear and discussion with his exhibitions. These exhibitions consisted of two parts – first, a horrible – possible prophetic – cinema reel; and later some extraordinary experiments with scientific and electrical apparatus. . . . I seem to recall that Nyarlathotep was already in Providence; and that he was the cause of the shocking fear which brooded over all the people. I seem to remember that persons had whispered to me in awe of his horrors, and warned me not to go near him. . . . The terror [has] become a matter of conscious artistic creation.[6]

This was a nightmare Lovecraft could not exorcise, and it created a form of self-punishment which he wrote into his story *The Case of Charles Dexter Ward*:

From a private hospital for the insane near Providence, Rhode Island, there recently disappeared an exceedingly singular person. He bore the name of Charles Dexter Ward, and was placed under restraint most reluctantly by the *grieving father* who had watched his aberration grow from a eccentricity to a dark mania involving both a possibility of murderous tendencies and a peculiar change in the apparent contents of his mind. Doctors confess themselves quite baffled by his case, since it presented oddities of a general physiological as well as psychological character.

(emphasis mine)

It is clear that Lovecraft brought deeply personal material to his work, and this may account for his low output of stories and high output of confessional letters.

Another area of 'neurosis' for him was his relationship with the ordinary modern world in the United States of the 1920s and 1930s. Lovecraft's background was essentially Anglophile and of provincial New England. As a young man he published a magazine called *The Conservative*.[7] Self-educated and outside the New England college world, Lovecraft yearned for a past age into which he could escape. In 1923 he wrote self-mockingly:

> Nothing must disturb my undiluted Englishry – God Save the King! I am naturally a Nordic – a chalk-white, bulky Teuton of the Scandinavian or North-German forests – a Viking – a berserk killer – a predatory rover of the blood of Hengist and Horsa – a conqueror of Celts and Mongols and founder of Empires – a son of the thunders and the arctic winds, and brother to the frosts and the auroras – a drinker of foemen's blood from newpicked skulls . . .[8]

And in 1929, in another letter, he tells us, 'my writing soon became distorted – till at length I wrote only as a means of re-creating around me the atmosphere of my 18th century favourites'.[9] After his marriage, he moved to Brooklyn and travelled, in a limited fashion, visiting the older colonial USA: Philadelphia, Richmond, Williamsburg and Yorktown. When his marriage failed he returned to Providence and the world of his aunts. Indeed, when previously offered the editorship of *Weird Tales*, then published in Chicago, Lovecraft refused to commit himself on the grounds of having just arrived in New York (which he refers to as 'venerable New-Amsterdam').[10] Moreover, his stories are usually set in a just-surviving seventeenth-century America. For instance, in his tale 'The Survivor' his narrator tells us,

> I came to Providence, Rhode Island, in 1930, intending to make only a brief visit and then go on to New Orleans. But I saw the Charriere house on Benefit Street, and was drawn to it as only an antiquarian would be drawn to any unusual house isolated in a New England street of a period not its own, a house clearly of some age . . . indefinable aura that both attracted and repelled. . . . I saw it first as an antiquarian, delighted to discover set in a row of staid New England houses a house which was manifestly of a seventeenth-century Quebec style, and thus so different from its neighbours as to attract immediately the eye of any passer-by. I

had made many visits to Quebec, as well as to other old cities of the North American continent, but on this first visit to Providence, I had not come primarily in search of ancient dwellings.

'The Peabody Heritage', too, is architecturally specific: 'the dwelling itself was the product of many generations. It had been built originally in 1787, at first as a simple colonial house, with severe lines, an unfinished second story, and four impressive pillars at the front.'

Lovecraft's desperation for a gentlemanly existence was set against a background of rapid social change. Although married to a Jew, he continually poured vitriol on the incoming waves of immigrants, reserving a special hatred for the new Jewish immigrants, whom he called 'beady eyed rat-faced Asiatics'.[11] Moreover, his wife Sonia recalls that, when he actually came face to face with them in New York, 'Howard would become livid with rage. He seemed almost to lose his mind.'[12] This distinctly unusual behaviour Lovecraft could not deal with in direct terms, choosing rather a 'black magic' science fiction which transformed social fears into fantasy nightmares.[13] New York is also suitably transformed into a fantastical realm of historical and 'species' degeneracy:[14]

> I saw a vista which will ever afterward torment me in dreams. I saw the heavens verminous with strange flying things, and beneath them a hellish black city of giant stone terraces with impious pyramids flung savagely to the moon, and devil-lights burning from un-numbered windows. And swarming loathsomely on aerial galleries I saw the yellow, squint-eyed people of that city, robed horribly in orange and red and dancing insanely to the pounding of fevered kettle-drums. . . . I have gone home to the pure New England lanes up which fragrant sea-winds sweep at evening.
>
> ('He')

Elsewhere this becomes more explicit, and a New York police detective finds himself amid the degenerate hoards of the metropolitan heart:

> He had for some time been detailed to the Butler Street station in Brooklyn when the Red Hook matter came to his notice. Red Hook is a maze of hybrid squalor near the ancient waterfront

opposite Governor's Island, with dirty highways climbing the hill from the wharves to that higher ground where the decayed lengths of Clinton and Court Streets lead off towards the Borough Hall. Its houses are mostly of brick, dating from the first quarter to the middle of the nineteenth century. . . . The population is a hopeless tangle and enigma; Syrian, Spanish, Italian, and negro elements impinging upon one another, and fragments of Scandinavian and American belts lying not far distant. It is a babel of sound and filth.

('The Horror at Red Hook')

In his long tale 'At the Mountains of Madness', a 'fetid black' monster which Lovecraft called a 'Shoggoth' is likened to the 'Boston–Cambridge tunnel' subway train. Yet the Shoggoths 'whatever they had been . . . were men'.

This is evidence enough of Lovecraft's peculiar brand of horror – a transposition of his social fears about new immigrant groups into a cosmic battle in which the evil *Üntermenschen* are constantly defeating the less numerous *Übermenschen*. Many critics stop at this point, believing Lovecraft's horror to be purely racist, but this is perhaps only half the story, for the majority of Lovecraft's tales depict Anglo-Saxon degeneracy among the rural white poor, not the newly arrived passengers of the steerage. Two examples must suffice:

He paused exhausted, as the whole group of natives stared in a bewilderment not quite crystallized into fresh terror. Only old Zebulon Whateley, who wanderingly remembered ancient things but who had been silent heretofore, spoke aloud.

'Fifteen year' gone,' he rambled, 'I heered Ol' Whateley say as haow some day we'd hear a child o' Lavinny's a callin' its father's name on the top o' Sentinel Hill. . . .'

But Joe Osborn interrupted him to question the Arkham men anew.

'What was it, *anyhaow*, an' haowever did young Wizard Whateley call it aout o' the air it come from?'

Armitage chose his words very carefully. . . . I'm going to burn his accursed diary, and if you men are wise you'll dynamite that altar-stone up there, and pull down all the rings of standing stones on the other hills.

('The Dunwich Horror')

Or:

> Sir William, standing with his searchlight in the Roman ruin,
> translated aloud the most shocking ritual I have ever known; and
> told of the diet of the antediluvian cult which the priests of Cybele
> found and mingled with their own. Norrys, used as he was to
> the trenches, could not walk straight when he came out of the
> English building. It was a butcher shop and kitchen – he had
> expected that – but it was too much to see familiar English im-
> plements in such a place, and to read familiar English *graffiti*
> there, some as recent as 1610.
>
> ('The Rats in the Wall')

On one side Lovecraft was faced with an invasion of 'Asiatics', but
on the other he witnessed another form of degeneracy – that of his
own race. In 1926, when Lovecraft produced his largest body of
work, he would have been witness to an amazing growth of rural
religious fervour. In 1925 an article on the rise of the 'Holy Rollers'
painted this picture of rural enthusiasm:

> The song became a dirge and the dirge became a fiendish thing,
> rising in howls and wails and moanings that stilled the wild
> things of the night. Preacher Joe Leffew preached. 'Some folks
> thinks as how as we-uns are funny people. They come here, poor
> sinners that they are, to mock an' revile us. Here's our word of
> Scripture. "An' Christ reeled to an' fro, as a drunken man." Now,
> children, dear children, some folks think that means the Lamb
> was a drunkard. T'aint so at all. It says "as a drunken man". You
> cain't tell me God's son ever went home all soused up.'
>   Preacher Joe Leffew assailed education. 'I ain't got no learnin'
> an' never had none,' said Preacher Joe Leffew. 'Glory be to the
> Lamb! Some folks work their hands off'n up 'n to the elbows to
> give their young-uns education, and all they do is send their
> young-uns to hell.'[15]

This needs to be added to the growth of the 'know-nothing' intolerance of the Ku-Klux-Klan, which had been recently 'revived' in
the 1920s. In 1926, the year of Lovecraft's most prolific outpouring,
Hiram Wesley Evans, Imperial Wizard of the Klan, had this to say
about Americanness:

We are a movement of the plain people, very weak in matter of culture, intellectual support, and trained leadership. We are demanding, and we expect to win, a return of power into the hands of the everyday, not highly cultured, . . . but entirely unspoiled and not de-Americanized, average citizen of the old stock. Our members and leaders are all of this class – the opposition of the intellectuals and liberals. . . .

The Klan . . . has now come to speak for the great mass of Americans of the old pioneer stock. . . .

These are . . . a blend of various peoples of the so-called Nordic race . . . the Klan does not try to represent any people but these. . . .

[Now] we [have] found our great cities and the control of much of our industry and commerce taken over by strangers. . . .

So the Nordic American today is a stranger in large parts of the land his fathers gave him.[16]

In 1928 the Klan's rise in Indiana was described by Morton Harrison in terms reminiscent of Lovecraft's monster gods. The Klan is addressed by its leader:

Here in this uplifted hand, where all can see, I bear an official document addressed to the Grand Dragon, Hydras, Great Titans, Furies, Giants, Kleagles, Exalted Cyclops, Terrors, and All Citizens of the Invisible Empire of the Realm of Indiana. It is done in the executive chambers of His Lordship, the Imperial Wizard, in the Imperial City of Atlanta.[17]

This side of Lovecraft's fears is not mentioned by any critics who deal with his work. That Lovecraft pictured himself as a barbarian Nordic type was purely ironic given his frailty and lack of physicality; that he was a rationalist materialist, whose hobby was astronomy, added to his distaste for cults based on ignorance (he was, after all, an eighteenth-century gentleman).

In order to cope with racial alienation from both directions Lovecraft turned his social fears into nightmare fantasies. His *real* nightmares then returned upon themselves and fictional fantasy returned to its origins. To suggest, as most critics do, that Lovecraft's social fears were simply translated into fantasy ignores the fact that his fantasy life (his dreams) ran parallel to his social experience and was not just an internalization of that social experience: Holy Roller, Ku-Klux-Klan Grand Wizard, Nyarlathotep, Father trace

Lovecraft's concern with origins – origins in family and in America that literally paralysed him. Unable to cope with marriage, with city life, with work of any sort, Lovecraft finally could not exist in temperatures lower than 80°F, actually fainting when the heat dropped to 60°. In his stories the seeker after origins either is destroyed or goes mad; the 'Old Ones', for example, are decapitated ('At the Mountains of Madness'). Indeed, in 1929 Lovecraft wrote of his inability to escape the literary influence of either Poe or Dunsany: 'where', he asks, 'are my Lovecraft pieces?'[18] During March 1937 he died of cancer. Lin Carter's 1972 biographical obituary remarks,

> He lived like a hermit, a recluse, in self-imposed exile from his own world and his age, neither of which he enjoyed. Far rather would he have been born a cosmopolitan Roman of the late Empire, or an English squire in his beloved 18th century, or a colonial gentleman of the days before the Revolution. Alas, he was none of these things, except in his extraordinarily vivid dreams.[19]

After Lovecraft's death August Derleth made it a lifelong work of love to keep the master's writings available; yet the collections of Lovecraft work did not sell well. *Weird Tales* also went into decline. Stephen King drily comments,

> During and after the war years, horror fiction was in decline. The age did not like it. It was a period of rapid scientific development and rationalism – they grow very well in a war atmosphere, thanks – and it became a period which is now thought of by fans and writers alike as the 'golden age of science fiction'. . . . *Weird Tales* plugged grimly along, holding its own but hardly reaping millions (it would fold in the mid-fifties after a down-sizing from its original gaudy pulp size to a digest form failed to effect a cure for its ailing circulation).[20]

Nevertheless, Lovecraft's pantheon of gods steadily grew as other writers embellished the 'Cthulhu mythos', as it is called. The cult status of Lovecraft was becoming an inescapable fact. For many who loathed his excesses and 'poverty' of style, but for whom Lovecraft stories were an addiction there was also a problem. Stephen King says that Lovecraft has been called a hack, a description I would dispute vigorously, but whether he was or wasn't, and whether he was a writer of popular fiction or a writer of so-called 'literary fiction' (depending on your critical bent), really doesn't matter very much in this context, because either way, the man himself took his work seriously.[21]

David Punter confesses, 'perhaps little more needs to be said about Lovecraft: his writing is crude, repetitive, compulsively readable, the essence of pulp fiction'.[22]

In order to understand this ambivalence over Lovecraft's work it is necessary to see that Lovecraft's personal traumas were, in fact, the *social traumas* of the group from which his work emerged and to which his work was addressed. While that group of readers has evolved over the years since his death and the specific milieu in which he wrote belongs to the past, it is, nevertheless, still possible to identify some broader cultural issues which stop his work from being of purely historical interest.

Lovecraft's work emerged at a certain point coincident with the emergence of modern mass literacy in America and the growth of vocational self-improvement and literary escapism. Magazines such as *Weird Tales* met these needs following the decline of dime novels. The adolescent, mostly male readership that emerged during this period looked to magazines which included petit-bourgeois writers such as themselves who represented the world of a class and a culture that felt it had no voice. This was a class that saw itself as neither proletarian nor bourgeois and that felt itself exploited by bourgeois cultural requirements. (Lovecraft emerged from such a class, being self-educated, aspiring to be an eighteenth-century gentleman yet the son of a travelling salesman.) This petit-bourgeois-generated antagonism left it feeling bewildered and disenfranchised (hence Lovecraft's hatred of others, especially aliens). The readership of one class unknowingly united with another readership of fantasy tales – the bourgeois intelligentsia, who also felt (and feel) disenfranchised. In both classes a desire for a period before technological specialization (the very period from which these classes emerge) led to an alliance among the pages of *Weird Tales*. Such an alliance manifests itself in a distaste for money (Lovecraft's disinterest in publishing fiction or editing magazines) and a paradoxical love of ostentatious consumption (Lovecraft's taste for the life of a gentleman and, in his tales, for 'empires' and for prehistoric gods and 'heroes', who do not have to earn a living). This paradox is represented in the fiction by a 'revival' of a mythic past, a romanticized past of Gothic or feudal origins and a whole mythology of warring gods being a rewriting in fantasy terms of the myth of Genesis.

This construction of another (quite separate) history to the world other than the official bourgeois history reflects the petit-bourgeois belief in a conspiracy by 'those at the top'. This conspiracy involves the translation of social factors into black magic and occult forces which because they are about to return suggest they are outside human (therefore bourgeois) control. The immanence of archaic elements about to irrupt into modern life always brings the bourgeoisie near to defeat, but they can always recover and this allows the petit-bourgeoisie also to survive, for total defeat of the bourgeoisie would lead to total dissolution of the petit-bourgeoisie. These dangerous archaic elements represent anti-bourgeois forces, but they embody petit-bourgeois ideas about the bourgeoisie controlling everything. Hence Lovecraft's 'good' monsters have pyramidal heads covered with all-encompassing tentacles. Being buried under pyramids of power ('Imprisoned with the Pharaohs') suggests social pyramids, but, again, paradoxically, the monsters are always at the very bottom of the pyramid, beneath history and therefore outside it. What is seen to be at the top is represented as being underneath.

Such a representation of life also involves (despite Lovecraft's distaste for Holy Rollers) a strongly religious notion, but one that has become scientifically objectified: a materialist belief system. The class to which Lovecraft belonged had 'liberated' itself from an old-style religion, but was unable to go back to the superstitions beliefs of the lumpenproletariat or rural peasantry. Lovecraft instead turned to his hobby of astronomy in order to create stories about *astrology* and black magic bringing real monsters from the stars as star-spawn. Moreover, this quasi-religiosity which is fatalistic and deterministic rests on a scientific understanding of phenomena, at once upholding the incredible but defeated by it ('At the Mountains of Madness'). Objective, materialist science is used to defeat itself: it recognizes what it cannot control – the other, the Absolute, ultimately the gods or God (but the gods are mad).

We return to the question of origins – of the cosmos, of man, of the petit-bourgeoisie. The identification of those origins is bound to the textual unravelling of a riddle, which once deciphered offers Truth – not merely a set of truths, but an absolute reassurance of the impossibility of *change*, both capitalist and bourgeois; for the Truth is that the 'Old Ones' and their enemies will always exist and battle for the universe. Hence, history stops in eternal recurrence. In order to stop history it is necessary to travel back in time to find it and to disturb it, thereby discovering that it exists not merely as the past but also in the present as a threat. For the return of the past reassures us of permanence even as it acts to threaten the very class representatives (and hence the whole class) who go in search of it. Indeed, the other place for history fantasized by the petit-bourgeoisie is actually the place of archaic feudal relations, the relations of autocrat to peasant – the very class relationships that must not return if the petit-bourgeois (servants of the bourgeoisie) are to survive. Questioning the cosmic order (the social order) may lead to destruction, but it also leads to an answer: there is a need for order and a need to 'know one's place'. Hence, hatred of the new coincides with hatred of the old and ends in personal and class paralysis.

This paralysis is the result of the nature of the quest and the quester. It is not a metaphysical quest, but a materialist quest for metaphysical certainties. The hero is a loner, disenfranchized in the modern world by his desire for lost knowledge. He is characterized by physicality and a distaste for psychology. His actions are character, as introversion by extension implies the bourgeois notion of individual control and the privacy of thought. The petit-bourgeois hero is always a man who acts publicly in the arena of activity allowed him (Lovecraft hated Freud). Yet this lone quester is, paradoxically, removed from socialized activity: he avoids women, and hates Black people and Jews (who are deeply socialized). His actions are public, but they are not the property of the group from which he emerges (he prefers communion with dead masters) nor of aliens (whom he avoids and whose alienation, ironically, destroys him). In Lovecraft's tales public action is public only because it indicates private motives which are openly represented by a character's hostility or withdrawal from public life.

Like the heroes of his tales, Lovecraft's life was public but always anonymous (conducted with many people but only by letter). Like his characters, the pulp-fiction author has no biography: his cult is that of a name to a text only. The author's authority is ensured by the repetition of his name on the cover of a work or magazine – a name without personality. Hence, like the tales of the fabulous that he produced, the author himself becomes fabulous, and this fabulousness is both projected away from and determined by his ordinary existence.

This fabulousness accords well with Lovecraft's lack of and distaste for professionalism (bourgeois work). Remaining anonymous Lovecraft imposes no bourgeois ethic of the artist: any writer can join in with the mythology and create new monsters. Lovecraft's name on his stories stands for a *type* of story which anybody can create and which allows a tradition to emerge: even in his lifetime he rewrote other people's stories, and August Derleth completed Lovecraft's unfinished works after the author's death. The essential element thus emerges which constitutes the industrial processes within which Lovecraft tales exist. Always different, 'Lovecraft's' stories (whoever writes them: Colin Wilson, Robert Bloch, August Derleth or Ramsay Campbell) are, at the same time, always the same: they reflect the need for a production-line process and an unchanging product in an unchanging world – a world whose unchangingness reassures as it terrifies. But it is a world where the production process is always out of control. For Lovecraft it invaded his dreams:

> The death of my grandmother plunged me into a gloom from which I never fully recovered. . . . I began to have nightmares of the most hideous description, peopled with *things* which I called 'nightgaunts' – a compound word of my own coinage.[23]

Lovecraft's monsters enjoy a horribly easy reduplication of bodily parts which are animal but function unnaturally. Lovecraft's nightmare was of 'things' which had a life of their own – things which act quasi-humanly in his stories. Lovecraft's nightmares are about the products of the production line – things with their own history: a production line that he exorcized and reproduced in his fiction.

11

Harry and Marianne: The Never Ending Supernatural Soap

> I do *not* like careless talk about what you call ghosts.
> 'Oh, Whistle, and I'll Come to You My Lad', M.R. James

Anyone interested in haunted houses will certainly be aware of the ghost hunter Harry Price. Since his death in 1948, however, his reputation as a trustworthy authority has been severely dented, most notably by Trevor H. Hall in *The Haunting of Borley Rectory* (1956) and the later biography *Search for Harry Price* (1978) in which he established Price as both a fraud and an egotist.[1] And yet, Price's name has a minor cult following and his two 'factual' works about the rectory in the hamlet of Borley, Essex, although sometimes out of print, are firmly established in the lists of books regularly borrowed from public libraries. Indeed, first editions of both, *'The Most Haunted House in England'* and *The End of Borley Rectory* command high prices when they appear on the second-hand market.[2]

For those unfamiliar with the story of Borley I shall offer an outline, but let it suffice for the moment to say that the Victorian rectory was supposed to be haunted by headless coachmen, a ghostly nun, good and evil poltergeists and many other bizarre psychic phenomena all of which finally ended in the fire that destroyed the place in 1939. Here were sex, sensation, murder and thrills.

Approaching Borley is rather bleak even in good weather: the lanes have deep ditches on either side, the land is dead flat and uniform and the area depopulated. As you approach the 'village' you are reminded of the atmosphere of an M.R. James short story or of the threatening isolation of Fenchurch St Paul in Dorothy L. Sayers's *The Nine Tailors*. This is the classic landscape of East Anglia.[3]

Borley itself consists of a church, and a small number of old houses and farm buildings. It neither threatens nor welcomes. Nowadays it is the church that is believed to be haunted and a

205

group in 1979 recorded spirit footsteps and whisperings near the old Waldegrave Monument. Indeed, there was a note pinned to the graveyard gate which read, 'No ghost hunters after dark.' (The note, alas, no longer exists and modern bungalows cover the site of the original rectory.) In its heyday this sleepy hamlet was a stop for curious tourists and charabanc parties. On 17 June 1929, the *Daily Mirror* reported,

> The Rectory continues to receive the unwelcome attention of hundreds of curious people, and at night the headlights of their cars may be seen for miles around. One 'enterprising' firm even ran a motor coach to the Rectory, inviting the public 'to come and see the Borley Ghost', while cases of rowdyism were frequent.
>
> (Hall)

The unwanted visits of noisy tourists must irritate those who have to live in Borley, but for those who do visit the place it takes on the strange, isolated atmosphere of Price's books, for even though Trevor H. Hall and others have 'proved' that Price indulged in a massive hoax there is still enough of the weird left to leave the visitor with that especially enjoyable *frisson* of doubt. The place and its stories have regularly appeared in the media: on radio, on television and in the press. Paul Tabori followed Price's own autobiography with his biographical account *Harry Price: The Biography of a Ghost-Hunter* (1950) and Price's books were reprinted.[4]

By 1975 (when Price's reputation was under investigation and when the memory of Borley was fading into a cosy nostalgia for the 1920s and 1930s), Business Travel World could still advertise 'Psychic Research Tours', a holiday package, including Borley, organized by Enjoy Britain and the World Ltd. The cost of the eight-day holiday was £145.

The questions raised by this minor and yet controversial figure and his quest for 'life beyond the grave' are, what the motivational forces were which established Price's dubious reputation and what it is in the nature of his work on Borley that makes these works classics of their kind, in spite of or maybe because of their disputed status as factual documents.

Harry Price was born in 1881. The 1880s and 1890s were crucial in establishing a thriving popular and sensationalist press which was consumed by a voracious and half-educated populace. Mass readership was now catered for by a large and well-organized press machine which 'homed in' on lower-middle-class and working-class readers. The thriving newspaper industry reached its zenith when reinforced by the appearance of radio and film, stories from one medium feeding to other two. Both George Orwell and Richard Hoggart record this process. By the late 1920s Price was established as a 'psychic journalist'. For a poor boy with big ambitions and with no prospect of higher education or 'preferment', the popular press offered a direct route to 'easy' money, fame and a recognized knowledge gained through the 'university of life'. Price, like his better known journalist/author contemporaries, chose this route to fame.[5] The life he chose spanned hack journalism and an acknowledged thirst for the thrill of showmanship. The life work of Harry Price was, perhaps, the promotion of 'self' based upon increasingly unusual means.

Price claimed throughout his life that his origins were rural and his stock a decayed middle-class respectable Shropshire family. This was not so. Hall has shown that Price's origins were humble, urban and hardly respectable. Rather than coming into the world the son of a 'well-known paper manufacturer' of Shrewsbury, he was in fact the son of Edward Ditcher Price, a commercial traveller for a London pen and ink manufacturer and failed one-time grocer. His mother, who came from Newington in South London, met his father at 14 and married him at 16 – Edward Price was 40. When his father died, he left virtually nothing. To cover these inadequacies Price began his career of deceit. In all of it, even and especially through his work on psychical research, he craved *respectability*. Ironically, the more sensationally and unlikely Price behaved the more this was done to gain that respect never accorded to Price's family and never accorded by the middle classes to that invisible 'underclass' of tradespeople from whom his family hailed. Far from being the 'solicitor' he pretended to be on the marriage certificate (professional, middle-class and having a position in society) Price's maternal grandfather was, in fact, a newspaper reporter (feckless, rootless and without respectability). Hall bluntly declared 'I was dealing with a family of liars', but in this drive toward respectability there may be more to consider.

Until his marriage Price scratched a living as a 'numismatic' journalist on a Kent newspaper, a photographer of grocery shops, a manufacturer of glues and a creator of patent medicine (alongside other quacks, such as Dr Crippen: the arch example of the type of lower-middle-class rootless male we are studying). In 1908, however,

Price finally found a degree of respectability in his marriage to
Constance Knight, the daughter of a wealthy 'perfumer' from
middle-class Brockley, a suburb of South London. His wife brought
middle-class respectability and the comforts of money. After this
date Price could live out his 'fantasy' version of the respectable life
of a middle-class gentleman and use his fantasy to promote his
own idea of becoming a household name. In this, Price combined
a peripheral knowledge of advertising know-how and commercial
sense with an inbred distaste for the very money that had eluded
his own family. Price's business knowledge was founded not on the
'solid' principles of engineering or paper manufacture (as he claimed)
but rather upon the fairground principles of the shyster or the
wartime 'spiv'. He combined this knowledge with a deep-seated
desire (I suggest) to live the life of an amateur gentleman collector
– an eccentric and rather cautious investigator and collector of cu-
riosities: a very special kind of English gentlemanly type. After his
marriage, Price could indulge a spurious knowledge of archaeology
(for which he was exposed), display a deceitful knowledge of nu-
mismatics (which he plagiarized) and gain expertise in the history
of magic and legerdemain (about which he was an expert but about
which he still felt the need to lie). These eccentric gentlemanly
pursuits failed to bring any real reward (Price craved respectable,
that is, institutional recognition). What nearly brought him what he
wanted was psychical research.

One important factor in Price's story is his constant need to 're-
write' his own history or to write in episodes at points that elsewhere he had included as occurring at another time or place. Hall
points out at least two of these incidents. Without a strong sense of
his own 'reality' or perhaps oppressed by too much of this reality,
Price created the history of his life as it suited him. In this he became, not a commercial failure and an impossibly ill-educated drifter,
but a lively, creative, middle-class boy with leanings towards engineering and the knowledge that he would inherit his father's business in Shrewsbury.

One incident recorded as true in his autobiography (and investigated by Hall and proved totally false!) was the visit Price 'witnessed' as an eight-year-old boy in the market place in Shrewsbury.
Here 'the Great Sequah' put on his medicine show. The show may
or may not have occurred and Price probably did not witness it
(although a 'Sequah' was actually an American called Hartley who
came to Britain; Price may have seen the show in London). It is of

great interest to us to find out why Price felt an especial need to record the effect of the incident in his life. It appears to have had a direct effect on his psychological growth – yet as a 'fictional' memory in his autobiography it also seems to serve to justify the darker side of Price's psychic makeup: the master showman, flamboyant, American, magical and charismatic. We are told,

One cold January morning the 'Great Sequah', with his brass bands, gilded chariots, and troop of 'boosters' in the garb of Mohawk Indians, pitched his tent – so to speak – in Shrewsbury's principal square. . . . During the whole of this eventful morning I stood, cold but happy, open-mouthed at this display of credulity, self-deception, auto-suggestion, faith-healing, beautiful showmanship, super-charlatanism, and 'magic'. The miracles of the market-place left me spellbound.

What is important here is the recording of 'miracles' and the knowledge of 'credulity' and 'self-deception'. The ambivalence is important – Price both 'knew' and did *not* know about his deceptive schizoid nature: a nature well placed to create two of the 'greatest' books on psychical investigation, themselves a mixture of miracles and self-deception. Here, Price became both 'Sequah' (to whom he added the revealing epithet 'Great') and the sceptical, aloof investigator. The description of the 'Great Sequah' which mixes, in the same paragraph, real astonishment at the 'truly' magical and a knowledge that this is all the product of a 'cheat' describes and reveals the Harry Price that Price himself would not have recognized. The fact that what left him 'spellbound' happened in 'the market-place' (the proper place of a tradesman's son?) is, perhaps, also revealing of the important relationship that the modern supernatural has with capitalism and consumerism. In the 'projected' figure of the 'Great Sequah', Price accomplished the fantasy of the gentleman collector (this was the moment Price became interested in magic) and the fantasy of the charismatic showman.

And this dual fantasy was worked upon all Price's life, not least in his gentleman's library with its 'fake' bookplates and its air of antiquarianism, but also in his association with psychic extravaganzas. The first instance was Price's opening (accompanied by national publicity) of the sealed box of the religious fanatic Joanna Southcott (who had died in 1814). Needless to say, the box, which was meant to contain items useful during a national emergency, contained nothing of interest. The second incident, which was played out to an international audience, was the attempt to raise the devil in 1932 in the Hartz Mountains. The devil failed to materialize. In both these instances, and through the creation of the National Laboratory of Psychical Research, Price hoped to establish his credentials as a 'scientific' investigator: one worthy of respect among academics. On the Brocken Mountain, Price had C.E.M. Joad with him, and in the investigation into the haunting of Borley a group of undergraduates from Cambridge had conducted experiments into the phenomena there. Price always hoped for a university chair, honorary doctorate and university department. He donated his collection of work on magic to the University of London, but he was deprived of what he considered his right: a department of psychical research. What emerges through these exploits is the curious way Price's life becomes a lived fiction and the overriding social (that is socialized) unconscious of the man and his need, at almost any cost, to project a public persona.

In turning to Price's best-known works, it is necessary to fill in the story of Borley as it is narrated in *'The Most Haunted House in England'* (*MHHE*) and *The End of Borley Rectory* (*EBR*). The narrative covers a series of bizarre supernatural occurrences that had persisted from the late nineteenth century until the Second World War. The 'plot' consists of Price's investigation into these occurrences from his initial acquaintance with the case in 1929 to the early 1940s. Through ghostly visitations, poltergeist activity, spontaneous 'spirit' writing and planchette sessions, a story emerges of kidnap, murder and secrecy: a story either of a love affair between a nun and a monk which ended in tragedy or (more plausibly, at least in terms of the 'evidence') a love affair between the lord of the manor and a French 'nun' during the seventeenth century which ended, somewhat obscurely, with a 'rape' and 'murder' and three centuries of secrecy. Included within this double narrative (which forms the detective thriller part of the two books) is another tale of the eccentric clerics and their families who occupied the rectory since the time of Henry Bull in the late nineteenth century. Both books consist of collected reports and anecdotes interlaced with possible explanations offered by Price's correspondents and fellow investigators, and the atmosphere of both books is that of the detective at his trade, indeed, Price says he was asked to 'take charge of the case' (*MHHE*).

From the miscellaneous anecdotes and reports that emerge the reader is quickly immersed in a story in which the laws of nature seem horribly in abeyance – the atmosphere is at once sinister and fascinating. Some examples of incidents from the many that are offered will give the reader a feeling for the books. One occupant, 'awoke suddenly and found an old man in dark, old fashioned clothes, wearing a tall hat, standing by her bed. On another occasion, the same figure was seen sitting on the bed' (*MHHE*). 'One early morning in 1919 [other occupants of the rectory cottage] . . . saw a black shape, in the form of a little man, running round their bedroom' (*MHHE*). Another occupant, Mr Foyster, recorded in his diary numerous poltergeist phenomena, including violent attacks on his wife, who psychically attracted 'spirit' messages on the walls! Price listed some of the phenomena:

The phenomena our observers were able to confirm included footsteps and similar sounds; raps, taps and knockings; displacement of objects; 'clicks' and 'cracks'; sounds as of a door closing; knocks, bumps, thuds, jumping or stamping; dragging noise; wailing sounds; rustling or scrabbling noises; 'metallic' sounds; crashing, as of crockery falling; wall-pencillings; 'appearance' of objects; luminous phenomenon; odours, pleasant and unpleasant; sensation of coldness; tactual phenomena; sensation of a 'presence'; and a fulfilled prediction. One observer says she saw the 'nun'.

(*MHHE*)

Finally a planchette message revealed that *Sunex Amures* would burn down the house and this sinister entity finally fulfilled his promise (*MHHE*). All of these strange activities centred on the fate of the spirit of the 'nun' and indeed certain unidentified human bones are finally found in the cellar. The nun emerges during the story as, 'a Mary Lairre . . . a French girl of nineteen years of age, who was a novice in a nunnery at Havre, . . . and was murdered (strangled) by "Waldegrave" on May 17, 1667' (*EBR*).

Both books end on a disturbing note of inconclusiveness. Even after the destruction of the rectory the weird phenomena continued and just as Price is ready to leave Borley for good he finds on a photograph of the ruins, the distinct outline of half a brick floating in mid air!

What makes a good ghost story? Price's story of Borley seems to contain the definitive recipe: a coach and *headless* horseman; a ghostly nun who walks the grounds (waiting for her lover?); an old, decayed and isolated rectory (without electricity and with deep, dark and damp cellars that hold a terrible secret); psychic occupants (Marianne Foyster); bizarre occurrences (the appearance of a monster insect in one episode and of an old coat in another); bells that ring without human agency; messages from the dead (via suburban planchette readings); a legendary past (of monasteries and nunneries and a secret tunnel); flying bricks, vanishing and reappearing household utensils and 'apports' (a French medallion and a gold wedding ring). All this on what appears an almost daily basis taking place in and around a 'cold' spot outside 'the Blue Room'. In every respect the case was sensational. Into this dramatic setting steps the one person able, like Holmes, to put the thing into perspective: the ghost hunter.

In case the reader may wish to know what a psychic investigator takes with him when engaged on an important case, I will enumerate some of the items included in a ghost-hunter's kit.

Into a large suitcase are packed the following articles: A pair of soft felt overshoes used for creeping, unheard, about the house in order that neither human beings nor paranormal 'entities' shall be disturbed when producing 'phenomena'; steel measuring tape for measuring rooms, passages, testing the thickness of walls in looking for secret chambers or hidey-holes; steel screw-eyes, lead post-office seals, sealing tool, strong cord or tape, and adhesive surgical tape, for sealing doors, windows or cupboards; a set of tools, with wire, nails, etc.; hank of electric flex, small electric bells, dry batteries and switches (for secret electrical contacts); 9cm. by 12cm. reflex camera, film-packs and flash-bulbs for indoor or outdoor photography; a small portable telephone for communicating with assistant in another part of building or garden; note book, red, blue and black pencils; sketching block and case of drawing instruments for making plans; bandages, iodine and a flask of brandy in case member of investigating staff or resident is injured or faints; ball of string, stick of chalk, matches, electric torch and candle; bowl of mercury for detecting tremors in room or passage or for making silent electrical mercury switches; cinematograph camera with remote electrical control, and films; a sensitive transmitting thermometer [etc, etc].

(*MHHE*)

From all this it emerges that the ghost hunter combines the qualities of a Sherlock Holmes, a master spy and a boy scout – he is both a psychic adventurer and a rather well equipped camper (of the 'Famous Five' type). One is irresistibly reminded of this quality of adventure (a cross between E. Phillips Oppenheim and Edgar Wallace) when, after his last visit, Price tells us 'although I have investigated many haunted houses, before and since, never have such phenomena so impressed me as they did on this historic day. Sixteen hours of thrills!' (*MHHE*). However, Price combined these elements of the psychic thriller in order to reinforce the message of respectability he wanted to convey. In the second of the two works, *The End of Borley Rectory*, Price brings his narrative to a halt with the repeated, yet contradictory assertions that, firstly science cannot explain everything and secondly it will be able to explain psychic phenomena.

Price's second book ends with quotations linking supernatural phenomena with the laws of thermodynamics (*EBR*), atomic energy (*EBR*) and abnormal psychology (*EBR*). Yet he does not quite end there, for the last chapter presents the evidence of the two books as if it were a murder trial and Price 'proves' the strength and coherence of his arguments in a 'literary' court of law. Despite Price's desire for his evidence to be taken seriously, it is entirely based on anecdotes, 'faked' experimental conditions, legend, clairvoyancy and planchette readings. Every time historical accuracy is invoked the text suppresses it.[6] Thus, because 'hard' evidence cannot be found in the records there must have been either a conspiracy to suppress the truth or all evidence was accidentally removed or erased. In every case, the evidence of history and of archaeology is suppressed in favour of the logic of numerous clairvoyant messages and the selection of evidence to fit certain 'physical' phenomena that were reported.

Did these weird events occur? In one sense, there is no need to ask the question in the terms posed by a cultural historian. Our question is why did they occur *when* they occurred and to *whom*. On another level, that of plain fact, rather than perceptual qualification, there are enough clues in the text to suggest that many of the events were possibly 'staged', that some did not occur, that others could be put down to natural phenomena. The way they are all placed in one universe suggests a tenuous relationship cemented not by fact but by the fiction of the planchette. These random events are then given a shape by equally random and variable planchette messages (even Price agreed that so much was dictated this way that the sitters needed wallpaper rolls) and much of what Price reprints has no basis in anything that can be checked. If these are ghosts, then, perhaps they are the ghosts of cultural necessity? Moreover, the way Price constructed his story by claiming for himself only an 'editorial' role (*MHHE*) makes it difficult to see when certain events happened historically and if they really were recorded outside Price's control. Even he admitted that most people left the rectory through natural reasons and not through terrorization.

What as cultural phenomena do the events of Borley and the status of Price's two books represent? In the previous chapter I considered this relationship between the sensational and the respectable: that odd mixture of the inexplicable and supernatural and the organized and the social. For want of a better definition I have characterized this attitude as essentially 'lower middle class', a perceptual framework exemplified by, but not specific to, those elements of society on the ragged edge of class division. Here, I am keen to insist that 'class' represents a perceptual space inhabited by a whole spectrum of society and not wholly confined to income. This space is the space of the *disinherited*, culturally and economically. Typically, this is why popular fictions and alternative 'sciences' interest the intellectual and artistic classes as well as those who count themselves bereft of an education. At this period, prior to the Second World War, it is an attitude that is shared by the likes of W.B. Yeats, George Yeats, AE and the circle of the Golden Dawn, as well as the Society for Psychical Research and the 'ordinary' housewife in 'Alma', 'Coronation' or 'Balaclava' villas (or any such decayed suburb) who regularly visited a medium, read the tea leaves or attended a spiritualist meeting to be greeted by her long lost husband with a 'message'. T.S. Eliot satirized these attitudes with 'Madame Sosostris' in *The Waste Land*.

Because Price appealed to an essentially suburban and southern English audience (I suggest) his work should be seen against a background of rapid technological growth, suburban expansion and material progress. In the wealthy home counties of the late 1920s and 1930s (so different from the depressed north), the signs of material advancement could not be ignored. Against this a sense of *disorientation* among certain sectors would lead to the usual vacuum in spiritual needs for which Price's work would provide an ideal panacea: the phenomena (at Borley) could not be explained by science (materialism) but they demonstrated through relevance to the theological backwater of survival after death, that there *was* an explanation and an order which organized, and could not be controlled by, earthly powers.

In an age characterized by the masses and by mass means of control (radio (*EBR*), the loudspeaker, the factory-floor production line), an age in which commentators noted the 'loss' of individual control and sense of hope (see John Betjeman's 'Slough' or W.H. Auden's 'The Unknown Citizen'), and an age in which bureaucracy and state control appeared unstoppable (see Aldous Huxley's *Brave New World*) the 'ordinary' person could be comforted by a non-material explanation of circumstances. Borley's ghosts with their doctrine of survival suggested that one could exist (if only after death!) and preserve one's individualism (if only eccentrically as a 'nun' or 'headless' coachman) and willingly submit to an authority beyond oneself (via planchette messages). This is the best of both worlds, a theory of compensation that allowed the individual the freedom to be themself only if that selfhood had been granted by the authority of an agency outside the self. I am not suggesting (given the period) that Price's work acts as an analogue to the rise of fascism, indeed, given its essential Englishness and normalcy (a story of eccentric rectors in a corner of idyllic Essex) it would seem it acts as a 'mythic' compensation for the uncontrollable nature of world events.[7] The story begins in 1929 and ends during the Second World War. Throughout the narrative, Price insists that the events of Borley are a type of 'sign' of other worldliness (a prolonged miracle) that demands explanation. Borley itself is seen as of national importance, little less than a piece of English heritage.

Borley Rectory stands by itself in the literature of psychical manifestation. Wisely discarding theories of causation (which in these matters are little better than conjecture), the author, Mr Harry Price, sets out to prove by the cumulative evidence of eye-witnesses – recorded in a form which would be admissible in evidence in any court of law – the happening of events at Borley Rectory which it is impossible to explain by the operation of natural law.

The large number of the public who are interested in these things are under a debt of gratitude to him, for without his untiring energy and skilled experience as an investigator, a fascinating chapter in the history of psychical research would have been lost to the world.

(*EBR*)

In the end Harry Price never got his department at a university and never became Chair Professor of Parapsychology. For us Borley exists as merely a nostalgic memory, its site left unmarked except for the cryptic sign that once was nailed to the church gate. Ultimately, Price was a materialist who felt (genuinely?) that the domain of science could be widened to include occult subject matter. Despite the 'evidence' at Borley, the sensational could not be normalized into scientific experience and it remained both peripheral and trivial. A collector of books on magic tricks and a dabbler in the sensational, Price could not reconcile the sensational and the respectable any more than he could reconcile the supernatural and the temporal. For us, Price's life and his two major works represent an excursion into the forgotten, the trivial and the disenfranchised.

The phenomena at Borley proved to be subject matter for a story both sensational and respectable and Borley itself became a centre for a minor tourist industry based upon the illicit pleasures of the spectral. Although I have suggested the probable fraudulent nature of Harry Price's connection I have not yet pointed out the curious nexus of fictions that helped create Borley's legend and which allowed Price to place himself at the centre of the media's interest. For this we must look at Price's relationship with the inhabitants of the rectory.

It is probable that folk tales of ghostly carriages and suchlike had existed in Borley before the arrival of the Bull family who built the rectory, indeed the Bull sisters believed they 'saw' spectral phenomena as early as 28 July 1900.[8] Whether deceived or conniving the sisters began the belief in the haunted rectory. Their brother Henry (Harry) Bull later married Ivy Brackenbury who (probably for snobbish reasons) was disapproved of by the sisters. Harry Bull, a keen spiritualist, promised to return after death, and the sisters who accused Ivy of poisoning him (à la Mrs Maybrick) duly saw his apparition.

On 12 June 1929 Harry Price, working for the *Daily Mirror* arrived at Borley after correspondence about the hauntings with the next occupants, the Smiths. Yet what emerges from now on is not a tale of ghosts but a tale of ghost writers! Price, scenting a good story, had come to investigate, but had originally been written to by Mabel Smith for advice on finding a publisher for her thriller *Murder at the Parsonage*, which had clearly been inspired both by the accusations of the Misses Bull against their sister-in-law Ivy and the writings of Agatha Christie. Instead of advice Mabel got Price, who realized the potential of a story which played up the fiction of a haunted house mystery.

> The Smiths must have *wanted* publicity. They *wanted* to attract a reporter to Borley and watch him at work. What Mrs Smith was after was material for her supernatural thriller, which was based not only on the traditional legends, but also upon stories invented by the cruel and malicious Bull sisters. Any publicity they received as the residents of a haunted house would of course be of greater value when she tried to place her manuscript.[9]

Later when Lionel Foyster lived in the house with his wife Marianne, he too tried to publish a manuscript based on a haunted house mystery:

> he completed a manuscript, entitled *Fifteen Months in a Haunted House*. Foyster's book was a story about a clergyman and his wife and the vicissitudes of their life in a haunted rectory that is recognised as Borley.[10]

Neither Mabel Smith nor Lionel Foyster published their manuscripts, instead Price ruthlessly exploited their co-operation and published two best-selling accounts himself.

This peculiar fictionality which centred around Borley marked the place as 'text' rather than as psychical centre. The folklore readily accepted by the Bull sisters had quickly become intertwined with the story of their brother's 'poisoning' at the hands of a ruthless woman whose persona they possibly based on their 'memories' of the Maybrick trial and this in turn spawned an Agatha Christie-type novel, a Dennis Wheatley style thriller and two best-selling journalistic acounts. And these texts themselves were bolstered by séance messages, planchette writings and copious graffiti aimed at Lionel Foyster's mysterious wife Marianne.

And what of Mariane Foyster? Research by Trevor Hall and Robert Wood unkindly revealed her to be 'nymphomaniac and a pathological liar' and her husband a 'credulous old fool'.[11] Apparently unable to recognize fact from fiction and with a husband willing to be knowingly deluded about his wife's activities, Marianne became the centre for the most extraordinary and the wildest events at

Borley. Recognized as a fraud by Price, he nevertheless played along
with her in order to keep the story alive as material for *his* Borley
books.

Marianne vanished (at least she hoped to) in 1946 when she left
for America. She had a bizarre past, both in Canada where she may
have been involved with supernaturalism and in England where
she falsified her age, origins and marital status, lived in successive
ménages à trois at Borley, ill-treated her adopted children, banished
her real children and may have finally murdered her husband. It
was she who probably wrote the Marianne messages on the walls
(supposedly from the 'nun'). But what is most curious of all is her
own psychic makeup, for Marianne was a supreme story-teller – a
liar whom everybody was willing to believe. Marianne was simply
her own supreme creation – a living fiction played out for *others* as
entertainment. Many years after the events at Borley she told an
interviewer, Robert Swanson: 'those were flights of fancy; kind of
a soap opera. It seems so horribly silly, but it seemed a lot of fun
at the time – a continuous story.'[12]

Harry Price had found a kindred spirit. Finally, what of Sunex
Amores? Well this creature too becomes the centre of a fiction – the
creation of one Captain Gregson, last owner of Borley and an arson-
ist in search of insurance money and an alibi! What occurred at
Borley between 1900 and 1946 was not a convention of spirits so
much as a convention of authors and a web of texts which congre-
gated around an isolated house in Essex. In such circumstances it
is writing itself which takes on the form of the supernatural wherein
two inhabitants at least lived out Borley's fiction as the reality of
their own existence. Without substance herself, Marianne Foyster,
the fictional creation of her own fantasies and those of Lionel Foyster,
emerges as the real ghost of Borley's soap opera.

Part III
Requiescat

12

The Death of Cult Fiction and the End of Theory

Any requiem for pulp culture will inevitably also be the requiem for the old high literary culture that defined itself as its implacable enemy. Both required the conjunction of market forces (that is, commercialism), media cross-fertilization (especially with film and newspapers) and the need for a canon of taste using *contemporary* literary production as its benchmark. If serious fiction used mimesis for revelatory truth, so pulp used it for entertainment. Indeed, pulp turned information into entertainment for the urban, literate and democratic masses.

In the age of Hollywood, it was the movie that acted as the defining medium for the world of literature (just as much as any tradition of high art), for writers engaged in representing the modern world. The magnetic grip of Hollywood and its inability to accommodate great writers is well documented; what is less obvious is how commercial movie-making influenced writing *per se*. It was the movies as form that transfixed and fascinated not merely movie audiences but writers of all types and levels. Just as the camera had challenged painting, so Hollywood challenged writing; the advent of television did not affect writing as Hollywood did and continues to do. Indeed, television is a side issue in terms of the formal changes and challenges brought about by the studio system, the moving image and the star system. Moreover, it is instructive to note that during the 1920s that golden age of the pulp magazine as well as the height of modernistic experimentation, Hollywood's influence can be felt as a guiding principle. By comparing the work of two writers who occupy different and supposedly opposite sides of the cultural divide one can usefully see how movie-making affected literary form.

Both F. Scott Fitzgerald and Dashiell Hammett were drawn to Hollywood, could not reconcile their art nor their affections with its culture and suffered as a consequence. Both were involved with and affected by the concept of a script. Some sample passages from each author give a sense of the impossibility of writing modern literature (that is during the 1920s and after) without incorporating the formal conditions of mimesis dictated by film technique. Here is part of the celebrated guest list from *The Great Gatsby*:

> Once I wrote down on the empty spaces of a time-table the names of those who came to Gatsby's house that summer. It is an old time-table now, disintegrating at its folds, and headed 'This schedule in effect July 5th, 1922'. But I can still read the grey names, and they will give you a better impression than my generalities of those who accepted Gatsby's hospitality and paid him the subtle tribute of knowing nothing whatever about him.
>
> From East Egg, then, came the Chester Beckers and the Leeches, and a man named Bunsen, whom I knew at Yale, and Doctor Webster Civet, who was drowned last summer up in Maine. And the Hornbeams and the Willie Voltaires, and a whole clan named Blackbuck, who always gathered in a corner and flipped up their noses like goats at whosoever came near. And the Ismays and the Chrysties (or rather Hubert Auerbach and Mr Chrystie's wife), and Edgar Beaver, whose hair they say, turned cotton-white one winter afternoon for no good reason at all. . . .
>
> (chapter 4)

What appears to come across from this passage with its carnivalesque grotesquerie is the movement, vivacity and exuberance of Fitzgerald's style – a style which suggests carnival but does not deliver it, after all we are witnesses only to a static list, not a real party in which people would have to be introduced dramatically. The list is, in essence, a clever trick, a literary equivalent of the *trompe l'oeil*. It is no wonder then that this so movie-like of novels should have filmed so disastrously. Where a movie is essentially *mobile* such a novel is essentially *static*. Two more examples make the point:

> A sudden emptiness seemed to flow now from the windows and the great doors, endowing with complete isolation the figure of the host, who stood on the porch, his hand up in a formal gesture of farewell.
>
> (chapter 3)

There was nothing to look at from under the tree except Gatsby's enormous house, so I stared at it, like Kant at his church steeple, for half an hour.

(chapter 5; emphasis mine)

Here mood is produced through a language of immobility and existential inertia which recreates a panoramic experience more in common with eighteenth-century landscape painting and the use of perspective glasses than with contemporary movie-making. In other words the linguistic form is *nostalgic* for print: a novel unusable by Hollywood but unrecognized as such by everybody in the business. Fitzgerald thus defines his novel by what Hollywood cannot use. Ironically because the novel *reads* like a movie it was guaranteed success with the public. Fitzgerald knew only too well that movies defined form in a way no writer could (or can) ignore.

Reading like a movie but nevertheless unfilmable, *Gatsby* seemed the epitome of the great American novel and yet its static nature tied it to an older age. How curious that the book is all about recapturing the past! Equally how curious that Fitzgerald, despite his contempt for Hollywood, could not write a successful novel without incorporating the formal requirements of the movie theatre. Filmic cross-fertilization had movie-ized the novel, had hijacked the literary qualities of fiction (as basic formal properties) and transformed them.

Conversely, Dashiell Hammett's *The Maltese Falcon* cannot be itself without also being a creation of the age of the movie. Hammett's book is stripped down to essential moments of action. Character is defined not by contemplation but by acts of volition. Two passages clearly give this sense:

She got up from the settee and went to the fireplace to poke the fire. She changed slightly the position of an ornament on the mantelpiece, crossed the room to get a box of cigarettes from a table in a corner, straightened a curtain, and returned to her seat.

. . .

Spade's thick fingers made a cigarette with deliberate care, sifting a measured quantity of tan flakes down into curved paper, spreading the flakes so that they lay equal at the ends with a slight depression in the middle, thumbs rolling the paper's inner edge down and up under the outer edges as forefingers pressed

it over, thumbs and fingers sliding to the paper cylinder's ends
to hold it even while tongue licked the flap, left forefinger and
thumb pinching their end while right forefinger and thumb
smoothed the damp seam, right forefinger and thumb twisting
their end and lifting the other to Spade's mouth.

Both passages demonstrate the concept of character as defined by
action and if the first is pure stage direction then the second is a
type of philosophy by making. It is equally instructive to consider
the concept of description in the novel. In the next quote the panorama is not Long Island nor New York as in *Gatsby* but a man's face
defined by the functionalism, futurism and modernism of the engineered V-Strut:

> Samuel Spade's jaw was long and bony, his chin a jutting V
> under the more flexible V of his mouth. His nostrils curved back
> to make another smaller V. His yellow-grey eyes were horizontal.
> The V motif was picked up again by thickish brows rising out-
> ward from twin creases above a hooked nose, and his pale brown
> hair grew down – from high flat temples – in a point on his
> forehead. He looked rather pleasantly like a blond satan.

In this opening sequence of themed images the figure of Spade
reconciles the longshot and the close up in the defining moment of
celebrity: Spade's presence fills the scene as a star's close-up fills a
screen. Thus the nature of description itself and especially that of
central characters is determined by the Hollywood image of the
movie star: totally *present*, and defining character by the facial dex-
terity of eyes, mouth, muscle. Psychology returns to the moment of
the 'look' which expresses, but does not explain, the inner forces of
character and will.

Alexis de Tocqueville was one of the first commentators to notice
the importance of speech-patterns in a democracy and the implications that held for a transition from 'writerly' (that is aristocratic)
cultures. Nowhere is speech and writing more focused than in the
creation of novelistic characters, carrying as they do the moral weight
and narrative structure of fiction. Here again it is instructive to see
the transition from Fitzgerald to Hammett. In *Gatsby*, characteriza-
tion speaks of continuity, elegance and permanence and it creates
a purposive and accumulative narrative: built-up detail provides a
meaningful *totality* to the work. But the work, just like its central

character, is borne back into history; Daisy is the past returned to be relived in the future. A continuous past captures the work. Moreover, we can relate this concept of character and of the past to Nathanial Hawthorne's 'Wakefield', a tale in which a man, having left his wife, lives a parallel existence for so long that he is unable to return to her. The result for Hawthorne is a salutary lesson – leave the 'natural' order and you become an 'outcast of the universe': a cosmic as well as an ethical alien.

Such alienation dominates *Gatsby* and the eyes of 'T.J. Eckleburg' look down on a universe that has lost God. Like Hawthorne, Fitzgerald aligns character and history with moral consequences. The world of Tom, Daisy, Jay and Nick is moral precisely because it knows it has *lost* its place in the universe and because there once was a moral universe now destroyed. All this relates Fitzgerald's ideas to the world of the nineteenth century, only amoral Daisy links us to the contemporaneity of Hammett's new style.

In Hammett's Continental Op we find the genuine voice of the masculinely modern. It is at once inelegant, banal, ephemeral and anonymous and it is focused through a first-person narrative whose episodes are cumulative but not homogeneous. What links episodes is character not theme and that character lives in a continuous present of speed, violence and movement. Hammett's work too can be related to Hawthorne's 'Wakefield' and in *The Maltese Falcon* we are given a long Hawthornesque parable about a man called Flitcraft. Having found the universe to be meaningless and *random*, after a near fatal incident he leaves his wife and family of many years. Unlike Wakefield, he happily restarts a similar parallel life and lives happily ever after. The message, quite unlike Hawthorne's, is that in a random universe one can adapt without the slightest alienation to the caprice of circumstance and that the only meaning we make is the one we make unknowingly in the patterns of our mundane existence. Unlike Kafka's 'K', Flitcraft simply (and unknowingly) *conforms* to the conditions of the random and therefore survives. It is in searching for a meaning that Gatsby is destroyed. Nostalgia kills both character and structure.

Unlike the frenetic action in Fitzgerald's *Gatsby*, Hammett's *The Maltese Falcon* is essentially a *static* novel, and given its wordiness a surprisingly good novel to adopt for screen. John Huston's faithfully wordy third version defined a Hollywood style. What emerges from Hammett's book is a style cognizant of Hollywood and a language incorporating and embracing 'the movies' as both a form and a *grammar*. Hammett's work *is* a movie, by which I mean it is constituted by embracing movie technique *as* literature. Fitzgerald's language imitates Hollywood and is mimetic of its form while Hammett's form *is* Hollywood – a transitional language no longer tied to a nostalgia for print nor for representation. Look at how Hammett happily refuses Bridget O'Shaughnessy any 'real' identity, leaving us simply a series of 'fictional' names which act to fix her literary characteristics in a proper name. Far more than James Joyce's *Finnegans Wake*, Hammett's *The Maltese Falcon* marks the end of the traditional representational novel and the beginning of a new crossed medium existing alongside of, and usually despised by those nostalgic for a *pure* high literary culture.

In their different ways both *The Great Gatsby* and *The Maltese Falcon* epitomize the necessary and inherent relationship between fiction and the other emerging mediums of the twentieth century. The emergent relationship created between the various media provided space for a new hybrid literature. Pulp embraced hybridity whereas 'high' fiction sought to ignore it or attack it. This changing of the nature of the 'form' of the modern novel was as profound as the more obvious formal (and purely literary) experimentation of avant-gardism. The proliferation of media both changed, contained and redefined literature. Whereas, once, fiction (especially as encoded in the novel form) had stabilized structures of representation, now the novel had to negotiate its own structural requirements in the light of other media (and especially the film script).

The conditions which allowed the guardians of culture to define themselves by their control of a hierarchically determined literature had flourished precisely because only print acted as valued information. By the mid-twentieth century other media could claim a stake in culture, but were on the whole excluded because of the primacy of print's claim to exemplary status (in terms of representation of *value*). Twice excluded, once as being seen as a lower grade literature and once as being seen as not literature at all (a sort of 'printed' movie or television show), pulp was a type of infiltration by hackdom into the realm of the sacred (that is, the serious novel).

This devaluation of pulp literature helped give the serious novel its status in an age where print was no longer the dominant form of representation. And yet, this also led to the collapse of the conditions in which high art could claim a commanding role as the cultural arbiter of taste. High culture is now dead. It is dead not because it cannot still fulfil or enlighten its recipient, nor because it died of neglect amid the philistinism of the masses. It is dead because it no longer has the right environmental conditions to sustain its creation. Contemporary novels, poetry and drama under the pressures of technology have adapted and flourished. The narrative, linear taxonomies of the classic novel have been refashioned in the postmodern age.

It was not only technology's relentless pursuit of subject matter that killed high culture. This just made it easily available. Yet, in so doing it gave high culture technology's shape and made it conform to technology's rules. Technology de-emphasized the notion of creation and replaced it with the conditions of consumption. Yet what ended the age of high culture was the loss of a foundation. Its own material circumstances changed and so did the make-up of its recipients. The autonomous, enlightened individual of the classic novel ceased to exist as a valid intellectual concept or even as a contemporary human type. Ironically, popular art itself is becoming more self-referential and in so doing is effacing itself as 'popular' as it appropriates high literary style.

It needed a neurotic high art to define a confident pulp culture, but pulp culture, while illicit, always desires respectability. This is nowhere beter exemplified than in the work of Stephen King. The greatest market force in American publishing, King's name is more trade mark than signature, his awareness of other media total, and yet horror is still an illicit thrill and print still the only mark of real genius: horror cannot be literature. In the self-referential world of Stephen King pulp too is finally sung its requiem: high art and its 'dark' other are reblended in the new grammar of the market and the consumer. No less than high literature's guardians, pulp's fans also retain their nostalgia for the word and its taxonomic solidity. King's obsessional love of print is the sign of an unfulfilled and unfulfillable search for respectability, while his chosen genre is and remains the contradictory refusal of that respectability – this is King's misery.

His clearest exploration of the pulp writer's dilemma occurs in *Misery* where Annie Wilkes has become the final ghastly incarnation of the muse. Wilkes is the Calliope of horror – a monster masquerading as a nurse – who forces her victim into an endless slavery to the word. Literally crippled by her attentions, the writer hates her and wishes to kill her but also is shackled to her by more than physical restraints. Without her, without the muse, who is also his number one fan, the writer would simply cease to exist as these are actually the required projections of himself. The writer's addiction, the viral infection of the muse is logorrhoea. It is this addiction that King's *Misery* explores and exemplifies, containing, as it does, an adventure not only in horror but in the very nature of print.

For all those of you who can't afford a Stephen King typescript there's one free with every copy of *Misery* – just join the bookclub. The manuscript in *Misery* has the perfect level of a simulacrum. The whole book acts as such: a simulacrum of the art of fiction. Here is a How-To Book with examples enclosed. Bound in real simulated kid comes the Franklin Mint version of an authentic famous writer's typescript (yes, *type*, none of that WP print-out stuff for me). With handwritten corrections added as in the original. See the process of creation occur before your very eyes – subscribe today!

The whole of *Misery* is racked by doubt and contempt – doubt about the audience and contempt for that audience. King encloses his book 'within' a book to pastiche the very sensibilities he knows he caters for in the majority of his audience.

Even as King desperately fights the demons of self-doubt he cannot avoid the myth his fans demand and that haunts him (I suspect) as his alter ego (the romantic artist as hero/slave to his act). He is also haunted by a dream. For his fans this may be the reality they see of his own work; a *roman à clef* of the writer as writer – not the glamorous work they thought but difficult, dangerous and obsessed. Fine. It is also a dream to haunt King. Behind the book stalk the ghosts of Hemingway, Fitzgerald, Du Maurier and Fowles, but maybe and especially the young Mailer: *Fast Cars – An American Dream* revisited?[1]

King wants to be taken seriously – and why not? He longs for the myth of the American hero-writer: an old battered Remington or Royal, a trash can, a black and red typewriter ribbon, a motel room somewhere on the Mexican border (remember *Salem's Lot* and Ben's post-vampire novel) ready to send that manuscript to the New York editor in time to gain that Pulitzer that brings no pleasure – only the endless pain, the bottle and the crushed pack of Camels.

It is interesting to compare King's obsession with being taken seriously with passages from Robert James Waller's *The Bridges of Madison County*, a work of pulp sentiments which fictionalizes (for the uninitiated) the role of the artist (tortured, lonely genius). This is typical of the dialogue:

'That's the problem in earning a living through an art form. You're always dealing with markets, and markets – mass markets – are designed to suit average tastes. . . .

Sometime I'm going to do an essay called "The Virtues of Amateurism" for all of those people who wish they earned their living in the arts. The market kills more artistic passion than anything else. It's a world of safety out there, for most people. They want safety, the magazines and manufacturers give them safety, give them homogeneity, give them the familiar and comfortable, don't challenge them . . .'

Francesca supposed that, for Robert Kincaid, this was everyday talk. For her, it was the stuff of literature.

The pretentiousness of this dialogue makes it bad art and worse pulp. Its aspiration is towards that very middle-brow conformity it attacks in its readers (the Francescas of this world). Hardly surprising that Robert Kincaid ('the last cowboy') should pack the obligatory cartons of Camel cigarettes.

King is caught looking two ways. At the end of *Misery*, Paul (aka King) works on a computer which he little understands and with which he can hardly cope. Yet, the bestsellers (and *also* the *important* novels) still appear. Writing is hard enough. King needs it mystified for him to be able to function. King's world is 'if only' – if only Smallsville was still a nice place to live, if only there was no junk mail, if only they still showed 'chapter-plays', if only (as in *Salem's Lot*) you could still buy Aurora kits of Frankenstein and the Werewolf that glowed in the dark, and if only you could be a modernist in Paris – a serious writer with a big bank account. How do you do that?

Stephen King is the biggest selling US author of all time (probably) but will his work last and is it serious? Does he have the one great popular novel in him – is this King's nightmare? And whenever he wants to assuage the demon of doubt he can fall back on a personal nostalgia which coincides with his reader's desires. This nostalgia is for *the act of writing itself* exemplified by the myth of Hemingway, an old typewriter, a bottle of hooch and a pack of Camels. King's oeuvre is suffused with nostalgia for the modernist writer as mythic alienated hero and with a nostalgia for schlock horror films and the popular culture of his youth. In that he is especially American.

Misery is a nostalgic book, an 'if only' book, despite the horror in
it. The real horror is the fear deep inside that the age of the serious
novel is long gone and that all novels are merely the raw screen-
play of yet another film. One long compromise. King works a nostalgic picture of the writer's trade – his own nostalgia is for the
innocence of creativity, an older, better period when popular books
could be serious books.

In *Tropic of Cancer* Henry Miller proposed the end of writing. In
Finnegans Wake, Joyce practised it. In these books what is proposed
is the end of *serious* fiction – the fiction of *reality*. In *Misery* what is
recorded is the *end of popular fiction* now gone cold, old and self-
conscious: the feminists get *Carrie* and the postmodernists get
Misery. Stephen King is taken seriously now *because* he is a popular
writer. Only Annie knows what a travesty this is – only Annie
knows that popular fiction is in big shit (She's the NUMBER ONE
FAN AN' SHE KNOWS). This is, in a weird way, the 'end' of the
popular fictionalist's trade: both knowing too much and yet also
too little. It is, after all, a book about pretend people and yet pretend people *can* die. In the book *Misery* must 'live'. Buried alive, she
is dug up and reanimated by the fictionalist's hand. Revival is nostalgia – the impossible is the return. Gothic nostalgia revives the
dead and lets them walk. But, when all is said and done – dead is
dead.

Like Annie Wilkes and her neighbours the Roydmans, King craves
recognition and recognition brings *respectability*. King's bizarre
worlds are the symptom of a need for *respectability*, the polite acquaintance of scholars with the antiquarian touch (Barlow, the vampire, is an antique dealer). This nostalgia for innocence is nevertheless
disturbed and upheld by the violation required of the gothic genre
itself: King's vehicle for respectability.

The gothic moment occurs at a precise point in our recent history.
The naked power of the Sadean libertine goes hand in glove with
the naked heroic innocence of the Rousseauistic savage. By a process of instant osmosis the one *becomes* the other: innocent in his evil,
savage in his control. *Justine* records not merely the nostalgia for a
lost medieval myth but also the new Techno myth of the body. For
Sade, his heros and their victims are all pumping machines. Here
then the body becomes a machine, an automated process of control
and production. In this, the body's becoming machinelike predates
most *actual* machines. The body had gained its privacy and had
such privacy proved real by its violation all in one go. From now

on the body as a bit-part machine tool – as a non-organism and as an object – would dominate the metaphoric and symbolic space of actual machines. 'George Stark's' own fictional villains is, of course, called A(lexis) Machine.

Medieval nostalgia coincided with this new awareness of the body – but already built in was a nostalgia for the body as a 'whole' entity. As real bodies ceased to be racked, tortured and pulled to bits for public sport, so the bourgeois state in the name of autonomous individual freedoms brought in dissection in the name of health and private humiliation in the name of public order. The body was at once recognized as a totality and at the same time pulled into the components of its machine existence. Frankenstein's monster walks with the living dead.

The gothic has long sinced sloughed off its nostalgia for the medieval but its nostalgia for the full body – a body bloated to bursting with all these gloopy machine-like tubes and joints – all that fossil-fuel blood – has remained. With the rise of science fiction, the true gothic either compromised or simply died: H.P. Lovecraft compromised, while M.R. James represented the end of the line. With the nostalgia for the medieval gone, Dracula lost his sublimity and the transcendent element departed for good. All that remained was the body – elemental, full of the sticky wet mess of the soft machine. In the modern era, the full body is always to be emptied, evacuated of its interior, opened from its private place into the glare of the public gaze. Violation of moral innocence (the stock of the gothic) now goes hand in hand with violation of the *physical* innocence of the total body. In modern gothic the body is always and ever totally *there*: its thereness is its horror as an object. Thus it is always *too much* there, too much *in place*. The closer the body gets the more its claustrophobic presence invites its dissolution. We are obsessed with the thereness, the total presence of others and at that moment, overclose, they become less than human – threateningly similar to bit part objects. Paranoia of bodily space: read *American Psycho*.

The individual, (no longer obsessed with the body as presence, but obsessed with escaping from it – one to whom the body is a mere symbol or token) is the artist. Meet his brother the psycho. The serious nut is obsessed with the body as fetish: a reinforcement of his own 'thereness' in the vacated (because dead) space of the other.

Norman Bates keeps mum but knows Norman Mailer's white

negro intimately. Colin Wilson's outsider goes for tea with Peter Sutcliffe. Annie Wilkes sure likes Paul Sheldon. The psycho and the obsessive artist are the last remains of real individuals in a world gone Stepford through junk TV, junk diets, junk art. Only psychos and writers still enjoy *authenticity* in a world of simulation and deceit.

In this weird romantic alliance of the creative and the destructive we see the last vestiges of self-possession in a Brave New World where the concept of self-possession is (itself) unthinkable. In such a world the artist is as scary as a psycho and may actually be one. From *Psycho* to *The Silence of the Lambs*, from *American Psycho* to *Twin Peaks* and from *Twin Peaks* to *Misery* the psycho goes hand in hand with the artist into the *Black Lodge*: bad dreams of paranoiacs. Here there is all the nostalgia of the postmodern for individual autonomy and the complete body, but it is crossed by slavery and dismemberment and loss of control to the system of the machine. Despite being dismembered almost all of Paul Sheldon's life with Annie is recalled in the immobile inner world of the *mind*. It is Paul's mind which constantly registers the indignities to his body as if his body was merely an object to contemplate.

The novel of the techno-body, this full body waiting to burst open (remember *Alien*) and reveal the total works, is a novel which necessarily goes in for total visualization. Such a novel restricts imagination by doing away with it. Total visualization dispenses with partial description. Such writing is for a culture going cold on imagination yet which views body functions as grotesque and fearful. In this horror as in pornography there is no *modesty* (shall I chop off your foot Paulie? Shall I chop off your thumb Paulie? Shall I chop off your 'man gland' Paulie?) As George Orwell pointed out long ago there is only the fascist boot, the presence of broken flesh, subjection and slavery.[2] No one gets out of this funny farm. Techno-subservience is now served up as escapism. The age of modern post-war horror is the age of the post-war corporate hero: Zombie Man, Zombie Woman.

King's books display a special contradiction: a nostalgia for an earlier innocent authentic reality produced by a fiction of *imagination*. This fiction's reality was only ever 'suggested'. The project of writing has run its course because the project of the autonomous bourgeois imagination has done so too. When we say King has a weird imagination we mean exactly the opposite. King's tragedy is that his novels leave nothing unsaid because it is all always present. King knows that the age of the full body demands *total* representation: you cannot avoid the machine. In the old sense, in the 'Hemingway' mythic sense (which was never the reality of Hemingway but always the myth) in this sense, he will never write a 'serious' novel, for the project he desires to participate in has now become a false trail.

Even as cult fiction has become self-aware and thereby lost its nature as pulp, so theory, that most self-reflexive of activities, has been colonized unawares by the very sensational, erotic and violent language of the pulp enterprise. Does this double yet unequal movement signal the end of both pulp and theory?[3]

There is now a large (often academic) audience for pulp exemplified by a new respect for the kitsch movie-making of the 1950s and 1960s. Russ Meyer's elephantasized Vixens play art-house cinemas both sides of the Atlantic and his banal yet surreally named films (for example, *Faster Pussycat! Kill! Kill!*) have found a new and unexpected respect among the critically aware. Ed Wood, whose very name seems a type of parental satire (Edward Wood, shortened to Ed Wood) and who found fame of sorts by becoming the worst film-maker ever has also been granted posthumous legitimacy through the loving reverence of educated fans, including the much-celebrated film-maker Tim Burton. As one critic has pointed out, to be the worst is in a peculiarly apt way to personify 'a particularly high concept'.[4] It is here, in this inversion of culture, that the worst attracts the 'best' and it is here also that the language of culture uneasily shifts. Tim Burton's film is *homage*, indeed 'there's no mistaking it for anything but an art film'.[5]

Edward D. Wood, Jr. was born in 1924 and flourished in the second great age of pulp, the era of pulp's phase of horror comics and drive-in B movies. He made crude horror and science-fiction films and ended his days making pornography, attracting along the way a gallery of freakish actors and the burnt-out junkie shell of Bela Lugosi whose death on the set of *Plan 9 from Outer Space* (1959) is recorded (as it were) in a cut-away shot which allows Bela in one door of a house and an appallingly poor look-alike to emerge from another. Wood's stable of freak actors, from Lugosi to 'Criswell the television psychic' and from Vampira to Tor Johnson seems a parody before the fact of Andy Warhol's later factory.

From irrelevant and talentless film-maker, Wood has risen through the ranks and now commands a place as a 'respected' iconographer of the 1950s, a *Kitschmeister* without parallel, a sweatergirl cross-dresser, an artist-manqué whose lasting memorial is *The Rocky Horror Show* which, in its turn, celebrated in high-camp good humour the androgynous posing of a whole generation unaware of Wood's Cold War transvestite *fest Glen or Glenda* (1953).

But this is quite different from giving Wood's work a theoretically or artistically central place. If Tim Burton has indeed 'embalmed' 'living kitsch' and turned it into dead 'art' he is guilty of the sins of reverence and respect that kill pulp dead. Yet the critic is also guilty of another sin when, in attempting to salvage both Wood (as naive amusement) and high culture (lamenting the loss of irony in Burton's work and attacking the celebration of the 'lowest common denominator') they invoke the full weight of the post-modern, hence: 'Deliberately or not, Ed Wood served to *deconstruct* all manner of Hollywood pretence.'[6] (my emphasis)

Suddenly Wood is legitimized as a natural philosopher, a true *naif* – an incompetent who wears the word deconstruction as an accolade for an oeuvre entirely crass and yet entirely self-knowing, aware of its power of denial and refusal – the decentring of the Derridean gaze summed up in its crudeness, vulgarity and ineptitude. If Ed Wood did not know, then his films 'know', as they actively decentre the 'pretence' of Hollywood. It's as if the verbal imperative of 'deconstruct' was always *in* the films, their *raison d'être*, discovered many years after the fact as the core of their claim to legitimacy.

A new and wholly unexpected admiration is legitimized by a theoretical and often semiotic turn, itself both scorned by and courted by pulp producers. Through such means, fictions once ignored as illicit are transformed retrospectively into a repectable and stabilized field of study. The second move, however, is the only one of real interest as it retains its illicit and problematic status while courting respectability and legitimacy. In this move the very language of pulp 'invades' the legitimate field of theory – gives its theoretically dull language the edge of scandal but also the means to command respect. *Consciously* scandalous and anti-establishment, literary theory nevertheless is itself scandalized by a metaphoric language that is violent, erotic and unstable. Here is a language not merely descriptive of the modern condition but entirely conditioned by it and to a certain extent directed by it in parallel with the fictions it seeks to explain. What exactly is the status of the language used here (without irony?) by critic Arthur Kroker?

What is the bimodern condition? It is the contemporary human situation of living at the *violent* edge of *primitivism* and *simulation*, of an indefinite reversibility in the order of things wherein only the *excessive* cancellation of difference through *violence* re-energizes the process. The bimodern condition, then, as a time of *excessive* tendencies towards *violent* boredom and *suicidal nihilism*: driftworks between *ecstasy* and *terminal catatrophe*. Here, the horizon finally closes and we are left with the *fatal* residues of all the referents in the *ecstasy* of *ruins*. That *fatal* moment prophesied by Heidegger's reflections on the techological logic of the *death camps* as the genetic logic of the bimodern scene. And all this under the sign of *seduction*.[7]

(emphases mine)

Here, for instance, we find a combination of explicitly scandalous language and a covert language of scandal which speaks only as the 'unspoken' of the first language. The overt language's *intention* is to disrupt established complacencies and at the same time describe them. Kroker is not being metaphoric but literal. The second language using the words of the first is a celebration of the erotic, the violent and the scandalous: an aesthetic of fascistic style unnoticed by Kroker as the antithesis of his own overt liberal and humanist sentiments. Here language becomes a type of style enjoyed for its own sake, a sub-cultural fantasy of control through an erotic apocalypse and a type of legitimate obscenity, not subversive but illicit (at once respectable *and* shocking). The first language is an attempt to shock explicitly, the second language is that which speaks the first – a scandal within the expression of theory itself.

A second example, apparently quite different from the one just offered concerns one academic's memories of her childhood. Influenced we are told, by radical politics, Marxism, feminism, post-structuralism and psychoanalysis, Valerie Walkerdine goes on to state of an essentially provincial, conservative, working-class, traditional and *stable* upbringing that,

We are beginning to speak of our histories, and as we do it will be to reveal the burden of *pain* and *desire* that formed us, and, in so doing, expose the *terrifying fraudulence* of our *subjugation*.[8]

(emphases mine)

Isn't this the vocabulary of the sensational – forgotten, yet returned to give substance to an otherwise unexciting life? Here we find

revelations of pain and desire and the need to expose (an exposé)
subjugation. Notice too the peculiar shift of the unanchored adverb,
'terrifying' fixed rather to 'fraudulence' than where we might expect to find it attached to 'subjugation'. But what possibly could be
meant by such violent language when used in association with such
a wholly uneventful life as recorded by the writer? Here the banal
becomes sensationalized, the erotic and the violent ('desire' and
'pain' and 'subjugation') meeting in a world of terror and fraud: the
language of the post-structuralist critic becomes quite uncosciously
that of the tabloid and the pulp thriller.

My contention is that contemporary post-structuralist criticism is
the new 'pulp', that its metaphors and obsessions parallel that of
pulp fiction and that around the critical genre, modern criticism has
created a subculture at once arcane and escapist: a fantastic arena
in which the body, sexuality and violence underwrite the cult's
wildest fetishes. Such criticism toys with the idea of somehow going beyond, transcending and deconstructing the boundaries and
realities presented in those fictions we as academics are paid to
explain daily. I further contend that such literary theory is basically
a *nostalgia* for scandal, a basically conservative retro-ism defined by
a loose alliance of deconstructionists, feminists and liberal critics
whose relationship to the established order is that of a false opposition unknowingly renewing, by mysticism and obfuscation, current cultural, political and economic control, having substituted a
theology of the body for a politics of intervention: theory as escapism, dressed in the erotic language of horror. Their celebration of
broken taboos *in fiction* simply reinforces the stability of the taboo
in the world.

My reading of *Misery* suggested a crisis in popular writing which
was most apparent in Stephen King's ambiguous attitude not only
to the 'muse', his readers and the nature of publishing but was also
focused on his chosen genre: horror. The specific consideration I
gave to King was part of a larger argument centred on the historical
progress of the gothic and the changing form of its presentation. I
suggested there was a movement in the genre, from a literature of
revelation and annihilation obvious in writers such as M.R. James
but obvious too in Edgar Allan Poe (whose tale 'The Facts in the
Case of M. Valdemar' is an exemplary instance of a tale centred on
bodily functions ending in revelation and annihilation), to current

works which also concentrate on the body but for different purposes. For Poe the interior of the body is simply a sticky mess of undifferentiated organs – a type of interior slime. For current writers brought up in a photographic and technological era the body represents an anatomical structure and a fluid-filled machine. In this present literature, the body is cut, dissected, ripped, dismembered, always tortured and abject; it is emptied out, displayed; part human and part machine, visceral, fluid, sticky with blood, semen, faeces, urine. The body is monstrously *there* but already so alien as to constitute an horrific elsewhere both paradoxically supernaturalized and objectified. The vague image of London fog and a faceless assassin represents what previous generations wanted to know about the psychopathic dismemberment of the body: material horror of annihilation – the flash of a knife and the moment of truth. Yet it is the famous Scotland Yard *photograph* of Mary Kelly's eviscerated body which forms the first link in a chain which reaches to the Zapruder tape of Kennedy's assassination and beyond: the interior of the body suddenly and uncannily exposed to a fascinated and sensationalized gaze.

The central stalking horror of this literature is no longer the demon, hellish spectre or ghost but the psychopathic hero-villain not only of pulp fiction but also of supposedly serious writers who themselves stalk the popular imagination for their subject matter. Here is a metaphorical or virtual world of libidinous violence, incest, dismemberment, Sadeian fantasy, with a shopping list of broken taboos and of invented horrors for which no taboo exists to be broken.

We can trace four parallel and interelated incarnations of fiction concerned with the erotic, the sensational and the horrific. The first includes the early work of James Herbert, Stephen King, Clive Barker, Shaun Hutson and many other popular authors who work or are identified with the purely horrific. The second includes popular fiction which crosses genres, especially into that of detective or crime fiction. Thomas Harris's *Silence of the Lambs* cannot be overlooked here. Purportedly based on the psychopathology of known serial killers, the book owes just as much to its gothic horror origins with Clarice Starling acting the part of the heroine in a Radcliffe-like adventure pursued through a dungeon basement filled with death's head moths, bodily parts and terrified female victims cowering in an oubliette. Hannibal Lecter, with his deformities, gross appetite and ludicious knowledge is at once Dr Fu Manchu, Dr No, and

Count Dracula. Here the mundanity of the psychopath is super-naturalized for popular consumption.

The third incarnation concerns writers or artists whose work is recognized by academics as 'art' and who have utilized the sociopathic as a central theme. These writers are Booker Prize can didates or Palm D'Or winners who may have no real interest in the horror genre *per se*. Its ultimate expression would appear to be Bret Easton Ellis's *American Psycho*.

The fourth incarnation is not in fiction at all but in current cultural criticism.

American Psycho is the ultimate novel of body nostalgia, a final futile search for the innocent subject amid the charnel house of New York's postmodern decadence. I want to state, rather baldly, that the fourth incarnation of contemporary erotic horror sensationalism is the new fictional space of literary theory itself: pulp violence as the heart and controlling passion of cultural inquiry and intellectual concern. I further want to suggest that post-structualist criticism is itself a type of nostalgia *interlaced* with other forms of artistic expression so as to form a parallel discourse, self-contained and only occasionally an explanatory commentary. This is the horror in the library where the gothicization and occulting of the ordinary takes place amid the rococo of academia's ivory towers. Theory is pulp sensation, plagiarized without acknowledgement.

Richard Wagner wrote to Theodor Uhlig in 1849 that,

> artwork cannot be created at the present time, but only prepared
> – by a process of revolutionizing, of destroying and smashing
> everything that is worth destroying and smashing. That is our
> work, and only then will totally different people from us become
> the true creative artists.[9]

He was expressing the creed of a new intellectualism, that was based on struggle, apocalypse and renewal. This has remained the basic premise of the structure and project of *theory* ever since. It is quite irrelevant to this argument to point out that theory includes the Hegelian dialectic and its nemesis. What is at stake is the status of theory *per se*. Theory was both scandal and catastrophe – a radical disestablishment at the level of structuration. The specific nature of individual theories is not the central question and thus Wagner's relationships with Bakunin or Nietzsche become secondary issues, although it is an interesting footnote that just prior to becoming involved with 'Young Germany', Wagner had been adding material to Marschner's *Der Vampyr*.

Dis-composition then is particular to cultural theory. A recent critic has seen in Luis Buñuel's *Un Chien Andalou* another precursor of deconstruction, a film determined by Buñuel's and Dali's commitment to 'the dramatic themes of sexuality and eroticism, especially as they connect to forms of violence'.[10] Such ideas are themselves relatable to Buñuel's remark that the film was 'a desperate and passionate appeal to murder'.[11]

The violent discomposition of the body is the radical metaphoric language of pulp, surrealism and contemporary critical practice. The individual now finds himself or herself haunted by a ghostly *Doppelgänger* known only as the 'other' whose presence turns the self into a schizoid subject whose pronoun is 'it'. And the spectral language of this ruptured subject is the erased Derridean half-voice of its philosophic designation. Suffering from suture, this bricolaged subjectivity seeps the fluids of abjection on the altar of Phallic sacrifice. Its alternative, androgynous pleasure, far from being understood as an image of a mere freakishness which is both pathetic and absurd is now applauded and joined to the erotic frenzy of *jouissance*, itself the infantile excessiveness of highly rational intellectualism.

This pornutopia of freaks, drivelling irrationalism and obscene language exists in a world of Foucaultian imprisonment and Althusserian paranoia – its favourite authors being de Sade, Poe, Artaud and Céline. A runic semiology reads the signs.

And one should add into this mélange the project of linguistic feminism where we need include neither such eccentricity as Mary Daly's white witchcraft nor Luce Irigaray's bizarre obsession with the placenta. Rather such feminism by its nature is haunted, not by the misdeeds of real men and real women, but by a shadowy and inexplicably alien force called phallocentrism whose agents are real men unwittingly dedicated to fulfilling a conspiratorial and generalized male aggressivity. Aggression, duality, violence, eroticism, paranoia, imprisonment, dismemberment, the irrational, the displacement of the real, the supernatural, the body, the freak, the nature of death and the spectral afterlife – these are the component features of horror-porn-pulp and its collusive double, contemporary criticism.

It seems that current theory is both a partially descriptive analysis of contemporaneity and *implicity* involved with that which it describes. This reciprocal arrangement has allowed a new lease of life to much fiction and theory about fiction. I have pointed out that modern theory is descriptive of a *metaphysical nostalgia* for the full body and the self-sufficient ego. The modern pulp gothic seems, in parallel, to describe a similar trajectory. Such reciprocal parallelism has meant that post-structuralist language has *incorporated* the language of the pulp gothic within its own discourse. A language inherently metaphoric in pulp (gothic) fiction has been taken as literal (a description of actuality) in post-structuralism. Such analysis is drenched in the language of nostalgia – virally disturbed by its own rhetoric of violence, irrationality and death.

Perhaps analysis must again reinvent itself as both descriptive and prescriptive. As such, both popular literature and cultural criticism have reached their outer limits on the edge of a certain cybernetic imagination. Contemporary pulp is inherently nostalgic, postmodern theory is its retrospective twin.

The recent revival of post-structuralist attitudes among critics one might consider a parallel but not explanatory framework to the texts discussed here. And so, finally, here we are in a world of virtual violence and erotic fantasy practised by decent critics yet virtual psychopaths: killers like us, critics like us.

The illicit pleasures of pulp fiction.

Notes

CHAPTER 1: 'SCUSE ME MR H'OFFICER

1. Peter Hunt, quoted in Robert Leeson, *Reading and Righting* (London: Collins, 1985) p. 145.
2. Patricia Hollis, *The Pauper Press: a Study in Working-Class Radicalism of the 1830s* (Oxford: Oxford University Press, 1970) p. viii.
3. Ibid.
4. Howard Zinn, *A People's History of the United States* (Harlow: Longman, 1980) p. 280.
5. Ibid., p. 286.
6. Ibid.
7. See, for example, Stanley Harrison, *Poor Men's Guardians: a Survey of the Struggles for a Democratic Newspaper Press 1763–1973* (London: Lawrence & Wishart, 1974).
8. See comments on the censorious and authoritarian nature of the radical press in Ken Worpole, *Dockers and Detectives* (London: Verso, 1983) p. 17.
9. See Worpole above; also Janet Batsleer, Tony Davies, Rebecca O'Rourke and Chris Weedon, *Rewriting English: Cultural Politics of Gender and Class* (London: Methuen, 1985) and Roger Bromley, *Lost Narratives: Popular Fictions, Politics and Recent History* (London: Routledge, 1988).
10. Brian Stableford, foreword to Steve Holland, *The Mushroom Jungle: a History of Postwar Paperback Publishing* (Westbury, Wilts.: Zeon Books, 1994) p. x.

CHAPTER 2: THROWING RICE AT BRAD AND JANET

1. For the illicit pleasures of drink, smoking and drugs see John C. Burnham, *Bad Habits* (New York: New York University Press, 1993) and for the illicit pleasures of public spaces see David Nasaw, *Going Out: the Rise and Fall of Public Amusements* (New York: Harper Collins, 1993).
2. Jim Miller cited in Greil Marcus, *In the Fascist Bathroom: Writings on Punk 1977–1992* (Harmondsworth: Penguin, 1993) p. 169.
3. Nick Hornby, *Fever Pitch* (London: Victor Gollancz, 1992) p. 10. See also D.J. Taylor, *A Vain Conceit: British Fiction in the 1980s* (London: Bloomsbury, 1989) p. 21:

   Why read fiction? At heart I suppose – this applies whether the author is Proust or Catherine Cookson, and knocks away most of the arguments advanced in this book – you read fiction to escape, to bring into your own life the rewarding tensions that would otherwise be absent from it. Books, it scarcely needs saying, are life lived at one remove. I feel about novels the way I felt at twelve about association football, the way I felt at eighteen about rock and roll. At bottom the critic is nothing more than a fan – or a performer *manqué*.

4. Jonathan Mantle, *In for a Penny: The Unauthorised Biography of Jeffrey Archer* (London: Hamish Hamilton, 1979) p. 133.
5. Marcus, op.cit., p. 167.
6. See George Orwell, 'Raffles and Miss Blandish', in *Decline of the English Murder and other Essays* (Harmondsworth: Penguin [1946], 1979).
7. Eliot's interest in popular culture can be seen in his essays on the music hall artiste, his fascination with contemporary murder trials and his use of Sherlock Holmes references.

It's notorious that T.S. Eliot was a Sherlock Holmes fan who pinched a chunk of 'The Musgrave Ritual' for the Second Tempter scene in *Murder in the Cathedral* (there are other Sherlockian echoes in the play) and puzzled academics with the bit in 'East Coker' about being lost 'in a dark wood, in a bramble, On the edge of a grimpen, where is no secure foothold . . .' Those who'd searched at length and in vain for the Old English root of the obscure word were not best pleased to hear it was merely the great Grimpen Mire from *The Hound of the Baskervilles*. A further micro-reference that I've never seen mentioned in print is Eliot's arrangement of *A Choice of Kipling's Verse* (1941), where unrelated poems from 1902 and 1897 are carefully placed together. They are titled . . . 'Sussex' and 'The Vampire.'

(*Million*, Sept/Oct 1992)

8. Jeff Koons, *The Jeff Koons Handbook* (London: Thames & Hudson, 1992) pp. 50 and 54.
9. Ibid., p. 56.
10. Ibid., p. 98.
11. Ibid., p. 138.
12. A.P. Ryan, *Lord Northcliffe* (London: Collins, 1953) p. 42 onwards.
13. Peter Haining, ed., *The Fantastic Pulps* (London: Victor Gollancz, 1975) pp. 189–90.
14. J. Pacione, *A History of the Booker Prize*, unpublished M. Phil (Stirling, 1991) pp. 3–4.
15. Maurice Flanagan, *Paperbacks, Pulp and Comic Collector* (Vol. 1. 1994) p. 48.
16. Geoffrey O'Brien, *Hardboiled America: the Lurid Years of Paperbacks* (New York: Van Nostrand Reinhold, 1981) pp. 12–13.
17. Haining, op.cit., pp. 13–14.
18. Lee Server, *Danger is My Business* (San Francisco: Chronicle Books, 1993) p. 15.

19. Noelle Watson and Paul Shellinger, eds, *Twentieth Century Science Fiction Writers* (Chicago: St James Press, 1991) p. 299.
20. Patrick Parrinder, 'Scientists in Science Fiction: Enlightenment and After', in Rhys Garnett and R.J. Ellis, eds, *Science Fiction: Roots and Branches: Contemporary Critical Approaches* (London: Macmillan, 1990) p. 57.
21. Ibid., p. 63.
22. Steven Marcus, *The Other Victorians* (London: Weidenfeld & Nicolson, 1966) p. 46.
23. Ibid., pp. 240–1.
24. John McHale quoted in Gillo Dorfles, *Kitsch: an Anthology of Bad Taste* (London: Studio Vista, 1969) pp. 98 and 108.
25. Harold Rosenberg, in Dorfles, op.cit., p. 9.
26. Clement Greenberg in Dorfles, op.cit., p. 116.
27. Herman Broch, in Dorfles, op.cit., p. 61.
28. Ibid., p. 62.
29. Ibid., p. 63.
30. Ibid., pp. 64–5.
31. J.A. Sutherland, *Fiction and the Fiction Industry* (London: Athlone Press, 1978) p. 65.
32. Ibid., p. xi.
33. John St John, *William Heinemann: a Century of Publishing, 1890–1990* (London: Heinemann, 1990) p. 20.
34. O'Brien ibid., pp. 33 and 35.
35. Matthew Arnold in Ray Ginger, ed., *The Nationalizing of American Life 1877–1900* (New York: Free Press, 1965) p. 123.
36. S.J. Taylor, *Shock! Horror!: The Tabloids in Action* (London: Corgi, 1991) p. 240.
37. Ibid., p. 76.
38. Ibid., p. 77.
39. Ibid.
40. Ibid., p. 17.
41. Ibid.

CHAPTER 3: TURNING THE WORLD AROUND

1. See Frank MacShane, *The Life of Raymond Chandler* (Boston: G.K. Hall, 1976).
2. Ibid., p. 1.
3. Victor E. Neuberg, *Popular Literature: a History and Guide* (London: Woburn Press, 1977) p. 142.
4. See Ken Worpole, *Dockers and Detectives* (London: Verso, 1983). See pp. 14–15 for reader confusions even in the mid-twentieth century!
5. Robert Collison, *The Story of Street Literature* (London: Dent, 1973) p. 31.
6. Collison, p. 38: Newby p. 15.
7. Newby, p. 139.

8.   Ibid., pp. 139–40.
9.   Collison, p. 6.
10. Ibid., p. 6.
11. Ibid., p. 10.
12. See Cyril Pearl, *The Girl with the Swansdown Seat: An Informal Report on Some Aspects of Mid-Victorian Morality* (London: Robin Clark [1955], 1980).
13. Harriett Hawkins, *Classics and Trash* (Hassocks: Harvester/Wheatsheaf, 1990) p. 10.
14. Ibid., p. 6.
15. John Feather, *A History of British Publishing* (London: Routledge, 1988) p. 137.
16. J.A. Sutherland, *Victorian Novelists and Publishers* (Chicago: University of Chicago Press, 1976) p. 63.
17. Ibid., p. 30.
18. Ibid., p. 33.
19. Charles Knight quoted in Peter Haining, *The Penny Dreadful* (London: Gollancz, 1975) p. 7.
20. Feather, op.cit., p. 57.
21. See John Carey, *The Intellectuals and the Masses* (London: Faber & Faber, 1992) p. 5. See also Feather, op.cit., p. 29.
22. Sutherland, op.cit., pp. 24 and 27.
23. See Katherine Tillotson, *Novels of the Eighteen-Forties* (Oxford: Clarendon, 1955) p. 23.
24. Sutherland, op.cit., p. 10.
25. Amy Cruse, *The Victorians and their Books* (London: Allen & Unwin, 1935) p. 315.
26. Ibid., p. 321.
27. See Peter Keating, *The Haunted Study: a Social History of the English Novel, 1875–1914* (London: Secker & Warburg, 1989).
28. John Carey, op.cit., pp. 11–12.
29. Ibid., p. 6.
30. Quoted in Alan J. Lee, *The Origins of the Popular Press in England 1855–1914* (London: Croom Helm, 1976) p. 27.
31. Ibid., p. 29.
32. Ibid., p. 15.
33. Ibid., p. 37. As early as 1829, George Shillibeer's omnibus included the loan of a newspaper within the fare.
34. Ibid., p. 38.
35. Ibid., p. 293.
36. See Richard Hoggart, *The Uses of Literacy* (Harmondsworth: Penguin [1957], 1990).
37. Daniel Boorstin, *The Americans: the Democratic Experience* (New York: Vintage, 1993).
38. See Keating, op.cit., pp. 4–5.
39. Boorstin, op.cit., p. 198.
40. Ibid., p. 145.
41. See Shirley Harrison, *The Diary of Jack the Ripper* (London: Smith Gryphon, 1994) pp. 179–80.

42. Hillel Schwartz, 'Torque: the New Kinaesthetic of the Twentieth Century', in Jonathan Crary and Sanford Kwinter eds, *Incorporations* (New York: Zone, 1992) p. 95.
43. Ibid., pp. 95–6.
44. Robert Leeson, *Reading and Righting* (London: Collins, 1985) p. 116.
45. Ibid., p. 128.
46. See chapter 1 in David Trotter, *The English Novel in History 1895–1920* (London: Routledge, 1993).
47. See *Reader's Digest* (March 1988).
48. Ibid., p. 183.
49. Ibid.
50. Penelope Dell, *Nettie and Sissie: A Biography of Bestselling Novelist Ethel M. Dell and her Sister Ella* (London: Hamish Hamilton, 1977) p. 21.
51. Ibid.

CHAPTER 4: A RIVER SO DEEP

1. Quoted in Richard Brown, *Society and Economy in Modern Britain 1700–1850* (London: Routledge, 1991) p. 215.
2. Ibid., p. 216.
3. Ibid.
4. E.J. Hobsbawm, *The Age of Empire 1975–1914* (London: Weidenfeld and Nicolson, 1987) p. 30.
5. John Lawson and Harold Silver, *A Social History of Education in England* (London: Methuen, 1973) p. 258.
6. Ibid., p. 324.
7. *International Encyclopaedia of Social Science*, Vol. 9.
8. Jerry White, *The Worst Street in North London: Campbell Bunk, Islington between the Wars* (London: Routledge & Kegan Paul, 1986) p. 8.
9. Ibid., pp. 107–9.
10. Ibid., pp. 130–1. The twopenny 'barrow' library often reverted to other goods such as cigarettes if profits were down. See J. Partington, *The Crowded Life of a Lancashire Lad* (Manchester, 1972) p. 99.
11. Carl N. Degler, *Out of Our Past: The Forces that Shaped Modern America* (New York: Harper [1959], 1984), p. 50; p. 105.
12. Ibid., p. 105.
13. James Bowen, *A History of Western Education*, Vol. 3 (London: Methuen, 1981), pp. 310–12.
14. Daniel Boorstin, *The Americans*, Vol. 2 (New York: Random House [1958], 1974) p. 30.
15. Alexis de Tocqueville, *Democracy in America*, ed. J.P. Mayer; trans. George Lawrence (London: Fontana, 1994) p. 474.
16. Ibid., p. 474; p. 470.
17. Ibid., p. 471.
18. Ibid.
19. Ibid.
20. Bowen, p. 444.

21. Ibid.
22. Ibid.; *International Encyclopaedia of Social Science*, op.cit.
23. H.L. Mencken, *The American Language* (New York: Alfred Knopf [1919], 1941) p. vi.
24. Ibid., p. 4.
25. Witherspoon, quoted in ibid., p. 5.
26. Ibid.
27. Webster, quoted in ibid., p. 10.
28. de Tocqueville, pp. 477–8.
29. Ibid., p. 478.
30. Philip S. Bagwell and G.E. Mingay, *Britain and America 1850–1939: a Study of Economic Change* (London: Routledge & Kegan Paul, 1970) p. 1.
31. Ibid., p. 2.
32. Ibid.
33. Ibid., p. 5.
34. Wallace Stevens, quoted in *Modern Poets on Modern Poetry*, ed. James Scully (London: Fontana, 1966) p. 155.
35. William Carlos Williams, 'In the American Grain', in eds Ronald Gottesman et al., *The Norton Anthology of American Literature*, Vol. 2 (New York: W.W. Norton, 1979) pp. 1458–9.
36. Ibid., p. 1460.
37. Charles Olson, in Scully, p. 278.
38. Peter Lamarque and Stein Hangom Olsen, *Truth, Fiction and Literature* (Oxford: Clarendon, 1994) p. 270.
39. Degler, pp. 326–7; *Encyclopaedia Americana*, Vol. 17.

CHAPTER 5: OUTLAWS AGAINST THE LAW BADGE

1. See Peter Linebaugh, *The London Hanged: Crime and Civil Society in the Eighteenth Century* (Harmondsworth: Penguin, 1993).
2. Ibid., p. 135.
3. Ibid., p. 169.
4. Patricia Hollis, *The Pauper Press: A Study in Working-Class Radicalism of the 1830s* (Oxford: Oxford University Press, 1970) p. 47.
5. Ibid.
6. Ibid.
7. Ibid., p. 48.
8. Linebaugh, op.cit., p. 39.
9. Ibid., pp. 7–8.
10. Ibid., p. 205.
11. E.S. Turner, *Boys Will Be Boys* (Harmondsworth: Penguin [1948], 1975) p. 53.
12. Ibid., p. 51.
13. Ibid., p. 52.
14. David Vincent, 'Reading in the Working Class Home', in John K. Walton and James Walvin eds, *Leisure in Britain 1780–1939* (Manchester: Manchester University Press, 1983) pp. 207–26 (p. 211).

15. Ibid., p. 210.
16. Ibid., p. 211.
17. Ibid.
18. See introduction in Clive Bloom ed., *Literature and Culture in Modern Britain*, Vol. 1 1900–1929 (Harlow: Longman, 1993).
19. Stephen Humphries, *Hooligans or Rebels? Oral History of Working-Class Childhood and Youth 1889–1939* (Oxford: Basil Blackwell, 1981) p. 34.
20. John Lawson and Harold Silver, *A Social History of Education in England* (London: Methuen, 1973) p. 193.
21. Ibid., p. 25.
22. See comments by William Cobbett in Lawson and Silver op.cit., p. 260.
23. Ibid.
24. E.P. Thompson, *The Making of the English Working Class* (London: Gollancz, 1980) p. 54.
25. Ibid., p. 56.
26. Thomas Boyle, *Black Swine in the Sewers of Hampstead* (London: Hodder & Stoughton, 1990) p. 22.
27. See David Vincent, art. cit., p. 223.
28. See Joseph McAleer, *Popular Reading and Publishing in Britain 1914– 1950* (Oxford: Clarendon, 1992).
29. Ibid., p. 109.
30. R.C. Terry, *Victorian Popular Fiction 1860–80* (London: Macmillan, 1983) pp. 9, 11, 31. See also John St John, *William Heinemann: a Century of Publishing, 1890–1990* (London: Heinemann, 1990) pp. 10, 24, 37.
31. McAleer, op.cit., p. 114.
32. Deborah Cameron and Elizabeth Frazer, *The Lust to Kill* (London: Polity Press, 1989).
33. Ibid., p. 50.
34. Ibid.
35. *Modern Review* (Oct–Nov 1994) p. 5.
36. See Mary Cadogan, *Richmal Crompton: the Woman Behind William* (London: Allen & Unwin, 1986).
37. See David Trotter, *The English Novel in History 1895–1920* (London: Routledge, 1993).
38. Ibid., p. 151.
39. John St John, op.cit., p. 52.
40. Ibid.
41. Ibid., p. 50.
42. Ibid.
43. Quoted in Humphreys, op.cit., p. 43.
44. Ibid., p. 43.
45. See Michael Brake, *Comparative Youth Culture* (London: Routledge [1985], 1993).

CHAPTER 6: SMART LIKE US

1. Lawrence W. Levine, *Highbrow/Lowbrow: The Emergence of Cultural Hierarchy in America* (Cambridge Mass.: Harvard University Press, 1988) p. 233.
2. William Dean Howells, 'Novel Writing and Novel-Reading: an Impersonal Explanation', in Ronald Gottesman et al., eds, *The Norton Anthology of American Literature*, Vol. 2 (New York: W.W. Norton, 1979) p. 301.
3. Levine, p. 224.
4. I.A. Richard, *Principles of Literary Criticism* (London: Routledge [1924], 1976) pp. 25 and 195.
5. John Carey: *The Intellectuals and the Masses: Pride and Prejudice among the Literary Intelligentsia, 1880–1939* (London: Faber & Faber, 1992) p. 7.
6. Ibid., p. 6.
7. Ibid.
8. Harry Ritchie, *Success Stories: Literature and the Media in England, 1950–1959* (London: Faber & Faber, 1988) p. 4.
9. Ibid., p. 9.
10. Ibid., p. 14.
11. Ibid., p. 15.
12. Ibid., p. 19.
13. Ibid., p. 21.
14. For C.P. Snow's lecture and subsequent comments see, *The Two Cultures and a Second Look* (Cambridge: Cambridge University Press, 1965).
15. Ritchie, p. 15.
16. See Allan Bloom, *The Closing of the American Mind* (Harmondsworth: Penguin, 1988) and Harold Bloom, *The Western Canon* (London: Macmillan, 1995).
17. Alvin Kernan, *The Death of Literature* (New Haven: Yale University Press (1990) p. 6.
18. Robert Hughes, *Culture of Complaint: The Fraying of America* (New York: Oxford University Press, 1993) p. 103.
19. Kernan, p. 138.
20. Herbert I. Schiller, *Culture Inc.: The Corporate Takeover of Public Expressions* (New York: Oxford University Press, 1989) p. 33.
21. Paul Fussell, *BAD or, The Dumbing of America* (New York: Summit Books, 1991) pp. 59–60.
22. Richard Hoggart, *The Uses of Literacy* (Harmondsworth: Penguin [1957], 1990) pp. 247–8 and 250.
23. Q.D. Leavis, 'The Case of Miss Dorothy Sayers: *Gaudy Night* and *Busman's Honeymoon*' in *Scrutiny*, Vol. VI (1937).
24. Fussell, p. 13.
25. Q.D. Leavis, art. cit.
26. Ibid.
27. F.R. Leavis, 'The Literary Racket' in *Scrutiny*, Vol. 1 (1932).
28. For the full letter see *The Times Higher Education Supplement* (20. 11. 92).
29. Both plays can be found in James L. Smith ed., *Victorian Melodramas* (London: Dent, 1976).

30. Harriett Hawkins, *Classics and Trash* (Hassocks: Harvester/Wheat-sheaf, 1990) pp. 110–11.
31. Ibid., p. 111.
32. Martin Seymour-Smith, *Guide to Modern World Literature* (London: Macmillan, 1986) p. xxxiv.
33. Ibid., pp. xxxiv–xxxv.
34. Raymond Williams, *Towards 2000* (London: Chatto & Windus, 1983).
35. Levine, p. 7.
36. Peter Keating, *The Haunted Study: A Social History of the English Novel 1875–1914* (London: Secker & Warburg, 1989) pp. 350 and 354.
37. Geoffrey O'Brien, *Hardboiled America: The Lurid Years of Paperbacks* (New York: Van Nostrand Reinhold, 1981) pp. 5–6.
38. Ibid., pp. 94–5.
39. Eds Peter Humm, Paul Stigant and Peter Widdowson, *Popular Fictions: Essays in Literature and History* (London: Methuen, 1986) p. 5.
40. John G. Cawelti, *Adventure, Mystery and Romance* (Chicago: University of Chicago Press, 1976) pp. 1–2.
41. Cawelti, p. 3.
42. Colin Watson, *Snobbery with Violence* (Harmondsworth: Penguin, [1971], 1987); E.S. Turner, *Boys will be Boys* (Penguin [1948], 1976).
43. Stephen King, *Danse Macabre* (London: Futura, 1986).
44. Leslie A. Fielder, 'Towards a Definition of Popular Literature', in C.W.E. Bigsby ed., *Superculture* (London: Paul Elek, 1975) pp. 28–42 (p. 28).
45. Ibid., p. 30.
46. Ibid.
47. Introduction to Bigsby ed., pp. 24–5.
48. Ibid., p. 6.
49. Ibid.
50. Ibid., p. 15.
51. Walter Nash, *Language in Popular Fiction* (London: Routledge, 1990) pp. 1–2.
52. Ibid., pp. 2–3.
53. Christopher Pawling, *Popular Fiction/Social Change* (London: Macmillan, 1984) p. 12.
54. Ibid., p. 13.
55. Gina Wisker, *It's My Party: Reading Twentieth-Century Women's Writing* (London: Pluto, 1993) p. 4.
56. Derek Longhurst ed., *Gender, Genre and Narrative Pleasure* (London: Unwin Hyman, 1989) p. 5.
57. Humm, p. 11.
58. Cosmo Landesman in *Sunday Times* (14.11.93). *The Modern Review* was edited by Toby Young.

CHAPTER 7: LIVING IN TECHNICOLOR

1. Stan Lee quoted in Greg C. McCue with Clive Bloom, *Dark Knights: The New Comics in Context* (London: Pluto, 1993) p. 84. Brendan Behan recalled in 1958 how borstal boys, lacking books, would tell stories

called 'pictures' after their love of cinema. See Neil Philip ed., *The Penguin Book of English Folktales* (Harmondsworth: Penguin, 1985) p. xxx.

2. See, for examples, Anthony Delves, 'Popular Recreation & Social Conflict in Derby 1800–1850', in Eileen Yeo and Stephen Yeo, eds, *Popular Culture and Class Conflict 1590–1914* (Brighton: Harvester, 1981) chapter 4.

3. Cyril Pearl points out the restrictions put upon upper-class street activity during the late Victorian period. See Cyril Pearl, *The Girl with the Swansdown Seat: An Informal Report on Some Aspects of Mid Victorian Morality* (London: Robin Clark [1955], 1980).

4. John G. Cavelti, *Adventure, Mystery and Romance* (Chicago: Chicago University Press, 1976) p. 6.

5. Walter Nash, *Language in Popular Fiction* (London: Routledge, 1990) p. 8.

6. Vance Packard *The Hidden Persuaders* (Harmondsworth: Penguin [1957], 1960) p. 23.

7. Ibid., p. 29.

8. Ibid., p. 45.

9. Ron Goulart, *Over 50 Years of American Comic Books* (Lincolnwood, Ill.: Publications International, 1991) p. 195.

10. Ibid., p. 199.

11. Ibid., pp. 200–1.

12. McCue, pp. 29–30.

13. Ibid., pp. 30–1.

14. Ibid., p. 32.

15. Steve Holland, *The Mushroom Jungle: A History of Postwar Paperback Publishing* (Dilton Marsh, Wilts.: Zeon, 1993) p. 136.

16. Raymond Hoggart, *The Uses of Literacy* (Harmondsworth: Penguin [1957], 1990) pp. 258–9.

17. Holland, pp. 129–30.

18. Ibid., pp. 192–3.

19. Ibid., p. 135.

20. Ibid., p. 137.

21. Ibid., p. 147.

22. Ibid., p. 151.

23. Ibid., pp. 152–4.

24. Ibid., p. 157.

25. M. Montgomery Hyde, ed., *The Lady Chatterley's Lover Trial* (London: Bodley Head, 1990) pp. 4–5.

26. Geoffrey O'Brien, *Hardboiled America: The Lurid Years of Paperbacks* (New York: Van Nostrand Reinhold, 1981) p. 43.

27. Ibid., p. 42.

28. Henry James quoted in Sandor Gilman, *The Jew's Body* (London: Routledge, 1991) p. 31.

29. Pearl, p. 258.

30. Ibid., p. 261.

31. For a more fully developed argument see Clive Bloom ed., *Literature and Culture in Modern Britain* (Harlow: Longman, 1992) pp. 14–27.

32. See Jan Harold Brunvand, *The Vanishing Hitchhiker – Urban Legends and their Meanings* (London: Picador, 1981). The religious versions of the Vanishing Hitchhiker confirm rather than deny modern, urban semi-secular fears and superstitious attitudes behind much contemporary life. Equally the Mormon version of this tale confirms its relationship to modern religiousity (i.e. Mormonism) both capitalist and urban, rather than some left over from pre-urban, rural or medieval history.

33. See *Betty Page: Queen of Pin Up* (Cologne: Benedikt Taschen, 1993). After almost forty years of living in obscurity Page has recently emerged to sign the occasional autograph.

CHAPTER 8: THE RIPPER WRITING

1. 'In appearance, a paper of the 1890s was a product substantially the same as our own . . . the phrase "new journalism" was first used by the poet Matthew Arnold of the lively work of the *Pall Mall Gazette* and its competitors in the late 1880s. This was indeed the seedbed of the twentieth century commercial popular press. . . . There was also a new group of evening papers circulating in London and going out aggressively for new readers. . . . It was these evening papers which first educated the morning papers into editorial policies suitable for the masses. Kennedy Jones and Alfred Harmsworth (later Lord Northcliffe) worked out their ideas for mass journalism for there was a new generation emerging in the years after the Great Exhibition of 1851 which had great curiosity but little education' – Anthony Smith, *The Newspaper: An International History* (London: Thames & Hudson, 1979) pp. 153–4.

2. Letters quoted by C.M. McCleod in *The Criminologist*, no. 9 (1968) 120–7.

3. Stephen Knight, *Jack the Ripper: The Final Solution* (London: Grafton, 1976).

4. Alexander Kelly, 'Ripperana and Ripperature', *The Assistant Librarian*, 1973, pp. 3–6.

5. Kim Newman in *Million*, March/June 1993, p. 20.

6. Ibid., p. 20.

7. Tony Bennett and Janet Woollacott, *Bond and Beyond: The Political Career of a Popular Hero* (London: Macmillan, 1987) p. 14.

8. Robert Harris, 'Selling Hitler in *The Media Trilogy* (London: Faber & Faber [1986], 1994) p. 579.

9. Shirley Harrison, *The Diary of Jack the Ripper*, (London: Smith Gryphon, 1993) p. ix and 178. For further discussion of the authenticity of the evidence see the *Evening Standard* (13.12.94) p. 12.

10. Brian Augustyn, Michael Mignola, P. Craig Russell, David Hornung, introduced by Robert Bloch, *Gotham by Gaslight* (New York: DC Comics, 1989).

11. Ibid., p. 1.

12. T.A. Critchley, *A History of Policy in England and Wales* (London: Constable, 1978) p. 161.
13. James Berry, *My Life as an Executioner*, ed. Jonathan Goodman (Newton Abbot: David & Charles, 1972).
14. Ibid., p. 1.
15. Ibid., p. 11.
16. Ibid., p. 66.
17. Ibid., p. 95.
18. Ibid.
19. Michel Foucault, *Discipline and Punish*, tr. Alan Sheridan (London: Allen Lane, 1977) p. 53.
20. Gordon Honeycomb, *The Murders of the Black Museum 1870–1970* (London: Hutchinson, 1982).
21. Foucault, *Discipline and Punish*, p. 57.
22. René Girand, *Violence and the Sacred*, tr. Patrick Gregory (Baltimore: Johns Hopkins University Press, 1977).
23. Ibid., p. 1.
24. Ibid.
25. Ibid., p. 2.
26. Ibid., p. 9.
27. Ibid., p. 12.
28. Ibid.
29. Ibid., p. 4.
30. Ibid., p. 8.
31. Ibid., p. 4.
32. René Girard, 'Myth and Ritual in Shakespeare: *A Midsummer Night's Dream*' in *Textual Strategies*, ed. Josué V. Harrari (London: Methuen, 1980) pp. 189–212.
33. See Stewart Evans and Paul Gainey, *The Lodger: the Arrest and Escape of Jack the Ripper* (London: Century, 1995) for the latest 'factual' accretion.

CHAPTER 9: WEST IS EAST

1. D.J. Enright, introduction to *The Mystery of Dr Fu Manchu* (London: J.M. Dent, 1985) p. vii. All quotations are then taken from this edition. *The Hand of Dr Fu Manchu* and *The Return of Dr Fu Manchu* and quoted from *Fu Manchu: Four Classic Novels* (Secausus, NJ: Citadel, 1983).
2. Enright, introduction, p. viii.
3. Ibid., pp. xiv–xv.
4. Colin Watson, *Snobbery with Violence* (London: Methuen, 1987) p. 15.
5. Ibid., p. 16.
6. Ibid., p. 158.
7. Ibid., p. 117.
8. Ibid., p. 44.
9. Cay Van Ash and Elizabeth Sax Rohmer, *Master of Villainy: A Biography of Sax Rohmer* (Bowling Green, OH: Bowling Green University Popular Press, 1972) p. 68.

10. John Fisher, *Paul Daniels and the Story of Magic* (London: Cape, 1987) p. 4. My thanks to Clare Hudson of the Victoria and Albert Theatre Museum of London for help in locating this information.
11. Van Ash and Sax Rohmer, *Master of Villainy*, pp. 32–3.
12. Ibid., p. 115.
13. Ibid., p. 114.
14. Ibid.
15. Ibid., p. 73.

CHAPTER 10: THIS REVOLTING GRAVEYARD

1. Lin Carter, *Lovecraft: A Look behind the Cthulhu Mythos* (London: Panther, 1975) p. 21.
2. Ibid.
3. Colin Wilson, Introduction to George Hay ed., *The Necronomicon* (London: Corgi, 1980) p. 22.
4. Ibid., p. 149.
5. Quoted in David Punter, *The Literature of Terror* (London: Longman, 1980) p. 285.
6. Carter, *Lovecraft*, pp. 35–6.
7. Ibid., p. 23.
8. Ibid., pp. 52–3
9. Ibid., p. 82.
10. Ibid., p. 56.
11. Ibid., p. 57.
12. Ibid., p. 58.
13. Punter, *The Literature of Terror*, p. 285.
14. Ibid., p. 282.
15. Quoted in George E. Mowry ed., *The Twenties* (Englewood Cliffs, NJ: Prentice-Hall, 1963) p. 155.
16. Ibid., pp. 137–9.
17. Ibid., p. 146.
18. Quoted in Carter, *Lovecraft*, p. 82.
19. Ibid., p. 129.
20. Stephen King, *Danse Macabre* (London: Futura, 1986) p. 45.
21. Ibid., p. 17.
22. Punter, *The Literature of Terror*, p. 288.
23. Carter, *Lovecraft*, p. 25.

CHAPTER 11: HARRY AND MARIANNE

1. Trevor H. Hall, E.J. Dingwall and K.M. Goldney, *The Haunting of Borley Rectory: A Critical Survey of the Evidence* (London: Duckworth, 1956); Trevor H. Hall, *Search For Harry Price* (London: Duckworth, 1978). All biographical details of Harry Price's life are from Hall unless otherwise stated.

2. Harry Price, *'The Most Haunted House in England'* (London: Longman, 1940) hereinafter referred to as *MHHE*; *The End of Borley Rectory* (London: Harrap, 1946) hereinafter referred to as *EBR*.
3. Belchamp St Paul appears in 'Count Magnus' by M.R. James, in *Casting the Runes and Other Ghost Stories* (Oxford: Oxford University Press, 1987).
4. Paul Tabori, *Harry Price: The Biography of a Ghost-Hunter* (Worthing: Athenaeum, 1950).
5. See previous chapter.
6. See Hall ch. 7 and ch. 9.
7. See Price's chronology, *EBR* p. 335.
8. Robert Wood, *The Widow of Borley: A Psychical Investigation* (London: Duckworth, 1992) p. 11.
9. Ibid., p. 18.
10. Ibid.
11. Ibid., p. 66.
12. Ibid., p. 117.

CHAPTER 12: THE DEATH OF CULT FICTION AND THE END OF THEORY

1. It would be tedious to catalogue all the references to other authors in King's fiction. A perfect example rests in his tribute to Daphne du Maurier in *The Dark Half*. In both *Misery* and *The Dark Half*, King makes a point of featuring references to Ernest Hemingway. Again, King's interest in authorial ancestors and author *Doppelgängers* even extends to his 'borrowing' a character from another writer. See *The Dark Half* (London: Guild, 1989) afterword p. 412 facing. Alexis Machine is taken from *Dead City* by Shane Stevens.
2. See George Orwell, 'Raffles and Miss Blandish' in *Decline of the English Murder and other Essays* (Harmondsworth: Penguin [1944], 1988) pp. 63–79.
3. For a further discussion of the reciprocity between high and low culture see Andrew Ross, *No Respect: Intellectuals and Popular Culture* (London: Routledge, 1989) pp. 3 and 5.

> While it speaks enthusiastically to the feelings, desires, aspirations, and pleasures of ordinary people, popular culture is far from being a straightforward or unified expression of popular interests. It contains elements of disrespect, and even opposition to structures of authority, but it also contains 'explanations,' as I have suggested, for the maintenance of respect for those structures of authority. . . .
>
> To be truthful, we ought to admit that there is no such thing as a history from above, of intellectuals, or a history from below, of popular culture, although many such histories, of either kind, have been and will continue to be written. On the contrary, it is increasingly important (especially today, when the once politicized

divisions between high and low culture make less and less sense in a culture that ignores these divisions with official impunity) to consider what is dialectical about the historically fractious relationship between intellectuals and popular culture.

4. J. Hoberman, 'Ed Wood . . . Not', in *Sight and Sound* (May 1995) p. 13.
5. Ibid., p. 13.
6. Ibid., p. 14.
7. Arthur Kroker, *The Possessed Individual: Technology and Postmodernity* (London: Macmillan, 1992) pp. 18–19.
8. Valerie Walkerdine, 'Dreams from an Ordinary Life', in Liz Heron ed., *Truth, Dare or Promise: Girls Growing Up in the 50s* (London: Virago, 1985) p. 76.
9. Richard Wagner quoted in John Deathridge and Carl Dahlhaus, *The New Grove Wagner* (London: Macmillan, 1984) pp. 70–1.
10. Luis Buñuel quoted in Jean Vigo, *Un Chien Andalou* (London: Faber & Faber, 1994) p. v.
11. Ibid., p. ix.

Index

257